WRITINGS ON
ART AND LITERATURE

MERIDIAN

Crossing Aesthetics

Werner Hamacher
& David E. Wellbery
Editors

From The Standard Edition of the Complete
Psychological Works of Sigmund Freud,
edited by James Strachey

Stanford
University
Press

Stanford
California

WRITINGS ON
ART AND LITERATURE

Sigmund Freud

with a Foreword by Neil Hertz

Stanford University Press
Stanford, California

Reproduced by permission from James Strachey, ed.,
*The Standard Edition of the Complete Psychological Works
of Sigmund Freud*, 24 vols. (London, 1953–74)

Printed in the United States of America

CIP data appear at the end of the book

Last figure below indicates year of this printing:
09   08   07   06   05   04   03   02   01

Contents

Foreword

Neil Hertz

Werner Herzog's movie about Kaspar Hauser—*Every Man for Himself and God Against All* (1975)—begins with a mysterious tableau: Kaspar is shown in the gloomy cellar where he has been imprisoned throughout his childhood. A man in black—a father? a guardian? a jailer?—appears at the door, descends, steadies Kaspar in a sitting position, places a sheet of paper on a small stool in front of him, forces a pen into his fist, and then, standing close behind him and leaning over him, he grasps Kaspar's hand in his own and makes him trace lines on the paper. "Schreiben!" he whispers in Kaspar's ear, "Schrei-ben!" telling him, "This is called 'writing'" or, simply, "Write!"

The scene has a history. In 1814, one of Freud's predecessors, the German Romantic Gotthilf Heinrich Schubert, published a theory of dreaming, *Die Symbolik des Traumes*, in which he argued that our minds are continuously engaged with two languages, a daytime language of words and a nighttime language of images, the images that make up our dreams. There is absolutely no relation between these discourses, he believed: they go their separate ways, and our attention is ordinarily directed to either one or the other of the channels. At certain moments of half-slumber, however, we can sometimes accidentally tune in to both, and then the most nonsensical combinations will occur to us. For example, he continued, offering an instance of such absurdity, "we think of the word *schreiben* and immediately before us we have the image of two men, one man carrying the other on his back."[1]

One sign of the difference Freud's work has made in the way we read is that we can no longer share Schubert's confidence that this particular juxtaposition of a word and an image makes no sense. On the contrary, like Werner Herzog, we are more likely to find it strikingly indicative, if enigmatically so. Indicative of what? There is, first, in Herzog's version, the play of light and darkness, the enlightenment associated with the arrival of this dark man, a sinister, though possibly enabling, figure. He has come to lean over another man, younger than he, less instructed than he. The weight of the older man's body, the pressure of his will give substance to the voiced word: *schreiben* takes on its imperative force. To write, to join the world of the instructed, is to submit to that force, to feel it entering one's body and guiding one's hand. Writing, Freud would have us say, is Oedipal, a coming to terms with the Father, a shouldering of the burden of the past.

But here a slight complication needs to be taken into account: what we are watching is not just a representation of Kaspar's initiation into literacy. It is also the initial sequence of Herzog's film, a sequence that is hard not to read as emblematic, as Herzog signing in, the director figured both by the man in black, the person who is literally directing Kaspar's hand, and by Kaspar himself, the one whose hand is doing the marking. The possibility of such multiple identifications—and of such reversals of the vectors of influence and causation—is common in works of art; it does not so much mute the Oedipal resonance of the scene as skew and prolong its vibrations; it brings the Oedipal into touch with more general questions of representation. There is no doubt that this is a frequent source of the viewer's or reader's pleasure, but it can be a source of anxiety, too, if what one thinks is at issue is one's understanding of the work.

The essays on art and literature collected here testify to the

---

[1]Gotthilf Heinrich Schubert, *Die Symbolik des Traumes*, ed. G. Sauder (Heidelberg: Verlag Lambert Schneider, 1968 [1814], p. 5.

strength of Freud's commitment to understanding, to his will to interpret, but they also make clear that what interpreting meant to him was less assigning meanings to a work of art than accounting for why the reader or viewer had been "so powerfully affected" (p. 123) by it.[1] Hence these pieces frequently invoke both the pleasures and the epistemological anxieties attendant on aesthetic experience.

Freud's generic answer to the question of art's emotional power was that it tapped into, aroused, and reconfigured unconscious energies and investments already at work "within" viewers and readers. Interpretations of works of art, then, like those of neurotic symptoms or dreams or slips of the tongue, are bound to reveal unconscious operations that are not peculiar to artists. Among other things, this meant that Freud's essays on art could serve as convenient and engaging illustrations of his theories. Ever the canny explainer, he frequently used them in just this fashion: a reader seeking a brief, lucid introduction to the Freudian understanding of repression, or of displacement, or of transference, could do worse than to turn to the pages in this volume devoted to "Delusions and Dreams in Jensen's *Gradiva*."

But literature and art were at times more than merely illustrative for Freud. To read the letters he addressed to Wilhelm Fliess in the fall of 1897, when he was formulating the Oedipus complex, is to see works of literature—Sophocles' play, *Hamlet*, Grillparzer's *Die Ahnfrau* (The ancestress)—providing a significant part of the material, variously accommodating and recalcitrant, that Freud was working through for the first time. It is worth quoting some paragraphs from that correspondence here: as the earliest of Freud's texts on literature, they belong in this volume. They appear in a letter of October 15, 1897, in a passage that begins with Freud complaining of the difficulties of self-analysis:

[1] Page references in parentheses are either to essays collected in this volume or, when preceded by *SE*, to volumes of *The Standard Edition of the Complete Psychological Works of Sigmund Freud*, ed. James Strachey (London: Hogarth Press, 1953–74).

So far I have found nothing completely new, [just] all the complications to which I have become accustomed. It is by no means easy. Being totally honest with oneself is a good exercise. A single idea of general value dawned on me. I have found, in my own case too, [the phenomenon of] being in love with my mother and jealous of my father, and I now consider it a universal event in early childhood, even if not so early in children who have been made hysterical. (Similar to the invention of parentage [family romance] in paranoia—heroes, founders of religion). If this is so, we can understand the gripping power of *Oedipus Rex*, in spite of all the objections that reason raises against the presupposition of fate; and we can understand why the later "drama of fate" was bound to fail so miserably. Our feelings rise against any arbitrary individual compulsion, such as is presupposed in *Die Ahnfrau* and the like; but the Greek legend seizes upon a compulsion which everyone recognizes because he senses its existence within himself. Everyone in the audience was once a budding Oedipus in fantasy and each recoils in horror from the dream fulfillment here transplanted into reality, with the full quantity of repression which separates his infantile state from his present one.

Fleetingly, the thought passed through my head that the same thing might be at the bottom of *Hamlet* as well. I am not thinking of Shakespeare's conscious intention, but believe, rather, that a real event stimulated the poet in his representation, in that his unconscious understood the unconscious of his hero. How does Hamlet the hysteric justify his words, "Thus conscience does make cowards of us all"? How does he explain his irresolution in avenging his father by the murder of his uncle—the same man who sends his courtiers to their death without a scruple and who is positively precipitate in murdering Laertes? How better than through the torment he suffers from the obscure memory that he himself had contemplated the same deed against his father out of passion for his mother, and—"use every man after his desert, and who should 'scape whipping?" His conscience is his unconscious sense of guilt. And is not his sexual alienation in his conversation with Ophelia typically hysterical? And his rejection of the instinct that seeks to beget children? And, finally, his transferral of the deed from his own father to Ophelia's? And does he not in the end, in the same marvelous way as my hysterical patients, bring down punishment on himself by suffering the same fate as his father of being poisoned by the same rival?.[1]

Jean Starobinski has shown that *Hamlet* in particular was crucial to the elaboration of Freud's thought because it allowed him to apply the mythic Oedipal model, as Sophocles had presented it, to the actions of someone who, precisely, had *not* murdered his father or slept with his mother, to someone like Freud himself or his patients. Hamlet's procrastination could then be seen not as a lack of energy or will, but as a case of paralysis, analogous to the motor paralysis Freud had encountered in hysterics. This analogy not only, as Freud was to boast some years later, "at last explained" the mystery of *Hamlet*'s power,[2] but it illuminated Freud's clinical experience as well, by further confirming his sense of the vigorous but unconscious activity of forces whose vectors, canceling each other out, had immobilized his patients.[3]

Moments of immobilization—literal and figurative—are sufficiently frequent in Freud's writings to warrant our attention. The first text collected in the *Standard Edition*, Freud's 1886 "Report on My Studies in Paris and Berlin" (*SE*, 1, 5–15), mentions the work on hysterical paralysis he engaged in under the supervision of Jean-Martin Charcot at the Salpetrière Hospital in Paris: indeed he later produced for Charcot a paper on the etiology of paralysis ("Some

[1] *The Complete Letters of Sigmund Freud to Wilhelm Fliess, 1887–1904*, ed. J. M. Masson (Cambridge, Mass.: Harvard University Press, 1985), p. 272. The allusion to Hamlet's precipitation in "murdering Laertes" may be a Freudian slip, conflating Hamlet's final duel with Laertes with his "precipitous" killing of Polonius. In the original French version of his article (see note 3 below), Jean Starobinski speculates that this glancing gesture at fratricide may have been motivated by the fact that Freud was writing to Fliess, a close friend and, in 1897, a possible rival.

[2] In the introductory paragraphs of "The Moses of Michelangelo" (1914), reprinted below pp. 122–50.

[3] "Hamlet and Oedipus," in Jean Starobinski, *The Living Eye*, trans. Arthur Goldhammer (Cambridge, Mass.: Harvard University Press, 1989), pp. 148–70. This is a translation of "Hamlet et Freud," which first appeared in *Les Temps Modernes* 253 (June 1967), pp. 2113–35. It was written as a preface to the French translation of Ernest Jones's (1949) *Hamlet and Oedipus*, published as *Hamlet et Oedipe* (Paris: Gallimard, 1967).

Points for a Comparative Study of Organic and Hysterical Motor
Paralyses," *SE*, **I**, 155–72). But in later volumes of his collected
works, as we watch Freud's fields of inquiry multiply and expand
beyond his initial interest in the neuroses, we read less of literal
paralysis, whether caused organically or psychologically, and encounter more references to moments in which people are, as it
were, "paralyzed" (*gelähmt,* in German).

As the most stubbornly effective of inhibitions, paralysis is
linked to taboo and, in particular, to sexual taboos drawing their
power from the fear of castration. In an essay not included in this
collection, Freud praised the dramatist Hebbel for his unorthodox
retelling of the story of Judith, the Biblical heroine famed for
having beheaded Holofernes. "Beheading," Freud noted, "is well-
known to us as a symbolic substitute for castration." But Hebbel
has added another twist: in his version of the story, long before her
encounter with Holofernes, Judith's "first husband was paralysed
on the bridal night by a mysterious anxiety, and never again dared
to touch her." The beheading, then, can be seen as a deferred and
displaced act of revenge: "Judith is one of those women whose
virginity is protected by a taboo. . . . She is accordingly the woman
who castrates the man who has deflowered her." Freud credits
Hebbel with "the fine perception of a poet" for having sensed the
long-suppressed "ancient motive" at stake in the Biblical story and
for having then improvised this "uncanny wedding night" ("The
Taboo of Virginity," *SE*, **II**, 207).

Freud's reading assimilates the bridegroom's paralyzing anxiety
to Medusa-fear, that feeling that "there is something uncanny
about the female genital organs" (p. 221), the sight of which "makes
the spectator stiff with terror, turns him to stone" (p. 264).
But Freud's understanding of the Medusa's Head was that if "the
thing itself" was terrifying—"unpresentable," in the words of Phi-
lippe Lacoue-Labarthe[1]—its visual or verbal depictions served

[1]See "The Scene Is Primal" in *The Subject of Philosophy*, ed. Thomas Trezise
(Minneapolis: University of Minnesota Press, 1993), pp. 109–12. In this reading of
Freud's "Psychopathic Characters on the Stage," in the course of discussing the
death-drive, which he would locate at the origins of representation, Lacoue-

a defensive, apotropaic function, as wardings-off of the threat through symbolic representation.[1] Hebbel's play, then, can be thought of in those terms, as both an instance of castration-anxiety and a defense against it.

Freud of course never exempted himself from these terrors or these defenses. In one telling autobiographical passage from "On the History of the Psycho-Analytic Movement," literal and metaphorical paralysis can be found juxtaposed in a surprising and suggestive anecdote. Freud tells of half-overhearing Charcot talking quietly with another colleague about a young married woman's neurotic illness, then listening to his professor exclaim, "with great animation":

Labarthe links the "unpresentability" of death in Freud to the need to turn one's eyes away from the Medusa's Head: "Death cannot—any more than can the woman's or the mother's sex—present itself as such, 'in person,' as Lyotard would say. Just as there is an *apotropaic* structure to the feminine abyss (to obscenity), there is an unavoidable *necessity* to the re-presentation (staging, *mise en scene*, *Darstellung*) of death, and consequently to identification, to mimetism." Lacoue-Labarthe is writing in the wake of Jacques Derrida's ongoing interventions in discussions of psychoanalysis, beginning with his essay "Freud and the Scene of Writing" (1967), collected in *Writing and Difference*, trans. Alan Bass (Chicago: University of Chicago Press, 1978). My own emphasis on "paralysis" in Freud owes much to Derrida, most particularly to his discerning in the fictions of Maurice Blanchot a "desire of paralysis that never ceases, which confers movement, and does so without measure." I am translating from p. 74 of Derrida's *Parages* (Paris: Galilée, 1986), where his long essay on Blanchot, "Pas," was reprinted. It first appeared in the French review *Gramma 3/4* in 1976. More recently, in "Résistances" (1992, collected in *Résistances: de la psychanalyse* [Paris: Galilée, 1996]), Derrida has returned to this notion and, on p. 35, proposed a paradoxically energizing "logic of paralysis" to be distinguished from the traditional "logic" of psycho*analysis*.

A fine Derridean study of Freud's dealings with literature and the visual arts, including an extended discussion of the relevance of the death-drive, may be found in Sarah Kofman, *The Childhood of Art: An Interpretation of Freud's Aesthetics*, trans. Winifred Woodhull (New York: Columbia University Press, 1988).

[1]A lucid account of the apotropaic uses of symbolic representation can be found in Jean Laplanche's *Problematiques II: Castration, Symbolisations* (Paris: PUF, 1980), pp. 58–68; see also my "Medusa's Head: Male Hysteria Under Political Pressure" in *The End of the Line* (New York: Columbia University Press, 1985), pp. 160–215, which draws on Laplanche's work.

*'Mais, dans des cas pareils c'est toujours la chose génitale, toujours . . .
toujours . . . toujours';* [But in this sort of case it's always a question of
the genitals—always, always, always] and he crossed his arms over his
stomach, hugging himself and jumping up and down on his toes
several times in his own characteristically lively way. I know that for a
moment I was almost paralysed [*gelähmt*] with amazement and said to
myself: 'Well, but if he knows that, why does he never say so?' But the
impression was soon forgotten; brain anatomy and the experimental
induction of hysterical paralyses [*Paralysen*] absorbed all my interest. (*SE*, **14**, 14)

"A question of the genitals" is an accurate but a bland translation: *la
chose génitale* also connotes that thing, the thing itself, and Freud's
use of the word "paralysis" here can illustrate his own theories of
anxiety. For the point of the anecdote—it is one of a group of
three—is that Freud's "apparently original discovery" of the sexual
etiology of the neuroses was in fact not so original. Rather, it was
the belated bringing to consciousness of something he had taken
in, without quite registering it, years earlier, listening to some of his
teachers, who at the time were even less conscious than he of what
it was they were conveying: "These three men had all communicated to me a piece of knowledge which, strictly speaking, they
themselves did not possess."

Freud is always curious about how people—himself included—
come by their knowledge of the unconscious. He wonders—in the
case of Dora, for example[1]—how his patients know what they
know, and he wonders, in exactly the same tone, what sources of
knowledge imaginative writers like Jensen draw on in creating
works like *Gradiva* (p. 81). Here, in this story about the indirect,
overheard conveyance of a central tenet of psychoanalysis from the,
as it were, unconscious Charcot to the young, all-but-unconscious
Freud, the distances separating the analyst, the artist, and the
hysteric almost collapse: Freud's metaphorical paralysis aligns him
with the patients whose own acquisition of sexual knowledge was

[1]See the footnotes at *SE*, **7**, 36 and **7**, 120. I take up this issue more fully in
"Dora's Secrets, Freud's Techniques" in *The End of the Line*, pp. 122–43.

often literally paralyzing, and locates him in a mirror relation with interlocutors like Charcot and Jensen, who turn out to be only obliquely in touch with what they may, after the fact, be said to unconsciously have known all along. It is a noticeable turn in Freud that such moments of shared "unconsciousness," when important transmissions are taking place, are frequently figured as temporary immobilization, like the charged symmetrical stasis of the analytic hour, in which free associations issuing from a couch are picked up by the free-floating attention of a listener in an armchair.

It is in this context—of being brought to a standstill by the unconscious arousal of repressed affect, usually but not exclusively attached to sexual anxieties—that we can best engage the question of how Freud imagines the reception of works of art. "The dramatist can indeed, during the representation, overwhelm us by his art and paralyse our powers of reflection," Freud writes, in a discussion of *Macbeth*, "but he cannot prevent us from attempting subsequently to grasp its effect by studying its psychological mechanism" (pp. 164–65). Hence, in "The Moses of Michelangelo," Freud would liken his own interpretive procedures to those of the art historian Giovanni Morelli, who "insist[ed] that attention should be diverted from the general impression and main features" of a work to "the significance of minor details" (p. 134); "these [minor details]," Freud had remarked earlier, writing of the Moses in particular, "we usually fail to notice, being overcome by the total impression of the statue and as it were paralysed by it" (p. 130). The point, of course, is to break that spell, but the spell is crucial to one's experience of the work, as constitutive of it as the analytic effort that succeeds and dispels this "paralysis." Oddly, Michelangelo's Moses himself, according to an interpretation Freud had just cited in order to disagree with it, is described as fixed in a certain attitude by the "pain of mind" that still "dominates him and almost paralyses him" (p. 130).

Statues tend to be static, even when, as in the case of the Gradiva, they depict a bewitching mobility (pp. 6–7); Freud, however, goes to some length to insist that Michelangelo has not caught Moses in the midst of rising to his feet, as some scholars had surmised.

Freud's confident dismissal of this interpretation is arrived at in part by his reasoning that the Moses was intended as the center piece of the sculptural ensemble decorating the tomb of Pope Julius II and that a "figure in the act of instant departure would be utterly at variance with the state of mind which the tomb is meant to induce in us." But Freud also offers a more subjective account of the sources of his conviction:

> I can recollect my own disillusionment when, during my first visits to San Pietro in Vincoli, I used to sit down in front of the statue in the expectation that I should now see how it would start up on its raised foot, dash the Tables of the Law to the ground and let fly its wrath. Nothing of the kind happened. Instead, the stone image became more and more transfixed, an almost oppressively solemn calm emanated from it, and I was obliged to realize that something was represented here that could stay without change; that this Moses would remain sitting like this in his wrath for ever. (p. 132)

The longer Freud looks, the more "transfixed" does the *statue* become. For what takes place in that "oppressively solemn calm" is a set of exchanges and identifications in which the intentions Freud attributes to Moses can be read as functions of his own unconscious self-positioning in relation to this "stone image." "Sometimes," he recalls,

> I have crept cautiously out of the half-gloom of the interior as though I myself belonged to the mob upon whom his eye is turned—the mob which can hold fast no conviction, which has neither faith nor patience, and which rejoices when it has regained its illusory idols. (p. 124)

Here, Freud is imagining himself on the receiving end of "the angry scorn of the hero's glance" (p. 124). But his final understanding of the statue, as his editors remark in a footnote, may no longer entail his seeing himself in the mob of idolators; rather, he draws on his identification with the hero himself. For the statue had appeared to him, in its fixity, as the depiction of a costly and admirable compromise, of righteous anger overcome and checked by the counterthrust of Moses' sense of his mission: thus suspended, Freud concludes, Moses "remained immobilized, and in this attitude Michelangelo has portrayed him as the guardian of the tomb" (p. 142).

"The guardian of the tomb": that last phrase may come as a slight surprise. It is easy to forget that the statue of Moses, so compelling in itself and by itself, is a piece of tomb sculpture. Moreover, given the drama Freud has conjured up of Moses' restraint, of his choosing not to cast down the Tablets, one might have expected him to be characterized as "the guardian of the *Law*." But Death and the Law are close companions in Freud's thought, and Death, which the tomb at once conceals and connotes, is central to his thinking about art. His most condensed and poignant engagement with these issues is in the essay entitled "The Theme of the Three Caskets" (pp. 109–21), which begins by raising "a small problem" about some lines in *The Merchant of Venice* and concludes with a stunningly counterintuitive reading of the last scene of *King Lear*.

Like the *Gradiva* piece, this essay offers a bravura display of Freud's interpretive practice: as he moves step by step to trace what he suspected is a myth "back to its origins," Freud called his shots, pointing out the various ways an original content has undergone distortion—through displacement, through symbolic substitution, through the disguising of an element by its opposite, through the "wishful reversal" of active and passive roles, the replacement of necessity by choice. Working back down the line, a suitor's choice among three caskets turns into a choice among three lovely women, like the Judgment of Paris; that, in turn, is transformed into an old man's challenge to his three daughters, the loveliest of whom, Cordelia, is strangely silent. Her "dumbness" suggests to Freud the silence of death, of a dead woman, but that in turn, "thanks to a displacement that is far from infrequent," allows him to conjecture that she is an avatar of the Goddess of Death, one of the Three Fates, Atropos "the ineluctable," a figure of "the ineluctable severity of Law and its relation to death and dissolution." But how, Freud then wondered, did a myth about the inevitability of death turn into a story about choosing among three women, how could the third sister, "the fairest, best, most desirable and most lovable of women," come to stand in for that Goddess of Death? And it is here that he is led to invoke that "ancient ambivalence" about the Mother—as creator and destroyer, Goddess of Love and Goddess of Death—that fuels Medusa fears and the apotropaic maneuvers they require.

Freud's text is itself apotropaic in just this sense, a piece of artful defensive rhetoric as well as an analysis of the rhetoric of a myth or "theme." It concludes with a symbolic tableau that is powerful precisely because it is impossible to take in its two superimposed elements simultaneously. Freud first recalls Shakespeare's stage direction—"Reenter Lear with Cordelia dead in his arms"; he then replaces this image with another, of the Goddess of Death in one of her traditional roles, carrying the dead hero from the battlefield. *Lear* concludes, Freud concluded, with the King carried away by Death: "the third of the Fates alone, the silent Goddess of Death, will take him into her arms." There is no way a theatrical audience could see this second image. Nor can a reader visualize it: to imagine Cordelia holding Lear is grotesque; besides, it isn't Cordelia, but "the silent Goddess of Death" who takes him in her arms. This is a construction—at once a rhetorical construction of Freud's pen, and a reconstruction of the "primeval myth" he would discern behind or beneath the visible scene. It is a remarkable piece of work, and it has left many readers transfixed, aware of a busy play of energies—Shakespeare's, Freud's, the anonymous energies that go to build up a culture's unconscious investments, its elaborations and its defenses—but immobile in the face of the "paralyzing" powers of art.

Note on This Edition

The essays in this volume are reproduced from James Strachey, ed., *The Standard Edition of the Complete Psychological Works of Sigmund Freud,* 24 vols. (London, 1953–74) by arrangement with Sigmund Freud Copyrights and The Estate of Angela Harris. The editor's notes by James Strachey that precede the works and essays in *The Standard Edition,* as well as a bibliography of items cited in the footnotes to the essays, can be found at the end of this volume.

Bibliographic information on the location of an essay in *The Standard Edition* is given on the first page of that essay. The numbers in the margins indicate the page numbers in *The Standard Edition.*

WRITINGS ON
ART AND LITERATURE

§ Delusions and Dreams in Jensen's *Gradiva*

I

A GROUP of men who regarded it as a settled fact that the essential [7] riddles of dreaming have been solved by the efforts of the author of the present work[1] found their curiosity aroused one day by the question of the class of dreams that have never been dreamt at all— dreams created by imaginative writers and ascribed to invented characters in the course of a story. The notion of submitting this class of dreams to an investigation might seem a waste of energy and a strange thing to undertake; but from one point of view it could be considered justifiable. It is far from being generally be- lieved that dreams have a meaning and can be interpreted. Science and the majority of educated people smile if they are set the task of interpreting a dream. Only the common people, who cling to superstitions and who on this point are carrying on the convictions of antiquity, continue to insist that dreams can be interpreted. The author of *The Interpretation of Dreams* has ventured, in the face of the reproaches of strict science, to become a partisan of antiquity and superstition. He is, it is true, far from believing that dreams foretell the future, for the unveiling of which men have vainly striven from time immemorial by every forbidden means. But even

SOURCE: *Standard Ed.*, **9**, 7–95.
[1]See Freud, *The Interpretation of Dreams* (1990*a*).

3

he has not been able entirely to reject the relation of dreams to the future. For the dream, when the laborious work of translating it had been accomplished, revealed itself to him as a wish of the dreamer's represented as fulfilled; and who could deny that wishes are predominantly turned towards the future?

I have just said that dreams are fulfilled wishes. Anyone who is not afraid of making his way through an abstruse book, and who [8] does not insist on a complicated problem being represented to him as easy and simple in order to save him trouble and at the cost of honesty and truth, may find the detailed proof of this thesis in the work I have mentioned. Meanwhile, he may set on one side the objections which will undoubtedly occur to him against equating dreams and wish-fulfilments.

But we have gone a long way ahead. It is not a question yet of establishing whether the meaning of a dream can always be rendered by a fulfilled wish, or whether it may not just as often stand for an anxious expectation, an intention, a reflection, and so on. On the contrary, the question that first arises is whether dreams have a meaning at all, whether they ought to be assessed as mental events. Science answers 'no': it explains dreaming as a purely physiological process, behind which, accordingly, there is no need to look for sense, meaning or purpose. Somatic stimuli, so it says, play upon the mental instrument during sleep and thus bring to consciousness now one idea and now another, robbed of all mental content: dreams are comparable only to twitchings, not to expressive movements, of the mind.

Now in this dispute as to the estimation in which dreams should be held, imaginative writers seem to be on the same side as the ancients, as the superstitious public and as the author of *The Interpretation of Dreams*. For when an author makes the characters constructed by his imagination dream, he follows the everyday experience that people's thoughts and feelings are continued in sleep and he aims at nothing else than to depict his heroes' states of mind by their dreams. But creative writers are valuable allies and their evidence is to be prized highly, for they are apt to know a whole host of things between heaven and earth of which our philosophy has not yet let us dream. In their knowledge of the mind they are far in advance of us everyday people, for they draw upon sources which we have not yet opened up for science. If only this support given by writers in favour of dreams having a meaning were less ambiguous! A strictly critical eye might object that writers take their stand neither for nor against particular dreams having a [9] psychical meaning; they are content to show how the sleeping mind twitches under the excitations which have remained active in it as off-shoots of waking life.

But even this sobering thought does not damp our interest in the fashion in which writers make use of dreams. Even if this enquiry should teach us nothing new about the nature of dreams, it may perhaps enable us from this angle to gain some small insight into the nature of creative writing. Real dreams were already regarded as unrestrained and unregulated structures—and now we are confused by unfettered imitations of these dreams! There is far less freedom and arbitrariness in mental life, however, than we are inclined to assume—there may even be none at all. What we call chance in the world outside can, as is well known, be resolved into laws. So, too, what we call arbitrariness in the mind rests upon laws, which we are only now beginning dimly to suspect. Let us, then, see what we find!

There are two methods that we might adopt for this enquiry. One would be to enter deeply into a particular case, into the dream-creations of one author in one of his works. The other would be to bring together and contrast all the examples that could be found of the use of dreams in the works of different authors. The second method would seem to be far the more effective and perhaps the only justifiable one, for it frees us at once from the difficulties involved in adopting the artificial concept of 'writers' as a class. On investigation this class falls apart into individual writers of the most various worth—among them some whom we are accustomed to honour as the deepest observers of the human mind. In spite of this, however, these pages will be devoted to an enquiry

of the first sort. It happened that in the group of men among whom
the notion first arose there was one[1] who recalled that in the work
of fiction that had last caught his fancy there were several dreams
which had, as it were, looked at him with familiar faces and invited

[10]   him to attempt to apply to them the method of *The Interpretation
of Dreams*. He confessed that the subject-matter of the little work
and the scene in which it was laid may no doubt have played the
chief part in creating his enjoyment. For the story was set in the
frame of Pompeii and dealt with a young archaeologist who had
surrendered his interest in life in exchange for an interest in the
remains of classical antiquity and who was now brought back to
real life by a roundabout path which was strange but perfectly
logical. During the treatment of this genuinely poetic material the
reader had been stirred by all kinds of thoughts akin to it and in
harmony with it. The work was a short tale by Wilhelm Jensen—
Gradiva—which its author himself described as a 'Pompeian
phantasy'.

    And now I ought properly to ask all my readers to put aside this
little essay and instead to spend some time in acquainting themselves with *Gradiva* (which first appeared in the bookshops in
1903), so that what I refer to in the following pages may be familiar
to them. But for the benefit of those who have already read *Gradiva*
I will recall the substance of the story in a brief summary; and I
shall count upon their memory to restore to it all the charm of
which this treatment will deprive it.

    A young archaeologist, Norbert Hanold, had discovered in a
museum of antiquities in Rome a relief which had so immensely
attracted him that he was greatly pleased at obtaining an excellent
plaster cast of it which he could hang in his study in a German
university town and gaze at with interest. The sculpture represented a fully-grown girl stepping along, with her flowing dress a
little pulled up so as to reveal her sandalled feet. One foot rested
squarely on the ground; the other, lifted from the ground in the act

[1][This was Jung. See the Editor's Note for this essay.]

of following after, touched it only with the tips of the toes, while the sole and heel rose almost perpendicularly. It was probably the unusual and peculiarly charming gait thus presented that attracted the sculptor's notice and that still, after so many centuries, riveted the eyes of its archaeological admirer.

The interest taken by the hero of the story in this relief is the basic psychological fact in the narrative. It was not immediately explicable. 'Dr. Norbert Hanold, Lecturer in Archaeology, did not in fact find in the relief anything calling for special notice from the point of view of his branch of science.' (3.)[1] 'He could not explain to himself what there was in it that had provoked his attention. He only knew that he had been attracted by something and that the effect had continued unchanged ever since.' But his imagination was occupied with the sculpture without ceasing. He found something 'of to-day' about it, as though the artist had had a glimpse in the street and captured it 'from the life'. He gave the girl thus pictured as she stepped along the name of 'Gradiva'—'the girl who steps along'.[2] He made up a story that she was no doubt the daughter of an aristocratic family, perhaps 'of a patrician aedile,[3] who carried out his office in the service of Ceres', and that she was on her way to the goddess's temple. Then he found it hard to fit her quiet, calm nature into the busy life of a capital city. He convinced himself, rather, that she must be transported to Pompeii, and that somewhere there she was stepping across the curious stepping-stones which have been dug up and which made it possible to cross dry-foot from one side of the street to the other in rainy weather, though allowing carriage-wheels to pass between them as well. Her features struck him as having a *Greek* look and he had no doubt that she was of Hellenic origin. Little by little he brought the whole of his archaeological learning into the service of these and other phantasies relating to the original who had been the model for the relief.

[11]

[1][Plain numbers in brackets in the present translation are page references to Jensen, *Gradiva*, 1903.]

[2][The derivation of the name is further explained below, on p. 44.]

[3][A magistrate in charge of public buildings.]

But now he found himself confronted by an ostensibly scientific problem which called for a solution. It was a question of his arriving at a critical judgement as to 'whether Gradiva's gait as she stepped along had been reproduced by the sculptor in a life-like manner'. He found that he himself was not capable of imitating it, and in his quest for the 'reality' of this gait he was led 'to make observations of his own from the life in order to clear the matter up'. (9.) This, however, forced him into a course of behaviour that was quite foreign to him. 'Hitherto, the female sex had been to him no more than the concept of something made of marble or bronze, and he had never paid the slightest attention to its contemporary representatives.' Social duties had always seemed to him an unavoidable nuisance; he saw and heard young ladies whom he came across in society so little that when he next met them he would pass them by without a sign; and this, of course, made no favourable impression on them. Now, however, the scientific task which he had taken on compelled him, in dry, but more especially in wet, weather, to look eagerly in the street at women's and girls' feet as they came into view—an activity which brought him some angry, and some encouraging, glances from those who came under his observation; 'but he was aware of neither the one nor the other.' (10). As an outcome of these careful studies he was forced to the conclusion that Gradiva's gait was not discoverable in reality; and this filled him with regret and vexation.

Soon afterwards he had a terrifying dream, in which he found himself in ancient Pompeii on the day of the eruption of Vesuvius and witnessed the city's destruction. 'As he was standing at the edge of the forum beside the Temple of Jupiter, he suddenly saw Gradiva at no great distance from him. Till then he had had no thought of her presence, but now it occurred to him all at once and as though it was something natural that, since she was a Pompeian, she was living in her native town, and, *without his having suspected it, living as his contemporary.*' (12.) Fear of the fate that lay before her provoked him to utter a warning cry, whereupon the figure, as she calmly stepped along, turned her face towards him. But she then

[12]

proceeded on her way untroubled, till she reached the portico of
the temple;[1] there she took her seat on one of the steps and   [13]
slowly laid her head down on it, while her face grew paler and paler,
as though it were turning into marble. When he hurried after her,
he found her stretched out on the broad step with a peaceful expression, like someone asleep, till the rain of ashes buried her form.

When he awoke, the confused shouts of the inhabitants of
Pompeii calling for help still seemed to echo in his ears, and the
dull muttering of the breakers in the agitated sea. But even after his
returning reflection recognized the sounds as the awakening signs
of noisy life in a great city, he retained his belief for a long time in
the reality of what he had dreamt. When at length he had freed
himself of the notion that he himself had been present at the
destruction of Pompeii almost two thousand years earlier, he was
nevertheless left with what seemed a true conviction that Gradiva
had lived in Pompeii and been buried there with the others in the
year 79 A.D. The dream had as its result that now for the first time
in his phantasies about Gradiva he mourned for her as someone
who was lost.

While he was leaning out of the window, absorbed in these
thoughts, his attention was caught by a canary warbling its song
from a cage in the open window of the house opposite, Suddenly
something passed with a start through the mind of the young man,
who seems not yet to have fully woken from his dream. He thought
he saw in the street a form like his Gradiva, and thought he even
recognized her characteristic gait. Without thinking, he hurried
into the street so as to catch up with her; and it was only the
laughter and jeers of the passers-by at his early-morning attire that
quickly drove him back into his house. When he was in his room
again, the singing of the canary in its cage once more caught his
attention and suggested a comparison with himself. He too, so it
seemed to him, was like someone sitting in a cage, though it was
easier for him to escape from it. As though as a further aftermath of

[1][The Temple of Apollo.]

his dream, and perhaps, too, under the influence of the mild air of spring, a resolve took shape in him to make a spring-time journey to Italy. A scientific excuse for it soon presented itself, even though 'the impulse to make this journey had arisen from a feeling he could not name.' (24.)

[14]

Let us pause for a moment at this journey, planned for such remarkably uncogent reasons, and take a closer look at our hero's personality and behaviour. He still appears to us as incomprehensible and foolish; we have no idea how his peculiar folly will be linked to human feeling and so arouse our sympathy. It is an author's privilege to be allowed to leave us in such uncertainty. The charm of his language and the ingenuity of his ideas offer us a provisional reward for the reliance we place in him and for the still unearned sympathy which we are ready to feel for his hero. Of this hero we are further told that he was pre-ordained by family tradition to become an archaeologist, that in his later isolation and independence he was wholly absorbed in his studies and had turned completely away from life and its pleasures. Marble and bronze alone were truly alive for him; they alone expressed the purpose and value of human life. But nature, perhaps with benevolent intent, had infused into his blood a corrective of an entirely unscientific sort—an extremely lively imagination, which could show itself not only in his dreams but often in his waking life as well. This division between imagination and intellect destined him to become an artist or a neurotic; he was one of those whose kingdom is not of this world. Thus it was that it could come about that his interest was attached to a relief representing a girl stepping along in a peculiar fashion, that he wove his phantasies around her, imagined a name and origin for her, placed the figure he had created in the setting of the Pompeii that was buried more than eighteen hundred years before, and finally, after a strange anxiety-dream, magnified his phantasy of the existence and death of this girl named Gradiva into a delusion, which gained an influence over his actions. Such products of the imagination would seem to us

astonishing and inexplicable if we met them in someone in real
life. Since our hero, Norbert Hanold, is a fictitious person, we [15]
may perhaps put a timid question to his author, and ask whether
his imagination was determined by forces other than its own
arbitrary choice.

We had left our hero at the moment when he was apparently
being led by the song of a canary to decide on a journey to Italy, the
purpose of which was evidently not clear to him. We learn further
that he had no fixed plan or goal for his journey. An inner restlessness and dissatisfaction drove him from Rome to Naples and from
thence further still. He found himself among the swarm of honeymooners and was forced to notice the loving couples of 'Edwins'
and 'Angelinas',¹ but was quite unable to understand their goings-
on. He came to the conclusion that of all the follies of mankind
'getting married takes first place, as the greatest and most incomprehensible, and the senseless honeymoon trips to Italy are, in a
way, the crowning touch of this idiocy'. (27.) Having been disturbed in his sleep by the proximity of a loving couple in Rome, he
hurriedly fled to Naples, only to find other 'Edwins' and 'Angelinas'
there. Having gathered from their conversation that the majority of
these pairs of birds had no intention of nesting among the ruins of
Pompeii, but were flying towards Capri, he determined to do what
they did not, and only a few days after his departure found himself
'contrary to his expectation and intentions' in Pompeii.
But without finding there the repose he was in search of. The
part which had so far been played by the honeymoon couples, who
had troubled his spirits and harassed his thoughts, was now taken
over by the house-flies, which he was inclined to regard as the
incarnation of all that is absolutely evil and unnecessary. The two
sorts of tormenting spirits melted into a unity: some of the pairs [16]
of flies reminded him of the honeymooners, and he suspected that

¹['August' and 'Grete' in the original. The names recur frequently in the course
of the story and it has seemed best to replace them by those conventionally
applied to English honeymoon couples of the late Victorian age.]

they too were addressing each other in their language as 'dearest Edwin' and 'darling Angelina'. Eventually, he could not but realize that 'his dissatisfaction was not caused only by his surroundings but that its source was in part derived from within himself'. (42.) He felt that 'he was discontented because he lacked something, though it was not clear to him what'.

Next morning he passed through the '*Ingresso*' into Pompeii, and, after getting rid of the guide, strolled aimlessly through the town, without, strangely enough, remembering that only a short time before he had been present in his dream at its burial. When later on, at the 'hot and holy'[1] mid-day hour, which the ancients regarded as the hour of ghosts, the other visitors had taken flight and the heaps of ruins lay before him desolate and bathed in sunlight, he found that he was able to carry himself back into the life that had been buried—but not by the help of science. 'What it taught was a lifeless, archaeological way of looking at things, and what came from its mouth was a dead, philological language. These were of no help to an understanding through the spirit, the feelings, the heart—put it as you please. Whoever had a longing for that must stand here alone, the only living creature, in the hot silence of mid-day, among the relics of the past, and look, but not with bodily eyes, and listen, but not with physical ears. And then . . . the dead wakened and Pompeii began to live once more.' (55.)

While he was thus animating the past with his imagination, he suddenly saw the unmistakable Gradiva of his relief come out of a house and step trippingly over the lava stepping-stones to the other side of the street, just as he had seen her do in his dream the other night, when she had lain down as though to sleep, on the steps of the Temple of Apollo. 'And together with his memory something else came into his consciousness for the first time: without being aware himself of the impulse within him, he had come to Italy and had travelled on to Pompeii, without stopping in Rome or Naples, in order to see whether he could find any traces of her. And "traces"

[17]

---

[1] [*Gradiva*, 51.]

literally; for with her peculiar gait she must have left behind an imprint of her toes in the ashes distinct from all the rest.' (58.)

At this point the tension in which the author has hitherto held us grows for a moment into a painful sense of bewilderment. It is not only our hero who has evidently lost his balance; we too have lost our bearings in the face of the apparition of Gradiva, who was first a marble figure and then an imaginary one. Is she a hallucination of our hero, led astray by his delusions? Is she a 'real' ghost? or a living person? Not that we need believe in ghosts when we draw up this list. The author, who has called his story a 'phantasy', has found no occasion so far for informing us whether he intends to leave us in our world, decried for being prosaic and governed by the laws of science, or whether he wishes to transport us into another and imaginary world, in which spirits and ghosts are given reality. As we know from the examples of *Hamlet* and *Macbeth*, we are prepared to follow him there without hesitation. If so, the imaginative archaeologist's delusion would have to be measured by another standard. Indeed, when we consider how improbable it must be that a real person could exist who bore an exact resemblance to the antique sculpture, our list of alternatives shrinks to two: a hallucination or a mid-day ghost. A small detail in the account soon cancels the first possibility. A large lizard was lying motionless, stretched out in the sunshine, but fled at the approach of Gradiva's foot and darted away across the lava paving-stones. So it was no hallucination, but something outside our dreamer's mind. But could the reality of a *rediviva* startle a lizard?

Gradiva disappeared in front of the House of Meleager. We shall not be surprised to hear that Norbert Hanold pursued his delusion that Pompeii had come to life around him at the mid-day hour of [18] ghosts and supposed that Gradiva too had come to life again and had entered the house in which she had lived before the fatal August day in 79 A.D. Ingenious speculations upon the personality of its owner (after whom the house was probably named), and upon Gradiva's relationship to him, shot through his head, and proved that his science was now completely in the service of his imagination. He entered the house, and suddenly found the apparition once more, sitting on some low steps between two yellow columns. 'There was something white stretched out across her knees; he could not clearly discern what it was; it seemed to be a sheet of papyrus . . .' On the basis of his latest theories of her origin he addressed her in Greek, and waited with trepidation to learn whether, in her phantom presence she possessed the power of speech. Since she made no reply, he addressed her instead in Latin. Then, with a smile on her lips: 'If you want to speak to me', she said, 'you must do it in German.'

What a humiliation for us readers! So the author has been making fun of us, and, with the help, as it were, of a reflection of the Pompeian sunshine, has inveigled *us* into a delusion on a small scale, so that we may be forced to pass a milder judgement on the poor wretch on whom the mid-day sun was really shining. Now, however, that we have been cured of our brief confusion, we know that Gradiva was a German girl of flesh and blood—a solution which we were inclined to reject as the most improbable one. And now, with a quiet sense of superiority, we may wait to learn what the relation was between the girl and her marble image, and how our young archaeologist arrived at the phantasies which pointed towards her real personality.

But our hero was not torn from his delusion as quickly as we have been, for, as the author tells us, 'though his belief made him happy, he had to take the acceptance of quite a considerable number of mysteries into the bargain'. (140.) Moreover, this delusion probably had internal roots in him of which we know nothing and which do not exist in ourselves. In his case, no doubt, energetic treatment would seem necessary before he could be brought back to reality. Meanwhile all he could do was to fit his delusion into the wonderful experience he had just had. Gradiva, who had perished with the rest in the destruction of Pompeii, could be nothing other than a mid-day ghost who had returned to life for

[19]

the brief ghostly hour. But why was it that, after hearing her reply
delivered in German, he exclaimed 'I knew your voice sounded like
that'? Not only we, but the girl herself was bound to ask the
question, and Hanold had to admit that he had never heard it,
though he had expected to in his dream, when he called to her as
she lay down to sleep on the temple steps. He begged her to do the
same thing again as she had then; but now she rose, gave him a
strange look, and in a few paces disappeared between the columns
of the court. A pretty butterfly had shortly before fluttered round
her for a while; and he interpreted it as a messenger from Hades
reminding the dead girl that she must return, since the mid-day
hour of ghosts was at an end. Hanold still had time to call after the
girl as she vanished: 'Will you return here tomorrow at the mid-day
hour?' To us, however, who can now venture upon more sober
interpretations, it looks as though the young lady had seen something improper in the remark addressed to her by Hanold and had
left him with a sense of having been insulted; for after all she could
have known nothing of his dream. May not her sensibility have
detected the erotic nature of his request, whose motive in Hanold's
eyes lay in its relation to his dream?

After Gradiva's disappearance our hero had a careful look at all
the guests congregated for their mid-day meal at the Hotel Diomède and went on to do the same at the Hotel Suisse, and he was
then able to feel assured that in neither of the only two hotels
known to him in Pompeii was there anyone bearing the remotest
resemblance to Gradiva. He would of course have rejected as
nonsensical the idea that he might actually meet Gradiva in one of [20]
the two inns. And presently the wine pressed from the hot soil of
Vesuvius helped to intensify the whirl of feeling in which he spent
the day.

For the following day one thing only was fixed: that Hanold
must once more be in the House of Meleager at mid-day; and, in
expectation of that moment, he made his way into Pompeii by an
irregular route—over the ancient city wall. A sprig of asphodel,
hung about with its white bell-shaped blossoms, seemed to him
significant enough, as the flower of the underworld, for him to

pluck it and carry it with him. But as he waited, the whole science
of archaeology seemed to him the most pointless and indifferent
thing in the world, for another interest had taken possession of
him: the problem of 'what could be the nature of the bodily
apparition of a being like Gradiva, who was at once dead and, even
though only at the mid-day hour, alive'. (80.) He was fearful, too,
that he might not meet her that day, for perhaps her return could
be permitted only at long intervals; and when he perceived her
once again between the columns, he thought her apparition was
only a trick of his imagination, and in his pain exclaimed: 'Oh! if
only you still existed and lived!' This time, however, he had evidently been too critical, for the apparition possessed a voice, which
asked him if he was meaning to bring her the white flower, and
engaged him, disconcerted once again, in a long conversation.

To his readers, however, to whom Gradiva has already grown of
interest as a living person, the author explains that the displeased
and repelling look which she had given him the day before had
yielded to an expression of searching interest and curiosity. And
indeed she now proceeded to question him, asked for an explanation of his remark on the previous day and enquired when it was
that he had stood beside her as she lay down to sleep. In this way
she learnt of his dream, in which she had perished along with her
native city, and then of the marble relief and the posture of the foot
which had so much attracted the archaeologist. And now she
[21] showed herself ready to demonstrate her gait, and this proved that
the only divergence from the original portrait of Gradiva was that
her sandals were replaced by light sand-coloured shoes of fine
leather—which she explained as being an adaptation to the present
day. She was evidently entering into his delusion, the whole com-
pass of which she elicited from him, without ever contradicting it.
Only once did she seem to be distracted from the part she was
playing, by an emotion of her own; and this was when, with his
thoughts on the relief, he declared that he had recognized her at the
first glance. Since at this stage of their conversation she still knew
nothing about the relief, it was natural for her to misunderstand

Hanold's words; but she quickly recovered herself, and it is only to us that some of her remarks sound as though they had a double sense, as though besides their meaning in the context of the delusion they also meant something real and present-day—for instance, when she regretted that he had not succeeded in confirming the Gradiva gait in his experiments in the streets: 'What a pity! perhaps you would not have had to make the long journey here!' (89.) She also learned that he had given her portrait on the relief the name of 'Gradiva', and told him her real name, 'Zoe'. 'The name suits you beautifully, but it sounds to me like a bitter mockery, for Zoe means life.' 'One must bow to the inevitable', was her reply, 'and I have long grown used to being dead.' Promising to be at the same place again at the mid-day hour next day, she bade him farewell after once more asking him for the sprig of asphodel: 'to those who are more fortunate people give roses in the spring; but to me it is right that you should give the flower of forgetfulness.' No doubt melancholy suited some one who had been so long dead and had returned to life again for a few short hours.

We are beginning to understand now, and to feel some hope. If the young lady in whose form Gradiva had come to life again accepted Hanold's delusion so fully, she was probably doing so in order to set him free from it. There was no other way of doing so; [22] to contradict it would have put an end to any such possibility. Even the serious treatment of a real case of illness of the kind could proceed in no other way than to begin by taking up the same ground as the delusional structure and then investigating it as completely as possible. If Zoe was the right person for the job, we shall soon learn, no doubt, how to cure a delusion like our hero's. We should also be glad to know how such delusions arise. It would be a strange coincidence—but, nevertheless, not without an example or parallel—if the treatment of the delusion were to coincide with its investigation and if the explanation of its origin were to be revealed precisely while it was being dissected. We may suspect, of course, that, if so, our case of illness might end up as a 'commonplace' love-story. But the healing power of love against a delusion is not to be despised—and was not our hero's infatuation for his Gradiva sculpture a complete instance of being in love, though of being in love with something past and lifeless?

After Gradiva's disappearance, there was only a distant sound, like the laughing call of a bird flying over the ruined city. The young man, now by himself, picked up a white object that had been left behind by Gradiva: not a sheet of papyrus, but a sketch-book with pencil drawings of various scenes in Pompeii. We should be inclined to regard her having forgotten the book there as a pledge of her return, for it is our belief that no one forgets anything without some secret reason or hidden motive.

The remainder of the day brought Hanold all manner of strange discoveries and confirmations, which he failed to synthesize into a whole. He perceived to-day in the wall of the portico where Gradiva had vanished a narrow gap, which was wide enough, however, to allow someone unusually slim to pass through it. He recognized that Zoe-Gradiva need not have sunk into the earth here—an idea which now seemed to him so unreasonable that he felt ashamed of having once believed in it; she might well have used [23] the gap as a way of reaching her grave. A slight shadow seemed to him to melt away at the end of the Street of the Tombs in front of what is known as the Villa of Diomedes.

In the same whirl of feeling as on the previous day, and deep in the same problems, he now strolled round the environs of Pompeii. What, he wondered, might be the bodily nature of Zoe-Gradiva? Would one feel anything if one touched her hand? A strange urge drove him to a determination to put this experiment to the test. Yet an equally strong reluctance held him back even from the very idea.

On a sun-bathed slope he met an elderly gentleman who, from his accoutrements, must be a zoologist or botanist and who seemed to be engaged in a hunt. This individual turned towards him and said: 'Are you interested in *faraglionensis* as well? I should hardly have suspected it, but it seems to be quite probable that it occurs not only on the Faraglioni Islands off Capri, but has established itself on the mainland too. The method prescribed by our colleague Eimer[1] is a really good one; I have made use of it many times already with excellent results. Please keep quite still . . .' (96.) Here the speaker broke off and placed a snare made of a long blade of grass in front of a crack in the rocks out of which the small iridescent blue head of a lizard was peering. Hanold left the lizard-hunter with a critical feeling that it was scarcely credible what foolish and strange purposes could lead people to make the long journey to Pompeii—without, needless to say, including in his criticism himself and his intention of searching in the ashes of Pompeii for Gradiva's footprints. Moreover, the gentleman's face seemed familiar, as though he had had a glimpse of it in one of the two hotels; his manner of address, too, had been as though he were speaking to an acquaintance.

In the course of his further walk, he arrived by a side-road at a house which he had not yet discovered and which turned out to be a third hotel, the 'Albergo del Sole'.[2] The landlord, with nothing [24] else to do, took the opportunity of showing off his house and the excavated treasures it contained to their best advantage. He asserted that he had been present when the pair of young lovers had been found in the neighbourhood of the Forum, who, in the knowledge of their inevitable doom, had awaited death closely embraced in each other's arms. Hanold had heard of this before, and had shrugged his shoulders over it as a fabulous tale invented by some imaginative story-teller; but to-day the landlord's words aroused his belief and this was increased when a metal clasp was produced, covered with a green patina, which was said to have been retrieved from the ashes beside the girl's remains. He purchased this clasp without any further critical doubts, and when, as he left the *albergo*, he saw in an open window a nodding sprig of asphodel covered with white blossoms, the sight of the funeral flowers came over him as a confirmation of the genuineness of his new possession.

[1] [A well-known zoologist of the second half of the nineteenth century.]
[2] [The 'Hotel of the Sun'.]

But with the clasp a new delusion took possession of him, or rather the old one had a small piece added to it—no very good augury, it would seem, for the treatment that had been begun. A pair of young lovers in an embrace had been dug out not far from the Forum, and it was in that very neighbourhood, by the Temple of Apollo, that in his dream he had seen Gradiva lie down to sleep [p. 12 f.]. Was it not possible that in fact she had gone further along from the Forum and had met someone and that they had then died together? A tormenting feeling, which we might perhaps liken to jealousy, arose out of this suspicion. He appeased it by reflecting on the uncertainty of the construction, and brought himself to his senses far enough to be able to take his evening meal at the Hotel Diomède. There his attention was drawn by two newly-arrived visitors, a He and a She, whom he was obliged to regard as a brother and sister on account of a certain resemblance between them—in spite of the difference in the colour of their hair. They were the first people he had met on his journey who made a sympathetic impression on him. A red Sorrento rose worn by the [25] girl aroused some kind of memory in him, but he could not think what. At last he went to bed and had a dream. It was a remarkably senseless affair, but was obviously hashed up from his day's experiences. 'Somewhere in the sun Gradiva was sitting, making a snare out of a blade of grass to catch a lizard in, and said: "Please keep quite still. Our lady colleague is right; the method is a really good one and she has made use of it with excellent results."' He fended off this dream while he was still asleep, with the critical thought that it was utter madness, and he succeeded in freeing himself from it with the help of an invisible bird which uttered a short laughing call and carried off the lizard in its beak.

In spite of all this turmoil, he woke up in a rather clearer and steadier frame of mind. A branch of a rose-tree bearing flowers of the sort he had seen the day before on the young lady's breast reminded him that during the night someone had said that people give roses in the spring. Without thinking, he picked a few of the roses, and there must have been something connected with them that had a relaxing effect on his mind. He felt relieved of his

unsociable feelings, and went by the usual way to Pompeii, burdened with the roses, the metal clasp and the sketch-book, and
occupied with a number of problems concerning Gradiva. The old
delusion had begun to show cracks: he was beginning to wonder
whether she might be in Pompeii, not at the mid-day hour only,
but at other times as well. The stress had shifted, however, to the
latest addition, and the jealousy attaching to it tormented him in
all sorts of disguises. He could almost have wished that the apparition might remain visible to his eyes alone, and elude the perception of others: then, in spite of everything, he could look on her as
his own exclusive property. While he was strolling about, waiting
for the mid-day hour, he had an unexpected encounter. In the *Casa
del Fauno* he came upon two figures in a corner in which they must
have thought themselves out of sight, for they were embraced in
each other's arms and their lips were pressed together. He was
astonished to recognize in them the sympathetic couple from the   [26]
previous evening. But their behaviour now did not seem to fit a
brother and sister: their embrace and their kiss seemed to him to
last too long. So after all they were a pair of lovers, presumably a
young honeymoon couple—yet another Edwin and Angelina. Curiously enough, however, this time the sight of them caused him
only satisfaction; and with a sense of awe, as though he had
interrupted some secret act of devotion, he withdrew unobserved.
An attitude of respectfulness, which he had long been without, had
returned to him.

When he reached the House of Meleager, he was once more
overcome by such a violent dread of finding Gradiva in someone
else's company that when she appeared the only words he found to
greet her with were: 'Are you alone?' It was with difficulty that he
allowed her to bring him to realize that he had picked the roses for
her. He confessed his latest delusion to her—that she was the girl
who had been found in the Forum in a lover's embrace and who
had owned the green clasp. She enquired, not without a touch of
mockery, whether he had found the thing in the sun perhaps: the
sun (and she used the [Italian] word '*sole*') produced all kinds of
things like that. He admitted that he was feeling dizzy in his head,

and she suggested as a cure that he should share her small picnic meal with her. She offered him half of a roll wrapped up in tissue paper and ate the other half herself with an obviously good appetite. At the same time her perfect teeth flashed between her lips and made a slight crunching sound as they bit through the crust. 'I feel as though we had shared a meal like this once before, two thousand years ago', she said; 'can't you remember?' (118.) He could think of no reply, but the improvement in his head brought about by the food, and the many indications she gave of her actual presence, were not without their effect on him. Reason began to rise in him and to throw doubt on the whole delusion of Gradiva's being no more than a mid-day ghost—though no doubt it might be argued on the other hand that she herself had just said that she had shared a meal with him two thousand years ago. As a means of settling the conflict an experiment suggested itself: and this he carried out craftily and with regained courage. Her left hand, with its delicate fingers, was resting on her knees, and one of the houseflies whose impertinence and uselessness had so much roused his indignation alighted on it. Suddenly Hanold's hand was raised in the air and descended with a vigorous slap on the fly and Gradiva's hand.

This bold experiment had two results: first, a joyful conviction that he had without any doubt touched a real, living, warm human hand, but afterwards a reproof that made him jump up in a fright from his seat on the steps. For, from Gradiva's lips, when she had recovered from her astonishment, there rang out these words: 'There's no doubt you're out of your mind, Norbert Hanold!' As everyone knows, the best method of waking a sleeper or a sleep-walker is to call him by his own name. But unluckily there was no chance of observing the effects produced on Norbert Hanold by Gradiva's calling him by his name (which he had told no one in Pompeii). For at this critical moment the sympathetic pair of lovers from the *Casa del Fauno* appeared, and the young lady exclaimed in a tone of joyful surprise: 'Zoe! Are you here too? And on your honeymoon like us? You never wrote me a word about it!' In face of this new evidence of Gradiva's living reality, Hanold took flight.

[27]

Nor was Zoe-Gradiva very agreeably surprised by this unexpected visit, which interrupted her in what was apparently an
important task. But she quickly pulled herself together and made a
fluent reply to the question, in which she explained the situation to
her friend—and even more to us—and which enabled her to get rid
of the young couple. She congratulated them; but she was not on
her honeymoon. 'The young man who's just gone off is labouring,
like you, under a remarkable aberration. He seems to think there's a
fly buzzing in his head. Well, I expect everyone has some sort of
insect there. It's my duty to know something about entomology, so
I can help a little in cases like that. My father and I are staying at   [28]
the Sole. Something got into *his* head too, and the.brilliant idea
occurred to him besides of bringing me here with him on condition
that I amused myself on my own at Pompeii and made no demands
of any kind on him. I told myself I should dig out something
interesting here even by myself. Of course I hadn't counted on
making the find that I have—I mean my luck in meeting you,
Gisa.' (124.) But now, she added, she must hurry off, so as to be
company for her father at his lunch in the 'Sun'. And she departed,
after having introduced herself to us as the daughter of the zoologist and lizard-catcher and after having, by all kinds of ambiguous
remarks, admitted her therapeutic intention and other secret designs as well.

The direction she took, however, was not towards the Hotel of
the Sun, where her father was waiting for her. But it seemed to her
too as though a shadowy form was seeking its grave near the Villa of
Diomedes, and was vanishing beneath one of the monuments. And
for that reason she directed her steps toward the Street of the
Tombs, with her foot lifted almost perpendicularly at each step. It
was to this same place that Hanold had fled in his shame and
confusion. He wandered ceaselessly up and down in the portico of
the garden, engaged in the task of disposing of the remains of his
problem by an intellectual effort. One thing had become undeniably clear to him: that he had been totally without sense or reason
in believing that he had been associating with a young Pompeian
woman who had come to life again in a more or less physical shape.

It could not be disputed that this clear insight into his delusion was an essential step forward on his road back to a sound understanding. But, on the other hand, this living woman, with whom other people communicated as though she were as physically real as themselves, was Gradiva, and she knew his name; and his scarcely awakened reason was not strong enough to solve this riddle. He was hardly calm enough emotionally, either, to show himself capable of facing so hard a task, for he would have preferred to have [29] been buried along with the rest two thousand years before in the Villa of Diomedes, so as to be quite certain of not meeting Zoe-Gradiva again.

Nevertheless, a violent desire to see her again struggled against what was left of the inclination to flight still lingering in him.

As he turned one of the four corners of the colonnade, he suddenly recoiled. On a broken fragment of masonry was sitting one of the girls who had perished here in the Villa of Diomedes. This, however, was a last attempt, quickly rejected, at taking flight into the realm of delusion. No, it was Gradiva, who had evidently come to give him the final portion of her treatment. She quite correctly interpreted his first instinctive movement as an attempt to leave the building, and showed him that it was impossible for him to run away, for a terrific downpour of rain had begun outside. She was ruthless, and began her examination by asking him what he had been trying to do with the fly on her hand. He had not the courage to make use of a particular pronoun,[1] but he did have the courage for something more important—for asking her the decisive question:

'As someone said, I was rather confused in my head, and I must apologize for treating the hand . . . I can't understand how I could

[1] [The pronoun of the second person singular. The point of some of what follows is necessarily lost in English. In all his remarks to Gradiva hitherto, Hanold had used the second person singular, partly, no doubt, because that would be the classical usage. Now, however, that he was beginning to realize that he was talking to a modern German girl, he felt that the second person singular was far too familiar and affectionate. Gradiva, on the other hand, had used the second person singular throughout in speaking to him.]

be so senseless . . . but I can't understand either how its owner could point out my . . . my unreasonableness to me by my own name.' (134.)

'So your understanding has not got as far as that, Norbert Hanold. But I can't say I'm surprised at it, you've accustomed me to it so long. I needn't have come to Pompeii to discover it again, and you could have confirmed it a good hundred miles nearer home.

'A hundred miles nearer', she explained, as he still failed to   [30] understand, 'diagonally across the street from where you live—in the house at the corner. There's a cage in my window with a canary in it.'

These last words, as he heard them, affected him like a distant memory: that must have been the same bird whose song had given him the idea of his journey to Italy.

'My father lives in that house: the Professor of Zoology, Richard Bertgang.'

So, since she was his neighbour, she knew him by sight and by name. We feel a sense of disillusionment: the solution falls flat and seems unworthy of our expectations.

Norbert Hanold showed that he had not yet regained his independence of thought when he replied: 'So you[1] . . . you are Fräulein Zoe Bertgang? But she looked quite different . . .'

Fräulein Bertgang's answer shows us that all the same there had been other relations between the two of them besides their simply being neighbours. She could argue in favour of the familiar '*du*', which he had used naturally to the mid-day ghost but had drawn back from in speaking to the live girl, but on behalf of which she claimed ancient rights: 'If you find this formal mode of address more suitable, I can use it too. But I find the other comes to my lips more naturally. I don't know if I looked different in the early days when we used to run about together in a friendly way or sometimes, by way of

---

[1] ['*Sie*', the German pronoun of the third person plural, which is always used in formal speech instead of the '*du*' of the second person singular.]

a change, used to bump and thump each other. But if you[1] had even once looked at me attentively in recent years, it might have dawned on you that I've looked like this for quite a time.'

[31]   So there had been a childhood friendship between them—perhaps a childhood love—which justified the '*du*'. This solution, it may be, falls just as flat as the one we first suspected. We are brought to a much deeper level, however, when we realize that this childhood relationship unexpectedly explains a number of details in what has happened in their contemporary contact. Consider, for instance, the slapping of Zoe-Gradiva's hand. Norbert Hanold found a most convincing reason for it in the necessity for reaching an experimental answer to the problem of the apparition's physical reality. But was it not at the same time remarkably like a revival of the impulse for the 'bumping and thumping' whose dominance in their childhood was shown by Zoe's words? And think, again, of how Gradiva asked the archaeologist whether it did not seem to him that they had shared a meal like this two thousand years before. This unintelligible question suddenly seems to have a sense, if we once more replace the historical past by the personal one— childhood—, of which the girl still had lively memories but which the young man appeared to have forgotten. And now the discovery dawns upon us that the young archaeologist's phantasies about his Gradiva may have been an echo of his forgotten childhood memories. If so, they were not capricious products of his imagination, but determined, without his knowing it, by the store of childhood impressions which he had forgotten, but which were still at work in him. It should be possible for us to show the origin of the phantasies in detail, even though we can only guess at them. He imagined, for instance, that Gradiva must be of *Greek* origin and that she was the daughter of a respected personage—a priest of Ceres, perhaps. This seems to fit in pretty well with his knowing that she bore the Greek name of Zoe and that she belonged to the family of

[1][From this point to the middle of her next speech, when, as will be seen, she finally rebels, Zoe makes a valiant attempt to use the formal '*Sie*'.]

a Professor of Zoology. But if Hanold's phantasies were transformed memories, we may expect to find an indication of the
source of those phantasies in the information given us by Zoe
Bertgang. Let us listen to what she has to say. She has told us of
their intimate friendship in their childhood, and we shall now hear   [32]
of the further course taken by this childhood relationship.

'At that time, as a matter of fact, up to about the age when, I don't
know why, people begin to call us *"Backfisch"*,[1] I had got accustomed to being remarkably dependent on you and believed I
could never in the world find a more agreeable friend. I had no
mother or sister or brother, my father found a slow-worm in spirits
considerably more interesting than me; and everyone (and I include girls) must have *something* to occupy their thoughts and
whatever goes along with them. That was what you were then. But
when archaeology took hold of you I discovered—you must forgive
me, but really your polite innovation sounds to me *too* ridiculous
and, besides, it doesn't fit in with what I want to express—as I was
saying, it turned out that you'd[2] become an unbearable person who
(at any rate so far as I was concerned) no longer had any eyes in his
head or tongue in his mouth, or any memory, where my memory
had stuck, of our friendship when we were children. No doubt that
was why I looked different from before. For when from time to
time I met you in society—it happened once as recently as last
winter—you didn't see me, still less did I hear you say a word.
Not that there was any distinction for me in that, for you treated
everyone else alike. I was thin air for you, and you—with your tuft
of fair hair that I'd rumpled for you often enough in the past—you
were as dull, as dried-up, and as tongue-tied as a stuffed cocka-
too, and at the same time as grandiose as an—*archaeopteryx*—yes,
that's right, that's what they call the antediluvian bird-monstrosity
they've dug up. Only there was one thing I hadn't suspected: that

[1][Literally 'fish for frying'. The common German slang term equivalent to
'flapper' or 'teenager'.]
[2][From this point onwards she finally reverts to '*du*'.]

there was an equally grandiose phantasy lodged in your head of looking on me too, here in Pompeii, as something that had been dug up and come to life again. And when all at once there you were [33] standing in front of me quite unexpectedly, it took me quite a lot of trouble at first to make out what an incredible cobweb your imagination had spun in your brain. After that, it amused me and quite pleased me in spite of its lunacy. For, as I told you, I hadn't suspected it of you.'

Thus she tells us plainly enough what with the years had become of their childhood friendship. In her it grew until she was thoroughly in love, for a girl must have something to which she can give her heart. Fräulein Zoe, the embodiment of cleverness and clarity, makes her own mind quite transparent to us. While it is in any case the general rule for a normally constituted girl to turn her affection towards her father in the first instance, Zoe, who had no one in her family but her father, was especially ready to do so. But her father had nothing left over for her; all his interest was engrossed by the objects of his science. So she was obliged to cast her eyes around upon other people, and became especially attached to her young playmate. When he too ceased to have any eyes for her, her love was not shaken by it but rather increased, for he had become like her father, was, like him, absorbed by science and held apart by it from life and from Zoe. Thus it was made possible for her to remain faithful in her unfaithfulness—to find her father once more in her loved one, to include both of them with the same emotion, or, as we may say, to identify both of them in her feeling. What is our justification for this piece of psychological analysis, which might well seem arbitrary? The author has presented us with it in a single, but highly characteristic, detail. When Zoe described the transformation in her former playmate which had so greatly disturbed her, she abused him by comparing him to an archaeopteryx, the bird-like monstrosity which belongs to the archaeology of zoology. In that way she found a single concrete expression of the identity of the two figures. Her complaint applies with the same word to the [34] man she loved and to her father. The archaeopteryx is, we might say, a compromise idea or an intermediate idea[1] in which her thought about the folly of the man she loved coincided with the analogous thought about her father.

With the young man, things had taken a different turn. Archaeology took hold of him and left him with an interest only in women of marble and bronze. His childhood friendship, instead of being strengthened into a passion, was dissolved, and his memories of it passed into such profound forgetfulness that he did not recognize or notice his early playmate when he met her in society. It is true that when we look further we may doubt whether 'forgetfulness' is the correct psychological description of the fate of these memories in our young archaeologist. There is a kind of forgetting which is distinguished by the difficulty with which the memory is awakened even by a powerful external summons, as though some internal resistance were struggling against its revival. A forgetting of this kind has been given the name of 'repression' in psychopathology; and the case which our author has put before us seems to be an example of this repression. Now we do not know in general whether the forgetting of an impression is linked with the dissolution of its memory-trace in the mind; but we can assert quite definitely of 'repression' that it does not coincide with the dissolution or extinction of the memory. What is repressed cannot, it is true, as a rule make its way into memory without more ado; but it retains a capacity for effective action, and, under the influence of some external event, it may one day bring about psychical consequences which can be regarded as products of a modification of the forgotten memory and as derivatives of it and which remain unintelligible unless we take this view of them. We have already seemed to recognize in Norbert Hanold's phantasies about Gradiva derivatives of his repressed memories of his childhood friendship with Zoe Bertgang. A return like this of [35] what has been repressed is to be expected with particular regular-

---

[1][Ideas of this kind play an important part in dreams and, indeed, wherever the primary psychical process is dominant. See *The Interpretation of Dreams* (1900*a*) *Standard Ed.*, 5, 596. Some good examples are given in Chapter IV of *On Dreams* (1901*a*), ibid., 648 ff.]

ity when a person's erotic feelings are attached to the repressed impressions—when his erotic life has been attacked by repression. In such cases the old Latin saying holds true, though it may have been coined first to apply to expulsion by external influences and not to internal conflicts: 'Naturam expelles furca, tamen usque recurret.'[1] But it does not tell us everything. It only informs of the *fact* of the return of the piece of nature that has been repressed; it does not describe the highly remarkable *manner* of that return, which is accomplished by what seems like a piece of malicious treachery. It is precisely what was chosen as the instrument of repression—like the '*furca*' of the Latin saying—that becomes the vehicle for the return: in and behind the repressing force, what is repressed proves itself victor in the end. This fact, which has been so little noticed and deserves so much consideration, is illustrated— more impressively than it could be by many examples—in a well-known etching by Félicien Rops; and it is illustrated in the typical case of repression in the life of saints and penitents. An ascetic monk has fled, no doubt from the temptations of the world, to the image of the crucified Saviour. And now the cross sinks down like a shadow, and in its place, radiant, there rises instead the image of a voluptuous, naked woman, in the same crucified attitude. Other artists with less psychological insight have, in similar representations of temptation, shown Sin, insolent and triumphant, in some position alongside of the Saviour on the cross. Only Rops has placed Sin in the very place of the Saviour on the cross. He seems to have known that, when what has been repressed returns, it emerges from the repressing force itself.

[36]   It is worth while pausing in order to convince oneself from pathological cases how sensitive a human mind becomes in states of repression to any approach by what has been repressed, and how even trivial similarities suffice for the repressed to emerge behind the repressing force and take effect by means of it. I once had under medical treatment a young man—he was still almost a boy—who,

---

[1] ['You may drive out Nature with a pitchfork, but she will always return.' This is actually a line of Horace (*Epistles*, **I**, 10, 24). It is misquoted in the German editions.]

after he had first unwillingly become acquainted with the processes of sex, had taken flight from every sexual desire that arose in him. For that purpose he made use of various methods of repression: he intensified his zeal in learning, exaggerated his dependence on his mother, and in general assumed a childish character. I will not here enter into the manner in which his repressed sexuality broke through once more precisely in his relation to his mother; but I will describe a rarer and stranger instance of how another of his bulwarks collapsed on an occasion which could scarcely be regarded as sufficient. Mathematics enjoys the greatest reputation as a diversion from sexuality. This had been the very advice to which Jean-Jacques Rousseau was obliged to listen from a lady who was dissatisfied with him: 'Lascia le donne e studia la matematica!'[1] So too our fugitive threw himself with special eagerness into the mathematics and geometry which he was taught at school, till suddenly one day his powers of comprehension were paralysed in the face of some apparently innocent problems. It was possible to establish two of these problems: 'Two bodies come together, one with a speed of . . . etc.' and 'On a cylinder, the diameter of whose surface is *m*, describe a cone . . . etc.' Other people would certainly not have regarded these as very striking allusions to sexual events; but he felt that he had been betrayed by mathematics as well, and took flight from it too.

If Norbert Hanold were someone in real life who had in this way banished love and his childhood friendship with the help of archaeology, it would have been logical and according to rule that what revived in him the forgotten memory of the girl he had loved in his childhood should be precisely an antique sculpture. It would have been his well-deserved fate to fall in love with the marble portrait of Gradiva, behind which, owing to an unexplained similarity, the [37] living Zoe whom he had neglected made her influence felt.

Fräulein Zoe seems herself to have shared our view of the young archaeologist's delusion, for the satisfaction she expressed at the

[1] ['Give up women and study mathematics!']

end of her 'frank, detailed and instructive speech of castigation' could scarcely have been based on anything but a recognition that from the very first his interest in Gradiva had related to herself. It was *this* which she had not expected of him, but which, in spite of all its delusional disguise, she saw for what it was. The psychical treatment she had carried out, however, had now accomplished its beneficent effect on him. He felt free, for his delusion had now been replaced by the thing of which it could only have been a distorted and inadequate copy. Nor could he any longer hesitate to remember her and to recognize her as the kind, cheerful, clever playmate who in essentials was not in any way changed. But he found something else very strange—

'You mean', said the girl, 'the fact of someone having to die so as to come alive; but no doubt that must be so for archaeologists.' (141.) Evidently she had not forgiven him yet for the roundabout path by way of archaeology which he had followed from their childhood friendship to the new relation that was forming.

'No, I mean your name . . . Because "Bertgang" means the same as "Gradiva" and describes someone "who steps along brilliantly".'[1] (142.)

We ourselves were unprepared for this. Our hero was beginning to cast off his humility and to play an active part. Evidently he was completely cured of his delusion and had risen above it; and he proved this by himself tearing the last threads of the cobweb of his delusion. This, too, is just how patients behave when one has loosened the compulsion of their delusional thoughts by revealing [38] the repressed material lying behind them. Once they have understood, they themselves bring forward the solutions of the final and most important riddles of their strange condition in a number of ideas that suddenly occur to them. We had already guessed that the Greek origin of the imaginary Gradiva was an obscure result of the Greek name 'Zoe'; but we had not ventured to approach the name

[1][The German root '*bert*' or '*brecht*' is akin to the English 'bright'; similarly '*gang*' is akin to 'go' (in Scotland 'gang').]

'Gradiva' itself, and had let it pass as the untrammelled creation of Norbert Hanold's imagination. But, lo and behold! that very name now turns out to have been a derivative—indeed a translation—of the repressed surname of the girl he had loved in the childhood which he was supposed to have forgotten.

The tracing back of the delusion and its resolution were now complete. What the author now adds is no doubt designed to serve as a harmonious end to his story. We cannot but feel reassured about the future when we hear that the young man, who had earlier been obliged to play the pitiable part of a person in urgent need of treatment, advanced still further on the road to recovery and succeeded in arousing in her some of the feelings under which he himself had suffered before. Thus it was that he made her jealous by mentioning the sympathetic young lady who had previously interrupted their tête-à-tête in the House of Meleager, and by confessing that she had been the first woman for whom he had felt a very great liking. Whereupon Zoe prepared to take a chilly leave of him, remarking that everything had now returned to reason— she herself not least; he could look up Gisa Hartleben (or whatever she was now called) again and give her some scientific assistance over the purpose of her visit to Pompeii; she herself, however, must go back to the Albergo del Sole where her father was expecting her for lunch; perhaps they would meet again some time at a party in Germany or in the moon. But once more he was able to make the troublesome fly an excuse for taking possession first of her cheek and then of her lips, and to set in motion the aggressiveness which is a man's inevitable duty in love-making. Once only a shadow seemed to fall on their happiness, when Zoe declared that now she [39] really must go back to her father or he will starve at the Sole. 'Your father? . . . what will happen? . . .' (147.) But the clever girl was able swiftly to quiet his concern. 'Probably nothing will happen. I'm not an indispensable part of his zoological collection. If I had been, perhaps I shouldn't have been so foolish as to give my heart to you.' In the exceptional event, however, of her father taking a different view from hers, there was a safe expedient. Hanold need only cross to Capri, catch a *Lacerta faraglionensis* there (he could practise the technique on her little finger), set the creature free over here, catch it again before the zoologist's eyes, and let him choose between a *faraglionensis* on the mainland and his daughter. The scheme, it is easy to see, was one in which the mockery was tinged with bitterness; it was a warning, as it were, to her fiancé not to keep too closely to the model on which she had chosen him. Here again Norbert Hanold reassures us, by showing all sorts of apparently small signs the great transformation that had taken place in him. He proposed that he and his Zoe should come for their honeymoon to Italy and Pompeii, just as though he had never been indignant with the honeymooning Edwins and Angelinas. He had completely lost from his memory all his feelings against those happy pairs, who had so unnecessarily travelled more than a hundred miles from their German home. The author is certainly right in bringing forward a loss of memory like this as the most trustworthy sign of a change of attitude. Zoe's reply to the plan for the scene of their honeymoon suggested by 'her childhood friend who had also in a sense been dug out of the ruins again' (150) was that she did not feel quite alive enough yet to make a geographical decision of that sort.

The delusion had now been conquered by a beautiful reality; but before the two lovers left Pompeii it was still to be honoured once again. When they reached the Herculanean Gate, where, at the entrance to the Via Consolare, the street is crossed by some ancient [40] stepping-stones, Norbert Hanold paused and asked the girl to go ahead of him. She understood him, 'and, pulling up her dress a little with her left hand, Zoe Bertgang, Gradiva *rediviva*, walked past, held in his eyes, which seemed to gaze as though in a dream; so, with her quietly tripping gait, she stepped through the sunlight over the stepping-stones to the other side of the street.' With the triumph of love, what was beautiful and precious in the delusion found recognition as well.

In his last smile, however,—of the 'childhood friend who had been dug out of the ruins'—the author has presented us with the key to the symbolism of which the hero's delusion made use in disguising his repressed memory. There is, in fact, no better analogy for repression, by which something in the mind is at once made inaccessible and preserved, than burial of the sort to which Pompeii fell a victim and from which it could emerge once more through the work of spades. Thus it was that the young archaeologist was obliged in his phantasy to transport to Pompeii the original of the relief which reminded him of the object of his youthful love. The author was well justified, indeed, in lingering over the valuable similarity which his delicate sense had perceived between a particular mental process in the individual and an isolated historical event in the history of mankind.[1]

[1][Freud himself adopted the fate of Pompeii as a simile for representation in more than one later passage. See, for instance, the 'Rat Man, case history (1909*d*), written not long after the present work, *Standard Ed.*, **10**, 176–7.]

II

[41] BUT after all, what we really intended to do originally was only to investigate two or three dreams that are to be found here and there in *Gradiva* with the help of certain analytic methods. How has it come about, then, that we have been led into dissecting the whole story and examining the mental processes in the two chief characters? This has not in fact been an unnecessary piece of work; it was an essential preliminary. It is equally the case that when we try to understand the real dreams of a real person we have to concern ourselves intensively with his character and his career, and we must get to know not only his experiences shortly before the dream but also those dating far back into the past. It is even my view that we are still not free to turn to our proper task, but that we must linger a little more over the story itself and carry out some further preliminary work.

My readers will no doubt have been puzzled to notice that so far I have treated Norbert Hanold and Zoe Bertgang, in all their mental manifestations and activities, as though they were real people and not the author's creations, as though the author's mind were an absolutely transparent medium and not a refractive or obscuring one. And my procedure must seem all the more puzzling since the author has expressly renounced the portrayal of reality by calling his story a 'phantasy'. We have found, however, that all his descriptions are so faithfully copied from reality that we should not object if *Gradiva* were described not as a phantasy but as a psychiatric study. Only at two points has the author availed himself of the licence open to him of laying down premisses which do not seem to have their roots in the laws of reality. The first time is where he makes the young archaeologist come upon what is undoubtedly an ancient relief but which so closely resembles a person living long-afterwards, not only in the peculiarity of the posture of the foot as it [42] steps along but in every detail of facial structure and bodily attitude, that the young man is able to take the physical appearance of that person to be the sculpture come to life. And the second time is where he makes the young man meet the living woman precisely in

36

Pompeii; for the dead woman had been placed there only by his imagination, and the journey to Pompeii had in fact carried him away from the living woman, whom he had just seen in the street of the town in which he lived. This second provision of the author's, however, involves no violent departure from actual possibility; it merely makes use of chance, which unquestionably plays a part in many human histories; and furthermore he uses it to good purpose, for this chance reflects the fatal truth that has laid it down that flight is precisely an instrument that delivers one over to what one is fleeing from. The first premiss seems to lean more towards phantasy and to spring entirely from the author's arbitrary decision—the premiss on which all that follows depends, the far-reaching resemblance between the sculpture and the live girl, which a more sober choice might have restricted to the single feature of the posture of the foot as it steps along. We might be tempted here to allow the play of our own phantasy to forge a link with reality. The name of 'Bertgang' might point to the fact that the women of that family had already been distinguished in ancient days by the peculiarity of their graceful gait; and we might suppose that the Germanic Bertgangs were descended from a Roman family one member of which was the woman who had led the artist to perpetuate the peculiarity of her gait in the sculpture. Since, however, the different variations of the human form are not independent of one another, and since in fact even among ourselves the ancient types re-appear again and again (as we can see in art collections), it would not be totally impossible that a modern Bertgang might reproduce the shape of her ancient ancestress in all the other features of her bodily structure as well. But it would no doubt be wiser, instead of such speculations, to enquire from the [43] author himself what were the sources from which this part of his creation was derived; we should then have a good prospect of showing once again how what was ostensibly an arbitrary decision rested in fact upon law. But since access to the sources in the author's mind is not open to us,[1] we will leave him with an undiminished right to construct a development that is wholly true

[1] [Cf. the 'Postscript' to this work, p. 85 below.]

to life upon an improbable premiss—a right of which Shakespeare, for instance, availed himself in *King Lear*.[1]

Apart from this, it must be repeated, the author has presented us with a perfectly correct psychiatric study, on which we may measure our understanding of the workings of the mind—a case history and the history of a cure which might have been designed to emphasize certain fundamental theories of medical psychology. It is strange enough that the author should have done this. But how if, on being questioned, he were completely to deny any such purpose? It is so easy to draw analogies and to read meanings into things. Is it not rather we who have slipped into this charming poetic story a secret meaning very far from its author's intentions? Possibly. We shall come back to the question later. For the moment, however, we have tried to save ourselves from making any such tendentious interpretation by giving the story almost entirely in the author's own words. Anyone who compares our reproduction with the actual text of *Gradiva* will have to concede us that much.

Perhaps, too, in most people's eyes we are doing our author a poor service in declaring his work to be a psychiatric study. An author, we hear them say, should keep out of the way of any contact with psychiatry and should leave the description of pathological mental states to the doctors. The truth is that no truly creative writer has ever obeyed this injunction. The description of the human mind is indeed the domain which is most his own; he has from time immemorial been the precursor of science, and so too of scientific psychology. But the frontier between states of mind described as normal and pathological is in part a conventional one and in part so fluctuating that each of us probably crosses it many times in the course of a day. On the other hand, psychiatry would be doing wrong if it tried to restrict itself permanently to the study of the severe and gloomy illnesses that arise from gross injuries to the delicate apparatus of the mind. Deviations from health which

[44]

[1] [Some further comment on the 'improbable premiss' to *King Lear* will be found at the end of Freud's paper on 'The Theme of the Three Caskets' (1913*f*), *Standard Ed.*, **12**, 301.]

are slighter and capable of correction, and which to-day we can trace back no further than to disturbances in the interplay of mental forces, arouse its interest no less. Indeed, only through the medium of these can it understand either normal states or the phenomena of severe illness. Thus the creative writer cannot evade the psychiatrist nor the psychiatrist the creative writer, and the poetic treatment of a psychiatric theme can turn out to be correct without any sacrifice of its beauty.[1]

And it is really correct—this imaginative picture of the history of a case and its treatment. Now that we have finished telling the story and satisfied our own suspense, we can get a better view of it, and we shall now reproduce it with the technical terminology of our science, and in doing so we shall not feel disconcerted at the necessity for repeating what we have said before.

Norbert Hanold's condition is often spoken of by the author as a 'delusion', and we have no reason to reject that designation. We can state two chief characteristics of a 'delusion', which do not, it is true, describe it exhaustively, but which distinguish it recognizably from other disorders. In the first place it is one of the group of pathological states which do not produce a direct effect upon the body but are manifested only by mental indications. And secondly it is characterized by the fact that in it 'phantasies' have gained the [45] upper hand—that is, have obtained belief and have acquired an influence on action. If we recall Hanold's journey to Pompeii in order to look for Gradiva's peculiarly formed footprints in the ashes, we shall have a fine example of an action under the dominance of a delusion. A psychiatrist would perhaps place Norbert Hanold's delusion in the great group of 'paranoia' and possibly describe it as 'fetishistic erotomania', because the most striking thing about it was his being in love with the piece of sculpture and because in the psychiatrist's view, with its tendency to coarsen

[1][Another discussion by Freud of the use of psychopathological material by creative writers will be found in a posthumously published essay, 'Psychopathic Characters on the Stage' (1942*a*), probably written a year or two before the present work.]

everything, the young archaeologist's interest in feet and the postures of feet would be bound to suggest 'fetishism'. Nevertheless all such systems of nomenclature and classification of the different kinds of delusion according to their subject-matter have something precarious and barren about them.[1]

Furthermore, since our hero was a person capable of developing a delusion on the basis of such a strange preference, a strict psychiatrist would at once stamp him as a *dégénéré* and would investigate the heredity which had remorselessly driven him to this fate. But here the author does not follow the psychiatrist, and with good reason. He wishes to bring the hero closer to us so as to make 'empathy' easier; the diagnosis of '*dégénéré*', whether it is right or wrong, at once puts the young archaeologist at a distance from us, for we readers are the normal people and the standard of humanity. Nor is the author greatly concerned with the hereditary and constitutional preconditions of the state, but on the other hand he plunges deep into the personal mental make-up which can give rise to such a delusion.

In one important respect Norbert Hanold behaved quite differently from an ordinary human being. He took no interest in living women; the science of which he was the servant had taken [46] that interest away from him and displaced it on to women of marble or bronze. This is not to be regarded as a trivial peculiarity; on the contrary, it was the basic precondition of the events to be described. For one day it came about that one particular sculpture of that kind laid claim to the whole of the interest which is ordinarily directed only to a living woman, and with that his delusion was there. We then see unrolled before our eyes the manner in which his delusion is cured through a happy turn of events, and his interest displaced back from the marble to a living woman. The author does not let us follow the influences which led our hero to turn away from women; he only informs us that his attitude was not explained by his innate disposition, which, on the contrary,

[1] In point of fact, the case of N. H. would have to be described as a *hysterical* delusion, not a paranoic one. The indications of paranoia are absent from it.

included some amount of imaginative (and, we might add, erotic) needs. And, as we learn later in the story, he did not avoid other children in his childhood: he had a friendship at that age with a little girl, was her inseparable companion, shared his little meals with her, used to thump her too and let her rumple his hair. It is in attachments such as this, in combinations like this of affection and aggressiveness, that the immature erotism of childhood finds its expression; its consequences only emerge later, but then they are irresistible, and during childhood itself it is as a rule recognized as erotism only by doctors and creative writers. Our own writer shows us clearly that he too is of the same opinion; for he makes his hero suddenly develop a lively interest in women's feet and their way of placing them. This interest was bound to bring him a bad reputation both among scientists and among the women of the town he lived in, a reputation of being a foot-fetishist; but *we* cannot avoid tracing the interest back to the memory of his childhood playmate. For there can be no doubt that even in her childhood the girl showed the same peculiarity of a graceful gait, with her toes almost perpendicularly raised as she stepped along; and it was because it represented that same gait that an ancient marble relief acquired such great importance for Norbert Hanold. Incidentally we may add that in his derivation of the remarkable phenomenon of fetishism the author is in complete agreement with science. Ever since Binet [1888] we have in fact tried to trace fetishism back to erotic impressions in childhood.[1]

[47]

The state of permanently turning away from women produces a personal susceptibility, or, as we are accustomed to say, a 'disposition' to the formation of a delusion. The development of the mental disorder sets in at the moment when a chance impression arouses the childhood experiences which have been forgotten and which have traces, at least, of an erotic colouring. 'Arouses', how-

---

[1] [Binet's views on fetishism were described in Freud's *Three Essays on the Theory of Sexuality* (1905*d*), to which however he added a footnote in 1920 casting doubts on their adequacy. A number of references to other discussions of fetishism in Freud's own writings are given in another footnote to the same passage (*Standard Ed.*, 7, 154–5).]

ever, is certainly not the right description, if we take into account
what follows. We must repeat the author's accurate account in
correct psychological technical terms. When Norbert Hanold saw
the relief, he did not remember that he had already seen a similar posture of the foot in his childhood friend; he remembered
nothing at all, but all the effects brought about by the relief
originated from this link that was made with the impression of his
childhood. Thus the childhood impression was stirred up, it became active, so that it began to produce effects, but it did not come
into consciousness—it remained 'unconscious', to use a term which
has to-day become unavoidable in psychopathology. We are anxious that this unconscious shall not be involved in any of the
disputes of philosophers and natural philosophers, which have
often no more than an etymological importance. For the time
being we possess no better name for psychical processes which
behave actively but nevertheless do not reach the consciousness of
the person concerned, and that is all we mean by our 'unconsciousness'. When some thinkers try to dispute the existence of an
unconscious of this kind, on the ground that it is nonsensical,
we can only suppose that they have never had to do with the
[48]   corresponding mental phenomena, that they are under the spell
of the regular experience that everything mental that becomes
active and intense becomes at the same time conscious as well, and
that they have still to learn (what our author knows very well) that
there are most certainly mental processes which, in spite of being
intense and producing effects, none the less remain apart from
consciousness.

We said a little earlier [p. 34 ff.] that Norbert Hanold's memories
of his childhood relations with Zoe were in a state of 'repression';
and here we have called them 'unconscious' memories. So we must
now pay a little attention to the relation between these two technical terms, which, indeed, appear to coincide in their meaning. It is
not difficult to make the matter plain. 'Unconscious' is the wider
concept; 'repressed' is the narrower one. Everything that is repressed is unconscious; but we cannot assert that everything unconscious is repressed. If when Hanold saw the relief he had

remembered his Zoe's gait, what had earlier been an unconscious memory of his would have become simultaneously active and conscious, and this would have shown that it had not earlier been repressed. 'Unconscious' is a purely descriptive term, one that is indefinite in some respects and, as we might say, static. 'Repressed' is a dynamic expression, which takes account of the interplay of mental forces; it implies that there is a force present which is seeking to bring about all kinds of psychical effects, including that of becoming conscious, but that there is also an opposing force which is able to obstruct some of these psychical effects, once more including that of becoming conscious. The mark of something repressed is precisely that in spite of its intensity it is unable to enter consciousness. In Hanold's case, therefore, from the moment of the appearance of the relief onwards, we are concerned with something unconscious that is repressed, or, more briefly, with something repressed.

Norbert Hanold's memories of his childhood relations with the girl with the graceful gait were repressed; but this is not yet the correct view of the psychological situation. We remain on the surface so long as we are dealing only with memories and ideas. What [49] is alone of value in mental life is rather the feelings. No mental forces are significant unless they possess the characteristic of arousing feelings. Ideas are only repressed because they are associated with the release of feelings which ought not to occur. It would be more correct to say that repression acts upon feelings, but we can only be aware of these in their association with ideas.[1] So that it was Norbert Hanold's erotic feelings that were repressed; and since his erotism knew and had known no other object than Zoe Bertgang in his childhood, his memories of her were forgotten. The ancient relief aroused the slumbering erotism in him, and made his childhood memories active. On account of a resistance to erotism that was present in him, these memories could only become operative as unconscious ones. What now took place in him was a struggle

[1][Some of this would need to be expressed differently in order to fit in with Freud's later and more elaborate discussions of repression, which are to be found, for instance, in Sections III and IV of his paper on 'The Unconscious' (1915*e*).]

between the power of erotism and that of the forces that were repressing it; the manifestation of this struggle was a delusion.

Our author has omitted to give the reasons which led to the repression of the erotic life of his hero; for of course Hanold's concern with science was only the instrument which the repression employed. A doctor would have to dig deeper here, but perhaps without hitting upon the reason in this case. But, as we have insisted with admiration, the author has not failed to show us how the arousing of the repressed erotism came precisely from the field of the instruments that served to bring about the repression. It was right that an antique, the marble sculpture of a woman, should have been what tore our archaeologist away from his retreat from love and warned him to pay off the debt to life with which we are burdened from our birth.

The first manifestations of the process that had been set going in Hanold by the relief were phantasies, which played around the figure represented in it. The figure seemed to him to have something 'of to-day' about her, in the best sense of the words, and it was as though the artist had captured her 'from the life' stepping along the street. He gave the girl in the ancient relief the name of 'Gradiva', which he constructed on the model of an epithet of the war-god striding into battle—'Mars Gradivus'. He endowed her personality with more and more characteristics. She may have been the daughter of a respected personage, of a patrician, perhaps, who was connected with the temple-service of a deity. He thought he could trace a Greek origin in her features; and finally he felt compelled to remove her from the busy life of a capital and to transport her to the more peaceful Pompeii, and there he made her step across the lava stepping-stones which made it possible to cross from one side of the street to the other. [P. 11.] These products of his phantasy seem arbitrary enough, but at the same time innocently unsuspicious. And, indeed, even when for the first time they gave rise to an incitement to action—when the archaeologist, obsessed by the problem of whether this posture of the feet corresponded to reality, began to make observations from life in order to examine the feet of contemporary women and girls—even this action was

[50]

screened by conscious scientific motives, as though all his interest
in the sculpture of Gradiva had sprung from the soil of his profes-
sional concern with archaeology. [P. 12.] The women and girls in
the street, whom he chose as the subjects of his investigation, must,
of course, have taken another, crudely erotic view of his behaviour,
and we cannot but think them right. We ourselves can be in no
doubt that Hanold was as much in ignorance of the motives of his
researches as he was of the origin of his phantasies about Gradiva.
These, as we learned later, were echoes of his memories of his
youthful love, derivatives of those memories, transformations and
distortions of them, after they had failed to make their way into his
consciousness in an unmodified form. The ostensibly aesthetic
judgement that the sculpture had something 'of to-day' about it
took the place of his knowledge that a gait of that kind belonged to   [51]
a girl whom he knew and who stepped across the street *at the
present time.* Behind the impression of the sculpture being 'from the
life' and the phantasy of its subject being Greek lay his memory of
the name Zoe, which means 'life' in Greek. 'Gradiva', as we learn
from our hero himself at the end of the story, after he has been
cured of his delusion, is a good translation of the surname 'Bertgang' which means something like 'someone who steps along
brilliantly or splendidly'. [P. 37.] The details about Gradiva's father
originated from Hanold's knowledge that Zoe Bertgang was the
daughter of a respected teacher at the University, which can well be
translated into classical terms as 'temple-service'. Finally, his phantasy transported her to Pompeii, not 'because her quiet, calm
nature seemed to demand it', but because no other or better
analogy could be found in his science for his remarkable state, in
which he became aware of his memories of his childhood friendship through obscure channels of information. Once he had made
his own childhood coincide with the classical past (which it was so
easy for him to do), there was a perfect similarity between the
burial of Pompeii—the disappearance of the past combined with its
preservation—and repression, of which he possessed a knowledge
through what might be described as 'endopsychic' perception. In
this he was employing the same symbolism that the author makes

the girl use consciously towards the conclusion of the story: 'I told
myself I should be able to dig out something interesting here even
by myself. Of course I hadn't counted on making the find that I
have . . .' (124 [p. 28].) And at the very end she replied to Hanold's
plan for their honeymoon with a reference to 'her childhood friend
who had also in a sense been dug out of the ruins again'. (150
[p. 39].)

Thus in the very first products of Hanold's delusional phantasies
and actions we already find a double set of determinants, a derivation from two different sources. One of these is the one that was
manifest to Hanold himself, the other is the one which is revealed
[52]   to us when we examine his mental processes. One of them, looked
at from Hanold's point of view, was conscious to him, the other was
completely unconscious to him. One of them was derived wholly
from the circle of ideas of the science of archaeology, the other arose
from the repressed childhood memories that had become active in
him and from the emotional instincts attached to them. One might
be described as lying on the surface and covering the other, which
was, as it were, concealed behind it. The scientific motivation
might be said to serve as a pretext for the unconscious erotic one,
and science had put itself completely at the service of the delusion.
It should not be forgotten, however, that the unconscious determinants could not effect anything that did not simultaneously satisfy
the conscious, scientific ones. The symptoms of a delusion—phantasies and actions alike—are in fact the products of compromise between the two mental currents, and in a compromise account is
taken of the demands of each of the two parties to it; but each side
must also renounce a part of what it wanted to achieve. Where a
compromise comes about it must have been preceded by a struggle—in this case it was the conflict we have assumed between
suppressed erotism and the forces that were keeping it in repression. In the formation of a delusion this struggle is in fact unend-
ing. Assault and resistance are renewed after the construction of
each compromise, which is never, so to speak, entirely satisfying.
Our author too is aware of this, and that is why he makes a peculiar

unrest dominate this stage of his hero's disorder, as a precursor and guarantee of further developments.

These significant peculiarities—the double motivation of phantasies and decisions, and the construction of conscious pretexts for actions to whose motivation the repressed has made the major contribution—will meet us often, and perhaps more clearly, in the further course of the story. And this is just as it should be, for the author has thus grasped and represented the unfailing chief characteristic of pathological mental processes.

The development of Norbert Hanold's delusion proceeded with a dream which, since it was not occasioned by any new event, seems to have arisen entirely out of his mind, filled as it was by a conflict. But let us pause before we enquire whether, in the construction of his dreams, too, the author meets our expectation that he possesses a deep understanding. Let us ask first what psychiatric science has to say to his hypotheses about the origin of a delusion and what attitude it takes to the part played by repression and the unconscious, to conflict and to the formation of compromises. In short, let us ask whether this imaginative representation of the genesis of a delusion can hold its own before the judgement of science. [53]

And here we must give what will perhaps be an unexpected answer. In fact the situation is quite the reverse: it is science that cannot hold its own before the achievement of the author. Science allows a gulf to yawn between the hereditary and constitutional preconditions of a delusion and its creations, which seem to emerge ready-made—a gulf which we find that our author has filled. Science does not as yet suspect the importance of repression, it does not recognize that in order to explain the world of psychopathological phenomena the unconscious is absolutely essential, it does not look for the basis of delusions in a psychical conflict, and it does not regard their symptoms as compromises. Does our author stand alone, then, in the face of united science? No, that is not the case (if, that is, I may count my own works as part of science), since for a

number of years—and, until recently more or less alone[1]—I myself
have supported all the views that I have here extracted from Jensen's
Gradiva and stated in technical terms. I indicated, in most detail in
connection with the states known as hysteria and obsessions, that
the individual determinant[2] of these psychical disorders is the
suppression of a part of instinctual life and the repression of the
ideas by which the suppressed instinct is represented, and soon
afterwards I repeated the same views in relation to some forms of
delusion.[3] The question whether the instincts concerned in this
causation are always components of the sexual instinct or may be of
another kind as well is a problem which may be regarded as a
matter of indifference in the particular case of the analysis of
Gradiva; for in the instance chosen by our author what was at issue
was quite certainly nothing other than the suppression of erotic
feelings. The validity of the hypotheses of psychical conflict and of
the formation of symptoms by means of compromises between the
two mental currents struggling against each other has been demonstrated by me in the case of patients observed and medically treated
in real life, just as I have been able to in the imaginary case of
Norbert Hanold.[4] Even before me, Pierre Janet, a pupil of the great
Charcot, and Josef Breuer, in collaboration with me, had traced
back the products of neurotic, and especially of hysterical, illness to
the power of unconscious thoughts.[5]

When, from the year 1893 onwards, I plunged into investigations
such as these of the origin of mental disturbances, it would certainly never have occurred to me to look for a confirmation of my

[1]See Bleuler's important work, *Affektivität, Suggestibilität, Paranoia* and C. G.
Jung's *Diagnostische Assoziationsstudien*, both published in Zurich in 1906.—
[*Added* 1912:] To-day, in 1912, I am able to retract what is said above as being no
longer true. Since it was written, the 'psycho-analytic movement' started by me
has become widely extended, and it is constantly growing.

[2][As contrasted, presumably, with a more general, inherited factor.]

[3]See the author's *Sammlung kleiner Schriften zur Neurosenlehre*, 1906 [in
particular the second paper on 'The Neuro-Psychoses of Defence' (1896*b*)].

[4]Cf. 'Fragment of an Analysis of a Case of Hysteria' (1905*e*).

[5]Cf. *Studies on Hysteria* (Freud, 1895*d*, with Breuer).

findings in imaginative writings. I was thus more than a little surprised to find that the author of *Gradiva*, which was published in 1903, had taken as the basis of its creation the very thing that I believed myself to have freshly discovered from the sources of my medical experience. How was it that the author arrived at the same knowledge as the doctor—or at least behaved as though he possessed the same knowledge?

Norbert Hanold's delusion, as I was saying, was carried a step further by a dream which occurred in the middle of his efforts to discover a gait like Gradiva's in the streets of the town where he lived. It is easy to give the content of this dream in brief. The dreamer found himself in Pompeii on the day on which that unhappy city was destroyed, and experienced its horrors without being in danger himself; he suddenly saw Gradiva stepping along there, and understood all at once, as though it was something quite natural, that since she was a Pompeian, she was living in her native town, and 'without his having suspected it, living as his contemporary' [p. 12]. He was seized with fear on her account and gave a warning cry, whereupon she turned her face towards him for a moment. But she proceeded on her way without paying any attention to him, lay down on the steps of the Temple of Apollo, and was buried in the rain of ashes after her face had lost its colour, as though it were turning into white marble, until it had become just like a piece of sculpture. As he was waking up, he interpreted the noises of a big city penetrating into his bedroom as the cries for help of the despairing inhabitants of Pompeii and the thunder of the wildly agitated sea. The feeling that what he had dreamt had really happened to him would not leave him for some time after he had awoken, and a conviction that Gradiva had lived in Pompeii and had perished there on the fatal day was left over with him by the dream as a fresh starting-point for his delusion.

It is not so easy for us to say what the author intended with this dream and what caused him to link the development of the delusion precisely to a dream. Zealous investigators, it is true, have

[55]

collected plenty of examples of the way in which mental disturbances are linked to dreams and arise out of dreams.[1] It appears,
too, that in the lives of a few eminent men impulses to important
actions and decisions have originated from dreams. But these
analogies are not of much help to our understanding; so let us keep
to our present case, our author's imaginary case of Norbert Hanold
[56]   the archaeologist. By which end are we to take hold of a dream like
this so as to fit it into the whole context, if it is not to remain no
more than an unnecessary decoration of the story?

I can well imagine that at this point a reader may exclaim: 'The
dream is quite easily explained—it is a simple anxiety-dream,
occasioned by the noises of the city, which were misinterpreted into
the destruction of Pompeii by the archaeologist, whose mind was
occupied with his Pompeian girl.' In view of the low opinion
generally prevailing of the performances of dreams, all that is
usually asked from an explanation of one is that some external
stimulus shall be found that more or less coincides with a piece of
the dream's content. This external stimulus to dreaming would be
supplied by the noise which woke the sleeper; and with this,
interest in the dream would be exhausted. If only we had some
reason for supposing that the town was noisier than usual that
morning! If only, for instance, the author had not omitted to tell us
that Hanold, against his usual practice, had slept that night with
his windows open! What a pity the author did not take the trouble
to do that! And if only anxiety-dreams were as simple as that! But
no, interest in the dream is not so easily exhausted.

There is nothing essential for the construction of a dream in a
link with an external sensory stimulus. A sleeper can disregard a
stimulus of this kind from the external world, or he can allow
himself to be awakened by it without constructing a dream, or, as
happened here, he can weave it into his dream if that suits him for
some other reason; and there are numerous dreams of which it is
impossible to show that their content was determined in this way

[1]Sante de Sanctis (1899). [Cf. *The Interpretation of Dreams* (1900a), Chapter I,
Section H, *Standard Ed.*, 4, 88 ff.]

by a stimulus impinging on the sleeper's senses.[1] No, we must try another path.

We may perhaps find a starting-point in the after-effects left by the dream in Hanold's waking life. Up to then he had had a phantasy that Gradiva had been a Pompeian. This hypothesis now became a certainty for him, and a second certainty followed—that she was buried along with the rest in the year 79 A.D.[2] Melancholy feelings accompanied this extension of the delusional structure, like an echo of the anxiety which had filled the dream. This fresh pain about Gradiva does not seem very intelligible to us; Gradiva would have been dead for many centuries even if she had been saved from destruction in the year 79 A.D. Or ought we not to argue in this kind of way either with Norbert Hanold or with the author himself? Here again there seems no path to an understanding. Nevertheless it is worth remarking that the increment which the delusion acquired from this dream was accompanied by a feeling with a highly painful colouring.

Apart from that, however, we are as much at a loss as before. This dream is not self-explanatory, and we must resolve to borrow from my *Interpretation of Dreams* and apply to the present example a few of the rules to be found in it for the solution of dreams.

One of these rules is to the effect that a dream is invariably related to the events of the day before the dream.[3] Our author seems to be wishing to show that he has followed this rule, for he attaches the dream immediately to Hanold's 'pedestrian researches'. Now these had no meaning other than a search for Gradiva, whose characteristic gait he was trying to recognize. So the dream ought to have contained an indication of where Gradiva was to be found. And it does so, by showing her in Pompeii; but that is no novelty to us.

Another rule tells us that, if a belief in the reality of the dream-images persists unusually long, so that one cannot tear oneself out

[57]

---

[1][Cf. *The Interpretation of Dreams, Standard Ed.,* **4**, 224.]
[2]See the text of *Gradiva* (15).
[3][*The Interpretation of Dreams,* Chapter V, Section A, *Standard Ed.,* **4**, 165ff.]

of the dream, this is not a mistaken judgement provoked by the
vividness of the dream-images, but is a psychical act on its own: it is
an assurance, relating to the content of the dream, that something
in it is really as one has dreamt it;[1] and it is right to have faith in this
[58]   assurance. If we keep to these two rules, we must conclude that the
dream gave some information as to the whereabouts of the Gradiva
he was in search of, and that that information tallied with the real
state of things. We know Hanold's dream: does the application of
these two rules to it yield any reasonable sense?

Strange to say, it does. The sense is merely disguised in a particular way so that it is not immediately recognizable. Hanold learned
in the dream that the girl he was looking for was living in a town
and contemporaneously with him. Now this was true of Zoe
Bertgang; only in the dream the town was not the German university town but Pompeii, and the time was not the present but the
year 79 A.D. It is, as it were, a distortion by displacement: what we
have is not Gradiva in the present but the dreamer transported into
the past. Nevertheless, in this manner, the essential and new fact is
stated: *he is in the same place and time as the girl he is looking for.* But
whence come this displacement and disguise which were bound to
deceive both us and the dreamer over the true meaning and
content of the dream? Well, we already have the means at our
disposal for giving a satisfactory answer to that question.

Let us recall all that we have heard about the nature and origin of
the phantasies which are the precursors of delusions [p. 44 ff.].
They are substitutes for and derivatives of repressed memories
which a resistance will not allow to enter consciousness unaltered,
but which can purchase the possibility of becoming conscious by
taking account, by means of changes and distortions, of the resistance's censorship. When this compromise has been accomplished, the memories have turned into the phantasies, which can
easily be misunderstood by the conscious personality—that is,
understood so as to fit in with the dominant psychical current.
Now let us suppose that dream-images are what might be described

[1][Ibid., **4**, 187 and **5**, 372.]

as the creations of people's physiological [i.e. non-pathological] delusions—the products of the compromise in the struggle between what is repressed and what is dominant which is probably [59] present in every human being, including those who in the day-time are perfectly sound in mind. We shall then understand that dream-images have to be regarded as something distorted, behind which something else must be looked for, something *not* distorted, but in some sense objectionable, like Hanold's repressed memories behind his phantasies. We can give expression to the contrast which we have thus recognized, by distinguishing what the dreamer remembers when he wakes up as the *manifest content of the dream* from what constituted the basis of the dream before the distortion imposed by the censorship—namely, the *latent dream-thoughts.* Thus, interpreting a dream consists in translating the manifest content of the dream into the latent dream-thoughts, in undoing the distortion which the dream-thoughts have had to submit to from the censorship of the resistance. If we apply these notions to the dream we are concerned with, we shall find that its latent dream-thoughts can only have been: 'the girl you are looking for with the graceful gait is really living in this town with you.' But in that form the thought could not become conscious. It was obstructed by the fact that a phantasy had laid it down, as the result of an earlier compromise, that Gradiva was a Pompeian; consequently, if the real fact that she was living in the same place and at the same time was to be affirmed, there was no choice but to adopt the distortion: 'You are living at Pompeii at the time of Gradiva.' This then was the idea which was realized by the manifest content of the dream, and was represented as a present event actually being experienced.

    It is only rarely that a dream represents, or, as we might say, 'stages', a single thought: there are usually a number of them, a tissue of thoughts. Another component of the content of Hanold's dream can be detached, the distortion of which can easily be got rid of, so that the latent idea represented by it can be detected. This is a piece of the dream to which once again it is possible to extend the

assurance of reality with which the dream ended. In the dream
Gradiva as she steps along is transformed into a marble sculpture.
[60]   This is no more than an ingenious and poetical representation of
the real event. Hanold had in fact transferred his interest from the
living girl to the sculpture: the girl he loved had been transformed
for him into a marble relief. The latent dream-thoughts, which
were bound to remain unconscious, sought to change the sculpture
back into the living girl; what they were saying to him accordingly
was something like: 'After all, you're only interested in the statue of
Gradiva because it reminds you of Zoe, who is living here and
now.' But if this discovery could have become conscious, it would
have meant the end of the delusion.

Are we perhaps under an obligation to replace in this way each
separate piece of the manifest content of the dream by unconscious
thoughts? Strictly speaking, yes; if we were interpreting a dream
that had really been dreamt, we could not avoid that duty. But in
that case, too, the dreamer would have to give us the most copious
explanations. Clearly we cannot carry out this requirement in the
case of the author's creation; nevertheless, we shall not overlook the
fact that we have not yet submitted the main content of the dream
to the process of interpretation or translation.

For Hanold's dream was an anxiety-dream. Its content was
frightening, the dreamer felt anxiety while he slept and he was left
with painful feelings afterwards. Now this is far from convenient
for our attempt at an explanation; and we must once again borrow
heavily from the theory of dream-interpretation. We are warned by
that theory not to fall into the error of tracing the anxiety that may
be felt in a dream to the content of the dream, and not to treat the
content of the dream as though it were the content of an idea
occurring in waking life. It points out to us how often we dream the
most ghastly things without feeling a trace of anxiety. The true
situation, we learn, is quite a different one, which cannot be easily
guessed, but which can be proved with certainty. The anxiety in
anxiety-dreams, like neurotic anxiety in general, corresponds to a
[61]   sexual affect, a libidinal feeling, and arises out of libido by the

process of repression.[1] When we interpret a dream, therefore, we must replace anxiety by sexual excitement. The anxiety that originates in this way has—not invariably, but frequently—a selective influence on the content of the dream and introduces into it ideational elements which seem, when the dream is looked at from a conscious and mistaken point of view, to be appropriate to the affect of anxiety. As I have said, this is not invariably so, for there are plenty of anxiety-dreams in which the content is not in the least frightening and where it is therefore impossible to give an explanation on conscious lines of the anxiety that is felt.

I am aware that this explanation of anxiety in dreams sounds very strange and is not easy to credit; but I can only advise the reader to come to terms with it. Moreover it would be a very remarkable thing if Norbert Hanold's dream could be reconciled with this view of anxiety and could be explained in that way. On that basis, we should say that the dreamer's erotic longings were stirred up during the night and made a powerful effort to make conscious his memory of the girl he loved and so to tear him out of his delusion, but that those longings met with a fresh repudiation and were transformed into anxiety, which in its turn introduced into the content of the dream the terrifying pictures from the memories of his schooldays. In this manner the true unconscious content of the dream, his passionate longing for the Zoe he had once known, became transformed into its manifest content of the destruction of Pompeii and the loss of Gradiva.

So far, I think, it sounds plausible. But it might justly be insisted that, if erotic wishes constitute the undistorted content of the dream, it ought also to be possible to point at least to some recognizable residue of those wishes concealed somewhere in the [62] transformed dream. Well, even that may be possible, with the help of a hint from a later part of the story. When Hanold had his first meeting with the supposed Gradiva, he recollected the dream and

[1]Cf. my first paper on the anxiety neurosis (1895*b*) and *The Interpretation of Dreams.* [*Standard Ed.*, **4**, 160–2, and **5**, 582ff.—In his *Inhibitions, Symptoms and Anxiety* (1926*d*), Freud put forward an amended view of the origin of anxiety.]

begged the apparition to lie down again as he had seen her do then [p. 19].[1] Thereupon, however, the young lady rose indignantly and left her strange companion, for she had detected the improper erotic wish behind what he had said under the domination of his delusion. We must, I think, accept Gradiva's interpretation; even in a real dream we cannot always expect to find a more definite expression of an erotic wish.

The application of a few of the rules of dream-interpretation to Hanold's first dream has thus resulted in making it intelligible to us in its main features and in inserting it into the nexus of the story. Surely, then, the author must have observed these rules in creating it? We might ask another question, too: why did the author introduce a dream at all to bring about the further development of the delusion? In my opinion it was an ingenious notion and once again true to reality. We have already heard [p. 55] that in real illnesses a delusion very often arises in connection with a dream, and, after what we have learnt about the nature of dreams, there is no need to see a fresh riddle in this fact. Dreams and delusions arise from the same source—from what is repressed. Dreams are, as one might say, the physiological delusions of normal people. [Cf. p. 58] Before what is repressed has become strong enough to break through into waking life as a delusion, it may easily have achieved a first success, under the more favourable conditions of the state of sleep, in the form of a dream with persisting effects. For during sleep, along with a general lowering of mental activity, there is a relaxation in the strength of the resistance with which the dominant psychical forces [63] oppose what is repressed. It is this relaxation that makes the formation of dreams possible, and that is why dreams give us our best access to a knowledge of the unconscious part of the mind—except that, as a rule, with the re-establishment of the psychical cathexes of waking life, the dream once more takes to flight and the ground that had been won by the unconscious is evacuated once again.

[1]'No, I didn't hear you speak. But I called to you when you lay down to sleep, and I stood beside you then—your face was as peaceful and beautiful as marble. May I beg of you—lie down once more on the step as you did then.' (70.)

III

IN the further course of the story there is yet another dream, [64] which may perhaps tempt us even more than the first to try to translate it and insert it into the train of events in the hero's mind.[1] But we should save very little by diverging from the author's account and hurrying on immediately to this second dream; for no one who wishes to analyse someone else's dream can avoid turning his attention in the greatest detail to all the dreamer's experiences, both external and internal. It will probably be best, therefore, to keep close to the thread of the story and to intersperse it with our glosses as we proceed.

The construction of the fresh delusion about Gradiva's death during the destruction of Pompeii in the year 79 A.D. was not the only result of the first dream, which we have already analyzed. Immediately after it Hanold decided on his journey to Italy, which eventually brought him to Pompeii. But, before that, something else happened to him. As he was leaning out of the window, he thought he saw a figure in the street with the bearing and gait of his Gradiva. In spite of being insufficiently dressed, he hurried after her, but failed to overtake her, and was driven back into the house by the jeers of the passers-by. When he was in his room once more, the song of a canary from its cage in the window of a house opposite stirred up in him a mood in which he too seemed to be a prisoner longing for freedom; and his spring-time journey was no sooner decided on than it was carried out.

The author has thrown a particularly clear light on this journey of Hanold's and has allowed him to have a partial insight into his [65] own internal processes. Hanold of course found himself a scientific pretext for his journey, but this did not last long. After all, he was in fact aware that 'the impulse to make this journey had arisen from a feeling he could not name'. A strange restlessness made him dissat-

[1][The last phrase in this sentence, which, in a slightly different form, has already appeared in the preceding paragraph (p. 62), is an echo of the opening sentence of *The Interpretation of Dreams* (*Standard Ed.*, **4**, 1).]

isfied with everything he came across, and drove him from Rome to Naples and from there to Pompeii; but even at this last halting-place he was still uneasy in his mood. He was annoyed at the folly of the honeymooners, and enraged at the impertinence of the house-flies which inhabit Pompeii's hotels. But at last he could no longer disguise from himself 'that his dissatisfaction could not be caused solely by what was around him but that there was something that sprang from himself as well'. He thought he was over-excited, felt 'that he was discontented because he lacked something, but he had no idea what. And this ill-humour followed him about everywhere.' In this frame of mind he was even furious with his mistress—with Science. When in the heat of the mid-day sun he wandered for the first time through Pompeii, 'the whole of his science had not merely abandoned him, but had left him without the slightest desire to find her again. He remembered her only as something in the far distance, and he felt that she had been an old, dried-up, tedious aunt, the dullest and most unwanted creature in the world.' (55.)

And then, while he was in this disagreeable and confused state of feeling, one of the problems attaching to his journey was solved for him—at the moment when he first saw Gradiva stepping through Pompeii. Something 'came into his consciousness for the first time: without being aware himself of the impulse within him, he had come to Italy and had travelled on to Pompeii, without stopping in Rome or Naples, in order to see whether he could find any traces of her. And "traces" literally; for with her peculiar gait she must have left behind an imprint of her toes in the ashes distinct from all the rest.' (58 [p. 16f.].)

[66] Since the author has taken so much trouble over describing the journey, it must be worth while too to discuss its relation to Hanold's delusion and its position in the chain of events. The journey was undertaken for reasons which its subject did not recognize at first and only admitted to himself later on, reasons which the author describes in so many words as 'unconscious'. This is certainly taken from the life. One does not need to be suffering from a delusion in order to behave like this. On the contrary, it is

an event of daily occurrence for a person—even a healthy person—
to deceive himself over the motives for an action and to become
conscious of them only after the event, provided only that a conflict
between several currents of feeling furnishes the necessary condition for such a confusion. Accordingly, Hanold's journey was from
the first calculated to serve the delusion, and was intended to take
him to Pompeii, where he could proceed further with his search for
Gradiva. It will be recalled that his mind was occupied with that
search both before and immediately after the dream, and that the
dream itself was simply an answer to the question of Gradiva's
whereabouts, though an answer which was stifled by his consciousness. Some power which we do not recognize was, however, also
inhibiting him to begin with from becoming aware of his delusional intention; so that, for the conscious reasons of his journey, he
was left only with insufficient pretexts which had to be renewed
from place to place. The author presents us with a further puzzle by
making the dream, the discovery of the supposed Gradiva in the
street, and the decision to undertake the journey as a result of the
singing canary succeed one another as a series of chance events
without any internal connection with one another.

   This obscure region of the story is made intelligible to us by
some explanations which we derive from the later remarks of Zoe
Bertgang. It was in fact the original of Gradiva, Fräulein Zoe
herself, whom Hanold saw out of his window walking past in the
street (89) and whom he nearly overtook. If this had happened, the
information given him by the dream—that she was in fact living at
the same time and in the same town as he was—would by a lucky
chance have received an irresistible confirmation, which would   [67]
have brought about the collapse of his internal struggle. But the
canary, whose singing sent Hanold off on his distant journey,
belonged to Zoe, and its cage stood in her window diagonally
across the street from Hanold's house. (135 [p. 30].) Hanold, who,
according to the girl's accusation, had the gift of 'negative hallucination', who possessed the art of not seeing and not recognizing
people who were actually present, must from the first have had an
unconscious knowledge of what we only learned later. The indica-

tions of Zoe's proximity (her appearance in the street and her bird's singing so near his window) intensified the effect of the dream, and in this position, so perilous for his resistance to his erotic feelings, he took to flight. His journey was a result of his resistance gathering new strength after the surge forward of his erotic desires in the dream; it was an attempt at flight from the physical presence of the girl he loved. In a practical sense it meant a victory for repression, just as his earlier activity, his 'pedestrian researches' upon women and girls, had meant a victory for erotism. But everywhere in these oscillations in the struggle the compromise character of the outcome was preserved: the journey to Pompeii, which was supposed to lead him away from the living Zoe, led him at least to her surrogate, to Gradiva. The journey, which was undertaken in defiance of the latent dream-thoughts, was nevertheless following the path to Pompeii that was pointed out by the manifest content of the dream. Thus at every fresh struggle between erotism and resistance we find the delusion triumphant.

This view of Hanold's journey as a flight from his awakening erotic longing for the girl whom he loved and who was so close to him is the only one which will fit in with the description of his emotional states during his stay in Italy. The repudiation of erotism which dominated him was expressed there in his disgust at the honeymooners. A short dream which he had in his *albergo* in Rome, and which was occasioned by the proximity of a German loving couple, 'Edwin and Angelina', whose evening conversation he could not help hearing through the thin partition-wall, throws a retrospective light, as it were, on the erotic drift of his first major dream. In the new dream he was once again in Pompeii and Vesuvius was once again erupting, and it was thus linked to the earlier dream whose effects persisted during the journey. This time, however, among the people imperilled were—not, as on the former occasion, himself and Gradiva but—the Apollo Belvedere and the Capitoline Venus, no doubt by way of an ironical exaltation of the couple in the next room. Apollo lifted Venus up, carried her out, and laid her down on some object in the dark which seemed to be a

[68]

carriage or cart, since it emitted 'a creaking noise'. Apart from this, the interpretation of the dream calls for no special skill. (31.)

Our author, who, as we have long since realized, never introduces a single idle or unintentional feature into his story, has given us another piece of evidence of the asexual current which dominated Hanold during his journey. As he roamed about for hours in Pompeii, 'strangely enough it never once recurred to his memory that a short time before he had dreamt of being present at the burial of Pompeii in the eruption of 79 A.D.' (47.) It was only when he caught sight of Gradiva that he suddenly remembered the dream and became conscious at the same time of the delusional reason for his puzzling journey. How could this forgetting of the dream, this barrier of repression between the dream and his mental state during the journey, be explained, except by supposing that the journey was undertaken not at the direct inspiration of the dream but as a revolt against it, as an emanation of a mental power that refused to know anything of the secret meaning of the dream?

But on the other hand Hanold did not enjoy this victory over his erotism. The suppressed mental impulse remained powerful enough to revenge itself on the suppressing one with discontent and inhibition. His longings turned into restlessness and dissatisfaction, which made his journey seem pointless to him. His insight [69] into his reasons for the journey at the bidding of the delusion was inhibited and his relations with his science, which in such a spot should have stirred all his interest, were interfered with. So the author shows us his hero after his flight from love in a kind of crisis, in a state of complete confusion and distraction, in a turmoil such as we usually find at the climax of an illness, when neither of the two conflicting powers has any longer a sufficiently superior strength over the other for the margin between them to make it possible to establish a vigorous mental régime. But here the author intervenes helpfully, and smoothes things out by making Gradiva appear at this juncture and undertake the cure of the delusion. By the power he possesses of guiding the people of his creation towards a happy destiny, in spite of all the laws of necessity which he makes

them obey, he arranges that the girl, to avoid whom Hanold had
fled to Pompeii, shall be transported to that very place. In this way
he corrects the folly to which the young man was led by his
delusion—the folly of exchanging the home of the living girl whom
he loved for the burial-place of her imaginary substitute.

With the appearance of Zoe Bertgang as Gradiva, which marks
the climax of tension in the story, our interest, too, soon takes a
new direction. So far we have been assisting at the development of a
delusion; now we are to witness its cure. And we may ask whether
the author has given a purely fanciful account of the course of this
cure or whether he has constructed it in accordance with possibilities actually present. Zoe's own words during her conversation with
her newly-married friend give us a definite right to ascribe to her an
intention to bring about the cure. (124 [p. 27].) But how did she set
about it? When she had got over the indignation aroused in her by
his suggestion that she should lie down to sleep again as she had
'then', she returned next day at the same mid-day hour to the same
spot, and proceeded to entice out of Hanold all the secret knowledge her ignorance of which had prevented her from understand-
[70]   ing his behaviour the day before. She learnt about his dream, about
the sculpture of Gradiva, and about the peculiarity of gait which
she herself shared with it. She accepted the role of the ghost
awakened to life for a brief hour, a role for which, as she perceived,
his delusion had cast her, and, by accepting the flowers of the dead
which he had brought without conscious purpose, and by expressing a regret that he had not given her roses, she gently hinted in
ambiguous words at the possibility of his taking up a new position.
(90 [p. 21].)

This unusually clever girl, then, was determined to win her
childhood's friend for her husband, after she had recognized that
the young man's love for her was the motive force behind the
delusion. Our interest in her behaviour, however, will probably
yield for the moment to the surprise which we may feel at the
delusion itself. The last form taken by it was that Gradiva, who had
been buried in 79 A.D., was now able, as a mid-day ghost, to
exchange words with him for an hour, at the end of which she must

sink into the ground or seek her grave once more. This mental cobweb, which was not brushed away either by his perceiving that the apparition was wearing modern shoes or by her ignorance of the ancient languages and her command of German, which was not in existence in her day, certainly seems to justify the author's description of his story as a 'Pompeian phantasy', but it seems also to exclude any possibility of measuring it by the standards of clinical reality.

Nevertheless, on closer consideration this delusion of Hanold's seems to me to lose the greater part of its improbability. The author, indeed, has made himself responsible for one part of it by basing his story on the premiss that Zoe was in every detail a duplicate of the relief. We must therefore avoid shifting the improbability of this premiss on to its consequence—that Hanold took the girl for Gradiva come to life. Greater value is given to the delusional explanation by the fact that the author has put no rational one at our disposal. Moreover the author has adduced contributory and mitigating circumstances on behalf of his hero's excesses in the shape of the glare of the *campagna* sunlight and the [71] intoxicating magic of the wine grown on the slopes of Vesuvius. But the most important of all the explanatory and exculpatory factors remains the ease with which our intellect is prepared to accept something absurd provided it satisfies powerful emotional impulses. It is an astonishing fact, and one that is too generally overlooked, how readily and frequently under these psychological conditions people of even the most powerful intelligence react as though they were feeble-minded; and anyone who is not too conceited may see this happening in himself as often as he pleases. And this is far more so if some of the mental processes concerned are linked with unconscious or repressed motives. In this connection I am happy to quote the words of a philosopher, who writes to me: 'I have been noting down the instances I myself experience of striking mistakes and unthinking actions, for which one finds motives afterwards (in a most unreasonable way). It is an alarming thing, but typical, to find how much folly this brings to light.' It must be remembered, too, that the belief in spirits and ghosts and the return of the dead, which finds so much support in the religions to which we have all been attached, at least in our childhood, is far from having disappeared among educated people, and that many who are sensible in other respects find it possible to combine spiritualism with reason. A man who has grown rational and sceptical, even, may be ashamed to discover how easily he may for a moment return to a belief in spirits under the combined impact of strong emotions and perplexity. I know of a doctor who had once lost one of his women patients suffering from Graves' disease[1], and who could not get rid of a faint suspicion that he might perhaps have contributed to the unhappy outcome by a thoughtless prescription. One day, several years later, a girl entered his consulting-room, who, in spite of all his efforts, he could not help recognizing as the dead one. He could frame only a single thought: 'So after all it's true that the dead can come back to life.' His dread did not give way to shame till the girl introduced herself as the sister of the one who had died of the same disease as she herself was suffering from. The victims of Graves' disease, as has often been observed, have a marked facial resemblance to one another; and in this case this typical likeness was reinforced by a family one. The doctor to whom this occurred was, however, none other than myself; so I have a personal reason for not disputing the clinical possibility of Norbert Hanold's temporary delusion that Gradiva had come back to life. The fact, finally, is familiar to every psychiatrist that in severe cases of chronic delusions (in paranoia) the most extreme examples occur of ingeniously elaborated and well-supported absurdities.

[72]

After his first meeting with Gradiva, Norbert Hanold had drunk his wine first in one and then in the other of the two restaurants that he knew in Pompeii, while the other visitors were engaged in eating the main meal of the day. 'Of course it never came into his head to think of the nonsensical idea' that he was doing it in order to discover in which of the hotels Gradiva was living and taking her meals. But it is difficult to say what other sense his actions could have had. On the day after their second meeting in the House of

[1][Exophthalmic goitre.]

Meleager, he had all kinds of strange and apparently unconnected experiences. He found a narrow gap in the wall of the portico, at the point where Gradiva had disappeared. He met a foolish lizard-catcher who addressed him as though he were an acquaintance. He discovered a third hotel, in an out-of-the-way situation, the 'Albergo del Sole', whose proprietor palmed off on him a metal clasp with a green patina as a find from beside the remains of a Pompeian girl. And, lastly, in his own hotel he noticed a newly-arrived young couple whom he diagnosed as a brother and sister and whom he found sympathetic. All these impressions were afterwards woven together into a 'remarkably senseless' dream, which ran as follows:

'Somewhere in the sun Gradiva was sitting, making a snare out of a blade of grass to catch a lizard in, and said: "Please keep quite [73] still. Our lady colleague is right; the method is a really good one and she has made use of it with excellent results." ' [P. 25.]

He fended off this dream while he was still asleep, with the critical thought that it was utter madness, and cast around in all directions to get free from it. He succeeded in doing so with the help of an invisible bird, which uttered a short laughing call and carried off the lizard in its beak.

Are we to venture on an attempt at interpreting this dream too—that is, at replacing it by the latent thoughts from whose distortion it must have arisen? It is as senseless as only a dream can be expected to be; and this absurdity of dreams is the mainstay of the view which refuses to characterize dreams as completely valid psychical acts and maintains that they arise out of a purposeless excitation of the elements of the mind.

We are able to apply to this dream the technique which may be described as the regular procedure for interpreting dreams. It consists in paying no attention to the apparent connections in the manifest dream but in fixing our eyes upon each portion of its content independently, and in looking for its origin in the dreamer's impressions, memories, and free associations.[1] Since, however, we

[1][Cf. *The Interpretation of Dreams, Standard Ed.*, 4, 103–4.]

cannot question Hanold, we shall have to content ourselves with referring to his impressions, and we may very tentatively put our own associations in place of his.

'Somewhere in the sun Gradiva was sitting, catching lizards and speaking.' What impression of the previous day finds an echo in this part of the dream? Undoubtedly the encounter with the elderly gentleman, the lizard-catcher, who was thus replaced in the dream by Gradiva. He sat or lay 'on a sun-bathed slope' and he, too, spoke to Hanold. Furthermore, Gradiva's remarks in the dream were copied from this man's remarks: viz. 'The method prescribed by our colleague Eimer is a really good one; I have made use of it many times already with excellent results. Please keep quite still.' [P. 23.] Gradiva used much the same words in the dream, except that 'our colleague Eimer' was replaced by an unnamed 'lady colleague'; moreover, the 'many times' in the zoologist's speech was omitted in the dream and the order of the sentences was somewhat altered. It seems, therefore, that this experience of the previous day was transformed into the dream with the help of a few changes and distortions. Why this particular experience? And what is the meaning of the changes—the replacement of the elderly gentleman by Gradiva and the introduction of the enigmatic 'lady colleague'?

There is a rule in interpreting dreams which runs as follows: 'A speech heard in a dream is always derived from one that has been heard or made by the dreamer in waking life.'[1] This rule seems to have been observed here: Gradiva's speech is only a modification of the old zoologist's speech which Hanold had heard the day before. Another rule in dream-interpretation would tell us that when one person is replaced by another or when two people are mixed up together (for instance, by one of them being shown in a situation that is characteristic of the other), it means that the two people are being equated, that there is a similarity between them.[2] If we venture to apply this rule too to our dream, we should arrive at this translation: 'Gradiva catches lizards just like the old man; she is

[74]

---

[1] [Cf. *The Interpretation of Dreams*, Standard Ed., **5**, 418 ff.]
[2] [Ibid., **4**, 320 ff.]

skilled in lizard-catching just as he is.' This result cannot exactly be said to be intelligible as yet; but we have yet another puzzle to solve. To what impression of the previous day are we to relate the 'lady colleague' who in the dream replaces the famous zoologist Eimer? Fortunately we have very little choice here. A 'lady colleague' can only mean another girl—that is to say, the sympathetic young lady whom Hanold had taken for a sister travelling with her brother. 'She was wearing a red Sorrento rose in her dress, the sight of which reminded him of something as he looked across from his corner of [75] the dining-room, but he could not think what.' [P. 24 f.] This remark of the author's gives us a right to regard her as the 'lady colleague' in the dream. What Hanold could not recall were, it cannot be doubted, the words spoken by the supposed Gradiva, who had told him, as she asked him for the white flowers of the dead, that in the spring people give happier girls roses. [P. 21.] But behind those words there had lain a hint of wooing. So what sort of lizard-catching was it that the happier 'lady colleague' had carried out so successfully?

Next day Hanold came upon the supposed brother and sister in an affectionate embrace, and was thus able to correct his earlier mistake. They were in fact a pair of lovers, and moreover on their honeymoon, as we discovered later when they so unexpectedly interrupted Hanold's third interview with Zoe. If now we are willing to assume that Hanold, though consciously taking them for a brother and sister, had immediately recognized their true relationship (which was unambiguously betrayed next day) in his unconscious, Gradiva's speech in the dream acquires a clear meaning. The red rose had become the symbol of a love-relation. Hanold understood that the couple were already what he and Gradiva had yet to become; the lizard-catching had come to signify mancatching; and Gradiva's speech meant something like: 'Only let me alone: I know how to win a man just as well as the other girl does.'

But why was it necessary for this penetration of Zoe's intentions to appear in the dream in the form of the old zoologist's speech? Why was Zoe's skill in man-catching represented by the old gentleman's skill in lizard-catching? Well, we can have no difficulty in answering that question. We guessed long ago that the lizard-catcher was none other than Bertgang, the professor of zoology and Zoe's father, who, incidentally, must have known Hanold too—which explains how he came to address him as an acquaintance.

[76] Let us assume, once again, that in his unconscious Hanold at once recognized the Professor. 'He had a vague notion that he had already had a passing glimpse of the lizard-hunter's face, probably in one of the two hotels.' This, then, is the explanation of the strange disguise under which the intention attributed to Zoe made its appearance: she was the lizard-catcher's daughter and had acquired her skill from him.

The replacement of the lizard-catcher by Gradiva in the content of the dream is accordingly a representation of the relation between the two figures which was known to Hanold in his unconscious; the introduction of the 'lady colleague' instead of 'our colleague Eimer' allowed the dream to express Hanold's realization that she was wooing a man. So far the dream welded together ('condensed', as we say) two experiences of the previous day into one situation, in order to bring to expression (in a very obscure way, it is true) two discoveries which were not allowed to become conscious. But we can go further, we can diminish the strangeness of the dream still more and we can demonstrate the influence of his other experiences of the previous day on the form taken by the manifest dream.

We may declare ourselves dissatisfied with the explanation that has hitherto been given of why it was that precisely the scene of the lizard-catching was made into the nucleus of the dream, and we may suspect that still other elements of the dream-thoughts were bringing their influence to bear in the emphasis that was laid on the 'lizard' in the manifest dream. Indeed, it may easily have been so. It will be recalled [p. 22] that Hanold had discovered a gap in the wall at the point where Gradiva had seemed to vanish—a gap 'which was nevertheless wide enough to allow a form that was unusually slim' to slip through. This observation led him in daytime to make an alteration in his delusion—an alteration to the effect that when Gradiva disappeared from his sight she did not sink into the earth but used the gap as a way of reaching her grave. In his unconscious thoughts he may have told himself that he had now discovered the natural explanation of the girl's surprising disappearance. But must [77] not the idea of slipping through narrow gaps and disappearing in them have recalled the behaviour of lizards? Was not Gradiva herself in this way behaving like an agile little lizard? In our view, then, the discovery of the gap in the wall contributed to determining the choice of the element 'lizard' in the manifest content of the dream. The lizard situation in the dream represented this impression of the previous day as well as the encounter with Zoe's father, the zoologist.

And what if now, growing bold, we were to try to find a representation in the content of the dream of the one experience of the previous day which has not yet been exploited—the discovery of the third inn, the Albergo del Sole? The author has treated this episode at such length and has linked so many things to it that it would surprise us if it alone had made no contribution to the construction of the dream. Hanold went into this inn, which, owing to its out-of-the-way situation and its distance from the railway station, had remained unknown to him, to purchase a bottle of soda-water to cool his heated blood. The landlord took the opportunity of displaying his antiquities, and showed him a clasp which he pretended had belonged to the Pompeian girl who had been found in the neighbourhood of the Forum closely embraced by her lover. Hanold, who had never hitherto believed this often-repeated tale, was now compelled by a power unknown to him to believe in the truth of this moving story and in the genuineness of the find; he purchased the brooch and left the inn with his acquisition. As he was going out, he saw, standing in a glass of water in the window, a nodding sprig of asphodel covered with white blossoms, and took the sight of it as a confirmation of the genuineness of his new possession. He now felt a positive conviction that the green clasp had belonged to Gradiva and that she had been the girl who had died in her lover's arms. He quieted the jealousy which thereupon seized him, by deciding the next day he would show the clasp to Gradiva herself and arrive at certainty about his suspicion. It cannot be denied that this was a curious new piece of [78] delusion; yet are we to suppose that no trace of it was to be found in his dream of the same night?

It will certainly be worth while to explain the origin of this addition to the delusion and to look for the fresh piece of unconscious discovery which was replaced by the fresh piece of delusion. The delusion appeared under the influence of the landlord of the 'Sun Hotel' to whom Hanold behaved in such a remarkably credulous fashion that it was almost as though he had been given a hypnotic suggestion by him. The landlord showed him a metal clasp for a garment, represented it as genuine and as having belonged to the girl who had been found buried in the arms of her lover; and Hanold, who was capable of being sufficiently critical to doubt both the truth of the story and the genuineness of the clasp, was at once taken in, and purchased the highly dubious antique. Why he should have behaved in this way is quite incomprehensible, and there is nothing to suggest that the landlord's personality might offer us a solution. But there is yet another riddle about the incident, and two riddles often solve each other. As he was leaving the *albergo* he saw a sprig of asphodel standing in a glass in a window and took it as a confirmation of the genuineness of the metal clasp. How could that have come about? But fortunately this last point is easy to solve. The white flower was no doubt the one which he had given to Gradiva at mid-day, and it is perfectly true that something was confirmed by the sight of it in the window of the inn. Not, it is true, the genuineness of the clasp, but something else that had already become clear to him when he discovered this *albergo* after having previously overlooked it. Already on the day before he had behaved as though he was searching in the two Pompeii hotels to find the person who appeared to him as Gradiva. And now, since he had so unexpectedly come upon a third one, he must have said to himself in his unconscious: 'So *this* is where she is staying!' And added, as he was going out: 'Yes, that's right! There's [79]   the asphodel that I gave her! So that's her window!' This then was the new discovery which was replaced by the delusion, and which could not become conscious because its underlying postulate that Gradiva was a living person whom he had once known could not become conscious.

But how did the replacement of the new discovery by the delusion take place? What happened, I think, was that the sense of conviction attaching to the discovery was able to persist and was retained, while the discovery itself, which was inadmissible to consciousness, was replaced by another ideational content connected with it by associations of thought. Thus the sense of conviction became attached to a content which was in fact foreign to it and this, in the form of a delusion, won a recognition which did not apply to it. Hanold transferred his conviction that Gradiva lived in the house to other impressions which he had received in the house; this led to his credulity in regard to the landlord's remarks, the genuineness of the metal clasp and the truth of the anecdote about the discovery of the embracing lovers—but only through his linking what he heard in the house with Gradiva. The jealousy which was already latent in him seized upon this material and the consequence was the delusion (though it contradicted his first dream) that Gradiva was the girl who had died in her lover's arms and that the clasp he had bought had belonged to her.

It will be observed that his conversation with Gradiva and her hint at wooing him (her 'saying it with flowers') had already brought about important changes in Hanold. Traits of masculine desire—components of the libido—had awakened in him, though it is true that they could not yet dispense with the disguise of conscious pretexts. But the problem of the 'bodily nature' of Gradiva, which pursued him all that day [pp. 20 and 23], cannot disavow its origin in a young man's erotic curiosity about a woman's body, even if it is involved in a scientific question by the conscious insistence on Gradiva's peculiar oscillation between death and life. His jealousy was a further sign of the increasingly active aspect of Hanold's love; he expressed this jealousy at the beginning of their conversation [80] the next day and with the help of a fresh pretext proceeded to touch the girl's body and, as he used to do in the far-off past, to hit her.

But it is now time to ask ourselves whether the method of constructing a delusion which we have inferred from our author's account is one that is known from other sources, or whether, indeed, it is possible at all. From our medical knowledge we can only reply that it is certainly the correct method, and perhaps the sole method, by which a delusion acquires the unshakable conviction which is one of its clinical characteristics. If a patient believes in his delusion so firmly, this is not because his faculty of judgement has been overturned and does not arise from what is false in the delusion. On the contrary, there is a grain of truth concealed in every delusion,[1] there is something in it that really deserves belief, and this is the source of the patient's conviction, which is therefore to that extent justified. This true element, however, has long been repressed. If eventually it is able to penetrate into consciousness, this time in a distorted form, the sense of conviction attaching to it is over-intensified as though by way of compensation and is now attached to the distorted substitute of the repressed truth, and protects it from any critical attacks. The conviction is displaced, as it were, from the unconscious truth on to the conscious error that is linked to it, and remains fixated there precisely as a result of this displacement. The instance of the formation of a delusion which arose from Hanold's first dream is no more than a similar, though not identical, example of such a displacement. Indeed, the method described here by which conviction arises in the case of a delusion does not differ fundamentally from the method by which a convic-

[81] tion is formed in normal cases, where repression does not come into the picture. We all attach our conviction to thought-contents in which truth is combined with error, and let it extend from the former over the latter. It becomes diffused, as it were, from the truth over the error associated with it and protects the latter, though not so unalterably as in the case of a delusion, against deserved criticism. In normal psychology, too, being well-connected—'having influence', so to speak—can take the place of true worth.

I will now return to the dream and bring out a small but not uninteresting feature in it, which forms a connection between two of its provoking causes. Gradiva had drawn a kind of contrast

---

[1] [Freud expressed this view at many points throughout the whole course of his writings. It appears, for instance, in the first edition of the *Psychopathology of Everyday Life* (1901*b*), Chapter XII, Section C (*a*), and in *Moses and Monotheism* (1939*a*), Chapter III, Part II, Section G.]

between the white asphodel blossoms and the red rose. Seeing the asphodel again in the window of the Albergo del Sole became an important piece of evidence in support of Hanold's unconscious discovery, which was expressed in the new delusion; and alongside this was the fact that the red rose in the dress of the sympathetic girl helped Hanold in his unconscious to a correct view of her relation to her companion, so that he was able to make her appear in the dream as the 'lady colleague'.

But where in the manifest content of the dream, it will be asked, do we find anything to indicate and replace the discovery for which, as we have seen, Hanold's new delusion was a substitute— the discovery that Gradiva was staying with her father in the third, concealed Pompeii hotel, the Albergo del Sole? Nevertheless it is all there in the dream, and not even very much distorted, and I merely hesitate to point to it because I know that even those of my readers who have followed me patiently so far will begin to rebel strongly against my attempts at interpretation. Hanold's discovery, I repeat, is fully announced in the dream, but so cleverly concealed that it is bound to be overlooked. It is hidden behind a play upon words, an ambiguity. 'Somewhere in the sun Gradiva was sitting.' We have quite correctly related this to the spot where Hanold met her father, the zoologist. But could it not also mean in the 'Sun'—that is, [82] Gradiva is staying in the Albergo del Sole, the Sun Hotel? And was not the 'somewhere', which had no bearing on the encounter with her father, made to sound so hypocritically indefinite precisely because it introduced a definite piece of information about the place where Gradiva was staying? From my experience elsewhere of real dreams, I myself am perfectly certain that this is how the ambiguity is to be understood. But I should not in fact have ventured to present this piece of interpretative work to my readers, if the author had not at this point lent me his powerful assistance. He puts the very same play upon words into the girl's mouth when next day she saw the metal clasp: 'Did you find it in the sun, perhaps, which produces things of this kind?' [P. 26.] And since Hanold failed to understand what she had said, she explained that she meant the Sun Hotel, which they call 'Sole' here, and where she had already seen the supposititious antique.

And now let us make a bold attempt at replacing Hanold's 'remarkably senseless' dream by the unconscious thoughts that lay behind it and were as unlike it as possible. They ran, perhaps, as follows: 'She is staying in the "Sun" with her father. Why is she playing this game with me? Does she want to make fun of me? Or can it possibly be that she loves me and wants to have me as her husband?'—And no doubt while he was still asleep there came an answer dismissing this last possibility as 'the merest madness', a comment which was ostensibly directed against the whole manifest dream.

Critical readers will now justly enquire about the origin of the interpolation (for which I have so far given no grounds) of the reference to being ridiculed by Gradiva. The answer to this is given in *The Interpretation of Dreams*, which explains that if ridicule, derision, or embittered contradiction occurs in the dream-thoughts, this is expressed by the manifest dream being given a senseless form, by absurdity in the dream.[1] This absurdity does not mean, therefore, that there is any paralysis of psychical activity: it is a method of representation employed by the dream-work. As always happens at specially difficult points, the author once more comes to our help here. The senseless dream had a short epilogue, in which a bird uttered a laughing call and carried the lizard away in its beak. But Hanold had heard a similar laughing call after Gradiva's disappearance [p. 22]. It had in fact come from Zoe, who with this laugh was shaking off the gloomy seriousness of her underworld role. Gradiva had really laughed at him. But the dream-image of the bird carrying off the lizard may have been a recollection of the earlier dream, in which the Apollo Belvedere carried off the Capitoline Venus [p. 68].

[83]

There may still be some readers who feel that the translation of the situation of lizard-catching by the idea of wooing has not been sufficiently well established. Some further support for it may be afforded by the consideration that Zoe in her conversation with her newly-married friend admitted precisely what Hanold's thoughts

---

[1][*The Interpretation of Dreams, Standard Ed.,* **5**, 444–5.]

about her suspected—when she told her she had felt sure that she would 'dig out' something interesting in Pompeii. Here she was trespassing into the field of archaeology, just as he had trespassed, with his simile of lizard-catching, into the field of zoology; it was as though they were struggling towards each other and each were trying to assume the other's character.

Here then we seem to have finished off the interpretation of this second dream as well. Both of them have been made intelligible to us on the presupposition that a dreamer knows in his unconscious thoughts all that he has forgotten in his conscious ones, and that in the former he judges correctly what in the latter he misunderstands in a delusion. In the course of our arguments we have no doubt been obliged to make some assertions which have seemed strange to the reader because of their unfamiliarity; and we have probably often roused a suspicion that what we pretended was the author's meaning was in fact only our own. I am anxious to do all I can to [84] dissipate this suspicion, and for that reason I will gladly enter into more detail over one of the most delicate points—I mean the use of ambiguous words and phrases, such as: 'Somewhere in the Sun Gradiva was sitting.'

Anyone who reads *Gradiva* must be struck by the frequency with which the author puts ambiguous remarks into the mouths of his two principal characters. In Hanold's case these remarks are intended by him unambiguously and it is only the heroine, Gradiva, who is struck by their second meaning. Thus, for instance, when in reply to her first answer he exclaimed 'I knew your voice sounded like that' [p. 19], Zoe, who was still in ignorance, could not but ask how that could be, since he had not heard her speak before. In their second conversation the girl was for a moment thrown into doubt about his delusion, when he told her that he had recognized her at once [p. 21]. She could not help taking these words in the sense (correct so far as his unconscious was concerned) of being a recognition that their acquaintance went back to their childhood; whereas he, of course, knew nothing of this implication of his remark and explained it only by reference to his dominant delusion. On the other hand, the remarks made by the girl, whose personality shows the most lucid clarity of mind in contrast to Hanold's delusion, exhibit an *intentional* ambiguity. One of their meanings chimes in with Hanold's delusion, so as to be able to penetrate into his conscious understanding, but the other rises above the delusion and gives us as a rule its translation into the unconscious truth for which it stands. It is a triumph of ingenuity and wit to be able to express the delusion and the truth in the same turn of words.

Zoe's speech in which she explains the situation to her friend and at the same time succeeds in getting rid of the interrupter [p. 27 f.] is full of ambiguities of this kind. It is in reality a speech made by the author and aimed more at the reader than at Zoe's newly-married 'colleague'. In her conversations with Hanold the ambiguity is usually effected by Zoe's using the same symbolism that we [85] found in Hanold's first dream—the equation of repression and burial, and of Pompeii and childhood. Thus she is able in her speeches on the one hand to remain in the role for which Hanold's delusion has cast her, and on the other hand to make contact with the real circumstances and awaken an understanding of them in Hanold's unconscious.

'I have long grown used to being dead.' (90 [p. 21].) 'To me it is right that you should give the flower of forgetfulness.' [Ibid.] In these sentences there was a faint foretaste of the reproaches which broke out clearly enough later on in her final lecture to him, in which she compared him to an archaeopteryx. [Pp. 32f.] 'The fact of someone having to die so as to come alive; but no doubt that must be so for archaeologists.' [P. 37.] She made this last remark after the delusion had been cleared up, as though to give a key to her ambiguous speeches. But she made her neatest use of her symbolism when she asked: 'I feel as though we had shared a meal like this once before, two thousand years ago; can't you remember?' (118 [p. 26].) Here the substitution of the historical past for childhood and the effort to awaken the memory of the latter are quite unmistakable.

But whence comes this striking preference for ambiguous

speeches in *Gradiva*? It is no chance event, so it seems to us, but a necessary consequence of the premisses of the story. It is nothing other than a counterpart to the twofold determination of symptoms, in so far as speeches are themselves symptoms and, like them, arise from compromises between the conscious and the unconscious. It is simply that this double origin is more easily noticed in speeches than, for instance, in actions. And when, as is often made possible by the malleable nature of the material of speech, each of the two intentions lying behind the speech can be successfully expressed in the same turn of words, we have before us what we call an 'ambiguity'.

In the course of the psychotherapeutic treatment of a delusion or of an analogous disorder, ambiguous speeches of this kind are often produced by the patient, as new symptoms of the briefest duration; [86] and it can happen that the doctor finds himself too in the position of making use of them. In that way it not infrequently happens that with the meaning that is intended for the patient's conscious he stirs up an understanding of the meaning that applies to his unconscious. I know from experience that the part thus played by ambiguity is apt to raise the greatest objection in the uninitiated and to give rise to the greatest misunderstandings. But in any case our author was right in giving a place in his creation to a picture of this characteristic feature of what takes place in the formation of dreams and delusions.

IV

[87] THE emergence of Zoe as a physician, as I have already re-marked, arouses a new interest in us. We shall be anxious to learn whether a cure of the kind she performed upon Hanold is conceivable or even possible, and whether the author has taken as correct a view of the conditions for the disappearance of a delusion as he has of those for its genesis.

We shall unquestionably be met at this point by an opinion which denies that the case presented by the author possesses any such general interest and disputes the existence of any problem requiring solution. Hanold, it will be said, had no alternative but to abandon his delusion, after its subject, the supposed 'Gradiva' herself, had shown him that all his hypotheses were incorrect and after she had given him the most natural explanations of everything puzzling—for instance, of how it was that she had known his name. This would be the logical end of the matter; but since the girl had incidentally revealed her love to him, the author, no doubt to the satisfaction of his female readers, arranged that his story, a not uninteresting one otherwise, should have the usual happy ending in marriage. It would have been more consistent and equally possible, the argument will proceed, if the young scientist, after his error had been pointed out, had taken his leave of the lady with polite thanks and given as the reason for refusing her love the fact that he was able to feel an intense interest in antique women made of bronze or marble, and in their originals if they were accessible to contact, but that he did not know what to do with contemporary girls of flesh and blood. The author, in short, had quite arbitrarily tacked a love story on to his archaeological phantasy.

In rejecting his view as an impossible one, we observe in the first place that the beginnings of a change in Hanold were not shown only in his abandoning his delusion. Simultaneously, and indeed [88] before his delusion was cleared up, an unmistakable craving for love awakened in him, which found its outcome, naturally as it were, in his courting the girl who had freed him from his delusion. We have already laid emphasis on the pretexts and disguises under

78

which his curiosity about her 'bodily nature', his jealousy, and his brutal masculine instinct for mastery were expressed in the midst of his delusion, after his repressed erotic desire had led to his first dream. As further evidence of this we may recall that on the evening after his second interview with Gradiva a live woman for the first time struck him as sympathetic, though he still made a concession to his earlier horror of honeymooning couples by not recognizing her as being newly-married. Next morning, however, he was a chance witness of an exchange of endearments between the girl and her supposed brother, and he withdrew with a sense of awe as though he had interrupted some sacred act [p. 26]. His derision of 'Edwin and Angelina' was forgotten, and he had acquired a sense of respect for the erotic side of life.

Thus the author has drawn the closest link between the clearing up of the delusion and the outbreak of a craving for love, and he has paved the way for the inevitable outcome in a courtship. He knows the essential nature of the delusion better than his critics: he knows that a component of loving desire had combined with a component of resistance to it in bringing about the delusion, and he makes the girl who undertakes the cure sensitive to the element in Hanold's delusion which is agreeable to her. It was only this knowledge which could decide her to devote herself to the treatment; it was only the certainty of being loved by him that could induce her to admit her love to him. The treatment consisted in giving him back from outside the repressed memories which he could not set free from inside; but it would have had no effect if in the course of it the therapist had not taken his feelings into account and if her ultimate translation of the delusion had not been: 'Look, all this only means that you love me.'

The procedure which the author makes his Zoe adopt for curing her childhood friend's delusion shows a far-reaching similarity—no, a complete agreement in its essence—with a therapeutic [89] method which was introduced into medical practice in 1895 by Dr. Josef Breuer and myself, and to the perfecting of which I have since then devoted myself. This method of treatment, to which Breuer first gave the name of 'cathartic' but which I prefer to describe as 'analytic', consists, as applied to patients suffering from disorders analogous to Hanold's delusion, in bringing to their consciousness, to some extent forcibly, the unconscious whose repression led to their falling ill—exactly as Gradiva did with the repressed memories of their childhood relations. Gradiva, it is true, could carry out this task more easily than a doctor: in several respects she was in what may be described as an ideal position for it. The doctor, who has no pre-existing knowledge of his patient and possesses no conscious memory of what is unconsciously at work in him, must call a complicated technique to his help in order to make up for this disadvantage. He must learn how to infer with great certainty from the conscious associations and communications of the patient what is repressed in him, how to discover his unconscious as it betrays itself behind his conscious words and acts. He then brings about something like what Norbert Hanold grasped at the end of the story when he translated back the name 'Gradiva' into 'Bertgang'. [P. 37.] The disorder vanishes while being traced back to its origin; analysis, too, brings simultaneous cure.

But the similarity between Gradiva's procedure and the analytic method of psychotherapy is not limited to these two points—the making conscious of what has been repressed and the coinciding of explanation with cure. It also extends to what turns out to be the essence of the whole change—to the awakening of feelings. Every disorder analogous to Hanold's delusion, what in scientific terms we are in the habit of calling 'psychoneuroses', has as its precondition the repression of a portion of instinctual life, or, as we can safely say, of the sexual instinct. At every attempt to introduce the unconscious and repressed causes of the illness into consciousness, [90] the instinctual component concerned is necessarily aroused to a renewed struggle with the repressing powers, only to come to terms with them in the final outcome, often to the accompaniment of violent manifestations of reaction. The process of cure is accomplished in a relapse into love, if we combine all the many components of the sexual instinct under the term 'love'; and such a relapse is indispensable, for the symptoms on account of which the treatment has been undertaken are nothing other than precipitates of earlier struggles connected with repression or the return of the repressed, and they can only be resolved and washed away by a fresh high tide of the same passions. Every psycho-analytic treatment is an attempt at liberating repressed love which has found a meagre outlet in the compromise of a symptom. Indeed, the agreement between such treatments and the process of cure described by the author of *Gradiva* reaches its climax in the further fact that in analytic psychotherapy too the re-awakened passion, whether it is love or hate, invariably chooses as its object the figure of the doctor.

It is here that the differences begin, which made the case of Gradiva an ideal one which medical technique cannot attain. Gradiva was able to return the love which was making its way from the unconscious into consciousness, but the doctor cannot. Gradiva had herself been the object of the earlier, repressed love; her figure at once offered the liberated current of love a desirable aim. The doctor has been a stranger, and must endeavour to become a stranger once more after the cure; he is often at a loss what advice to give the patients he has cured as to how in real life they can use their recovered capacity to love. To indicate the expedients and substitutes of which the doctor therefore makes use to help him to approximate with more or less success to the model of a cure by love which has been shown us by our author—all this would take us much too far away from the task before us.

And now for the final question, whose answer we have already evaded more than once. [Cf. pp. 43 and 54.] Our views on repression, on the genesis of delusions and allied disorders, on the formation and solution of dreams, on the part played by erotic life, and on the method by which such disorders are cured, are far from being the common property of science, let alone the assured possession of educated people. If the insight which has enabled the author to construct his 'phantasy' in such a way that we have been able to dissect it like a real case history is in the nature of knowledge, we should be curious to learn what were the sources of that knowledge. One of our circle—the one who, as I said at the [91] beginning, was interested in the dreams in *Gradiva* and their possible interpretation [cf. footnote, p. 9]—approached the author with the direct question whether he knew anything of such scientific theories as these. The author replied, as was to be expected, in the negative, and, indeed, somewhat brusquely.[1] His imagination, he said, had inspired *Gradiva*, and he had enjoyed it; if there was anyone whom it did not please, let him simply leave it alone. He had no suspicion of how greatly it had in fact pleased his readers.

It is quite possible that the author's disavowal does not stop at this. He may perhaps altogether deny any knowledge of the rules which we have shown that he has followed, and he may repudiate all the purposes we have recognized in his work. I do not regard this as improbable; but if it is so, there are only two possible explanations. It may be that we have produced a complete caricature of an interpretation by introducing into an innocent work of art purposes of which its creator had no notion, and by so doing have shown once more how easy it is to find what one is looking for and what is occupying one's own mind—a possibility of which the strangest examples are to be found in the history of literature. Let every reader now make up his mind whether he is able to accept this explanation. We ourselves, of course, hold to the other view, the remaining alternative. Our opinion is that the author need have known nothing of these rules and purposes, so that he could [92] disavow them in good faith, but that nevertheless we have not discovered anything in his work that is not already in it. We probably draw from the same source and work upon the same object, each of us by another method. And the agreement of our results seems to guarantee that we have both worked correctly. Our procedure consists in the conscious observation of abnormal mental processes in other people so as to be able to elicit and announce their laws. The author no doubt proceeds differently. He directs his attention to the unconscious in his own mind, he listens to its possible developments and lends them artistic expression instead of suppressing them by conscious criticism. Thus he experiences from

[1][See, however, the Editor's Note, p. 270.]

himself what we learn from others—the laws which the activities of this unconscious must obey. But he need not state these laws, nor even be clearly aware of them; as a result of the tolerance of his intelligence, they are incorporated within his creations. We discover these laws by analysing his writings just as we find them from cases of real illness; but the conclusion seems inescapable that either both of us, the writer and the doctor, have misunderstood the unconscious in the same way, or we have both understood it correctly. This conclusion is of great value to us, and it is on its account that it has been worth while to investigate by the methods of medical psychoanalysis the way in which the formation and the cure of the delusions as well as the dreams are represented in Jensen's *Gradiva.*

We would seem to have reached the end. But an attentive reader might remind us that at the beginning [p. 7.] we threw out an assertion that dreams are wishes represented as fulfilled and that we gave no proof of this. Well, is our reply, what we have described in these pages might show how little justification there is for trying to cover the explanations we have to give of dreams with the single formula that dreams are wish-fulfilments. Nevertheless the assertion stands and can easily be proved too for the dreams in *Gradiva.* The latent dream-thoughts—we know now what is meant by them—may be of the most various kinds; in *Gradiva* they are 'days' residues', thoughts that have been left over unnoticed and undealt-with from the mental activities of waking life. But in order for a dream to develop out of them, the co-operation of a wish (usually an unconscious one) is required; this contributes the motive force for constructing the dream, while the day's residues provide the material. In Norbert Hanold's first dream two wishes competed with each other in making the dream; one of them was actually admissible to consciousness, while the other belonged to the unconscious and operated from out of repression. The first was a wish, understandable in any archaeologist, to have been present as an eye-witness at the catastrophe in the year 79 A.D. What sacrifice would an archaeologist think too great if this wish could be realized [93] in any way other than in a dream! The other wish, the other constructor of the dream, was of an erotic nature: it might be crudely and also incompletely stated as a wish to be there when the girl he loved lay down to sleep. This was the wish the rejection of which caused the dream to become an anxiety-dream. The wishes that were the motive forces of the second dream are perhaps less conspicuous; but if we recall its translation we shall not hesitate to describe them too as erotic. The wish to be taken captive by the girl he loved, to fall in with her wishes and to be subfected to her—for so we may construe the wish behind the situation of the lizard-catching—was in fact of a passive, masochistic character. Next day the dreamer hit the girl, as though he was dominated by the contrary erotic current . . . But we must stop here, or we may really forget that Hanold and Gradiva are only creatures of their author's mind.

Postscript to the Second Edition
(1912)

IN the five years that have passed since this study was completed,
psycho-analytic research has summoned up the courage to approach the creations of imaginative writers with yet another purpose in view. It no longer merely seeks in them for confirmations of
the findings it has made from unpoetic, neurotic human beings; it
also demands to know the material of impressions and memories
from which the author has built the work, and the methods and
processes by which he has converted this material into a work of
art. It has turned out that these questions can be most easily
answered in the case of writers who (like our Wilhelm Jensen, who
died in 1911) were in the habit of giving themselves over to their
imagination in a simple-minded joy in creating Soon after the
publication of my analytic examination of *Gradiva* I attempted to
interest the elderly author in these new tasks of psycho-analytic
research. But he refused his co-operation.

A friend of mine has since then drawn my attention to two other
of the author's short stories, which might stand in a genetic relation
to *Gradiva*, as preliminary studies or earlier attempts at a satisfactory poetical solution of the same problem in the psychology of
love. The first of these stories, 'Der rote Schirm',[1] recalls *Gradiva* by
the recurrence in it of a number of small *motifs*, such as white
flowers of the dead, a forgotten object (Gradiva's sketch-book), and
a significant small animal (the butterfly and the lizard in *Gradiva*),
but more especially by the repetition of the main situation—the
apparition in the mid-day glare of a summer's day of a girl who had
died (or was believed to have died). In 'Der rote Schirm' the scene
of the apparition is a ruined castle, just as are the ruins of the   [95]
excavated Pompeii in *Gradiva*. The other story, 'Im gotischen
Hause',[2] shows no such resemblances either to *Gradiva* or to 'Der
rote Schirm' in its manifest content. But the fact that it was given

[1]['The Red Parasol.']
[2]['In the Gothic House.']

an external unity with the latter story by being published with it under a common title[1] points unmistakably to their having a closely related latent meaning. It is easy to see that all three stories treat of the same theme: the development of a love (in 'Der rote Schirm' the inhibition of a love) as an after-effect of an intimate association in childhood of a brother-and-sister kind. I gather further from a review by Eva, Countess Baudissin (in the Vienna daily paper *Die Zeit* of February 11, 1912) that Jensen's last novel *Fremdlinge unter den Menschen*,[2] which contains much material from the author's own childhood, describes the history of a man who 'sees a sister in the woman he loves'. In neither of the two earlier stories is there a trace of the main *motif* of *Gradiva*: the girl's peculiarly charming gait with the nearly perpendicular posture of her foot.

The relief of the girl who steps along in this way, which Jensen describes as being Roman, and to which he gives the name of 'Gradiva', is in fact derived from the zenith of Greek art. It is in the Museo Chiaramonti in the Vatican (No. 644), and has been restored and interpreted by Hauser [1903]. By the combination of 'Gradiva' and some other fragments, in Florence and Munich, two reliefs were obtained, each representing three figures, who seem to be identified as the Horae, the goddesses of vegetation, and the deities of the fertilizing dew who are allied to them.[3]

---

[1] *Übermächte* [*Superior Powers*]. Two short stories by Wilhelm Jensen, Berlin, Emil Felber, 1892.

[2] [*Strangers among Men*, Dresden, C. Reissner, 1911.]

[3] [Hauser (loc. cit.) regards them as Roman copies of Greek originals of the latter part of the fourth century B.C. The 'Gradiva' relief is now (1959) in Section VII/2 of the Museo Chiaramonti and is numbered 1284.]

§ Psychopathic Characters on the Stage

IF, as has been assumed since the time of Aristotle, the purpose of drama is to arouse 'terror and pity'[1] and so 'to purge the emotions', we can describe that purpose in rather more detail by saying that it is a question of opening up sources of pleasure or enjoyment in our emotional life, just as, in the case of intellectual activity, joking or fun open up similar sources, many of which that activity had made inaccessible. In this connection the prime factor is unquestionably the process of getting rid of one's own emotions by 'blowing off steam'; and the consequent enjoyment corresponds on the one hand to the relief produced by a thorough discharge and on the other hand, no doubt, to an accompanying sexual excitation; for the latter, as we may suppose, appears as a by-product whenever an affect is aroused, and gives people the sense, which they so much desire, of a raising of the potential of their psychical state. Being present as an interested spectator at a spectacle or play[2] does for

SOURCE: *Standard Ed.*, 7, 305–10.
[1][The German '*Mitleid*' has the meaning of 'sympathetic suffering'.]

[2]['*Schauspiel*' is the ordinary German word for a dramatic performance. Freud writes it here with a hyphen, '*Schau-spiel*' to bring out the word's two components: '*Schau*', 'spectacle', and '*Spiel*', 'play' or 'game'. Freud returned to this topic in his subsequent paper on creative art and phantasy (1908*e*) and again, many years later, at the end of Chapter II of *Beyond the Pleasure Principle* (1920*g*).]

adults what play does for children, whose hesitant hopes of being able to do what grown-up people do are in that way gratified. The spectator is a person who experiences too little, who feels that he is a 'poor wretch to whom nothing of importance can happen', who has long been obliged to damp down, or rather displace, his ambition to stand in his own person at the hub of world affairs; he longs to feel and to act and to arrange things according to his desires—in short, to be a hero. And the playwright and actor enable him to do this by allowing him *to identify himself* with a hero. They spare him something, too. For the spectator knows quite well that actual heroic conduct such as this would be impossible for him without pains and sufferings and acute fears, which would almost cancel out the enjoyment. He knows, moreover, that he has only *one* life and that he might perhaps perish even in a *single* such struggle against adversity. Accordingly, his enjoyment is based on an illusion; that is to say, his suffering is mitigated by the certainty that, firstly, it is someone other than himself who is acting and suffering on the stage, and, secondly, that after all it is only a game, which can threaten no damage to his personal security. In these circumstances he can allow himself to enjoy being a 'great man', to give way without a qualm to such suppressed impulses as a craving for freedom in religious, political, social and sexual matters, and to 'blow off steam' in every direction in the various grand scenes that form part of the life represented on the stage.

[306]

Several other forms of creative writing, however, are equally subject to these same preconditions for enjoyment. Lyric poetry serves the purpose, more than anything, of giving vent to intense feelings of many sorts—just as was at one time the case with dancing. Epic poetry aims chiefly at making it possible to feel the enjoyment of a great heroic character in his hour of triumph. But drama seeks to explore emotional possibilities more deeply and to give an enjoyable shape even to forebodings of misfortune; for this reason it depicts the hero in his struggles, or rather (with masochistic satisfaction) in defeat. This relation to suffering and misfortune might be taken as characteristic of drama, whether, as happens in serious plays, it is only *concern* that is aroused, and afterwards allayed, or whether, as happens in tragedies, the suffering is actually realized. The fact that drama originated out of sacrificial rites (cf. the goat and the scapegoat) in the cult of the gods cannot be unrelated to this meaning of drama.[1] It appeases, as it were, a rising rebellion against the divine regulation of the universe, which is responsible for the existence of suffering. Heroes are first and foremost rebels against God or against something divine; and pleasure is derived, as it seems, from the affliction of a weaker being in the face of divine might—a pleasure due to masochistic satisfaction as well as to direct enjoyment of a character whose greatness is insisted upon in spite of everything. Here we have a mood like that of Prometheus, but alloyed with a paltry readiness to let oneself be soothed for the moment by a temporary satisfaction.

Suffering of every kind is thus the subject-matter of drama, and [307] from this suffering it promises to give the audience pleasure. Thus we arrive at a first precondition of this form of art: that it should not cause suffering to the audience, that it should know how to compensate, by means of the possible satisfactions involved, for the sympathetic suffering which is aroused. (Modern writers have particularly often failed to obey this rule.) But the suffering represented is soon restricted to *mental* suffering; for no one wants *physical* suffering who knows how quickly all mental enjoyment is brought to an end by the changes in somatic feeling that physical suffering brings about. If we are sick we have one wish only: to be well again and to be quit of our present state. We call for the doctor and medicine, and for the removal of the inhibition on the play of phantasy which has pampered us into deriving enjoyment even from our own sufferings. If a spectator puts himself in the place of someone who is physically ill he finds himself without any capacity for enjoyment or psychical activity. Consequently a person who is physically ill can only figure on the stage as a piece of stage-property and not as a hero, unless, indeed, some peculiar physical aspects of his illness make psychical activity possible—such, for

[1][The subject of the Hero in Greek tragedy was discussed by Freud in his *Totem and Taboo* (1912–13), in Section 7 of the fourth essay.]

instance, as the sick man's forlorn state in the *Philoctetes* or the hopelessness of the sufferers in the class of plays that centre round consumptives.

People are acquainted with mental suffering principally in connection with the circumstances in which it is acquired; accordingly, dramas dealing with it require some event out of which the illness shall arise and they open with an exposition of this event. It is only an apparent exception that some plays, such as the *Ajax* and the *Philoctetes*, introduce the mental illness as already fully established; for in Greek tragedies, owing to the familiarity of the material, the curtain rises, as one might say, in the middle of the play. It is easy to give an exhaustive account of the preconditions governing an event of the kind that is here in question. It must be an event involving conflict and it must include an effort of will together with resistance. This precondition found its first and grandest fulfilment in a struggle against divinity. I have already said that a tragedy of this kind is one of rebellion, in which the dramatist and the audience take the side of the rebel. The less belief there comes to be [308]   in divinity, the more important becomes the *human* regulation of affairs; and it is this which, with increasing insight, comes to be held responsible for suffering. Thus the hero's next struggle is against human society, and here we have the class of *social* tragedies. Yet another fulfilment of the necessary precondition is to be found in a struggle between individual men. Such are tragedies of *character*, which exhibit all the excitement of an '*agon*' [ἀγών, conflict], and which are best played out between outstanding characters who have freed themselves from the bond of human institutions— which, in fact, must have *two* heroes. Fusions between these two last classes, with a hero struggling against institutions embodied in powerful characters, are of course admissible without question. Pure tragedies of character lack the rebellious source of enjoyment, but this emerges once again no less forcibly in social dramas (in Ibsen for instance) than it did in the historical plays of the Greek classical tragedians.

Thus *religious* drama, *social* drama and drama of *character* differ essentially in the terrain on which the action that leads to the suffering is fought out. And we can now follow the course of drama on to yet another terrain, where it becomes *psychological* drama. Here the struggle that causes the suffering is fought out in the hero's mind itself—a struggle between different impulses, and one which must have its end in the extinction, not of the hero, but of one of his impulses; it must end, that is to say, in a renunciation. Combinations of any kind between this precondition and the earlier types are, of course, possible; thus institutions, for instance, can themselves be the cause of internal conflicts. And this is where we have tragedies of love; for the suppression of love by social culture, by human conventions, or the struggle between 'love and duty', which is so familiar to us in opera, are the starting-point of almost endless varieties of situations of conflict: just as endless, in fact, as the erotic day-dreams of men.

But the series of possibilities grows wider; and psychological drama turns into psychopathological drama when the source of the suffering in which we take part and from which we are meant to derive pleasure is no longer a conflict between two almost equally conscious impulses but between a conscious impulse and a repressed one. Here the precondition of enjoyment is that the spectator should himself be a neurotic, for it is only such people who can derive pleasure instead of simple aversion from the revelation and the more or less conscious recognition of a repressed impulse. In anyone who is *not* neurotic this recognition will meet only with aversion and will call up a readiness to repeat the act of repression which has earlier been successfully brought to bear on the impulse: for in such people a single expenditure of repression has been enough to hold the repressed impulse completely in check. But in neurotics the repression is on the brink of failing; it is unstable and needs a constant renewal of expenditure, and this expenditure is spared if recognition of the impulse is brought about. Thus it is only in neurotics that a struggle can occur of a kind which can be made the subject of a drama; but even in them the dramatist will provoke not merely an *enjoyment* of the liberation but a *resistance* to it as well.

[309]

The first of these modern dramas is *Hamlet*.[1] It has as its subject the way in which a man who has so far been normal becomes neurotic owing to the peculiar nature of the task by which he is faced, a man, that is, in whom an impulse that has hitherto been successfully suppressed endeavours to make its way into action. *Hamlet* is distinguished by three characteristics which seem important in connection with our present discussion. (1) The hero is not psychopathic, but only *becomes* psychopathic in the course of the action of the play. (2) The repressed impulse is one of those which are similarly repressed in all of us, and the repression of which is part and parcel of the foundations of our personal evolution. It is this repression which is shaken up by the situation in the play. As a result of these two characteristics it is easy for us to recognize ourselves in the hero: we are susceptible to the same conflict as he is, since 'a person who does not lose his reason under certain conditions can have no reason to lose'.[2] (3) It appears as a necessary precondition of this form of art that the impulse that is struggling into consciousness, however clearly it is recognizable, is never given a definite name; so that in the spectator too the process is carried through with his attention averted, and he is in the grip of his emotions instead of taking stock of what is happening. A certain amount of resistance is no doubt saved in this way, just as, in an analytic treatment, we find derivatives of the repressed material [310]   reaching consciousness, owing to a lower resistance, while the repressed material itself is unable to do so. After all, the conflict in *Hamlet* is so effectively concealed that it was left to me to unearth it.

It may be in consequence of disregarding these three preconditions that so many other psychopathic characters are as unserviceable on the stage as they are in real life. For the victim of a neurosis is someone into whose conflict we can gain no insight if we first meet it in a fully established state. But, *per contra*, if we recognize

[1][Freud's first published discussion of *Hamlet* was in *The Interpretation of Dreams* (Chapter V, Section D (*β*); *Standard Ed.*, **4**, 264 ff.).]
[2][Lessing, *Emilia Galotti*, Act IV, Scene 7.]

the conflict, we forget that he is a sick man, just as, if he himself recognizes it, he ceases to be ill. It would seem to be the dramatist's business to induce the same illness in *us*; and this can best be achieved if we are made to follow the development of the illness along with the sufferer. This will be especially necessary where the repression does not already exist in us but has first to be set up; and this represents a step further than *Hamlet* in the use of neurosis on the stage. If we are faced by an unfamiliar and fully established neurosis, we shall be inclined to send for the doctor (just as we do in real life) and pronounce the character inadmissible to the stage.

This last mistake seems to occur in Bahr's *Die Andere*,[1] apart from a second one which is implicit in the problem presented in the play—namely, that it is impossible for us to put ourselves with conviction into the position of believing that one particular person has a prescriptive right to give the girl complete satisfaction. So that her case cannot become ours. Moreover, there remains a third mistake: namely that there is nothing left for us to discover and that our entire resistance is mobilized against this predetermined condition of love which is so unacceptable to us. Of the three formal preconditions that I have been discussing, the most important seems to be that of the diversion of attention.

In general, it may perhaps be said that the neurotic instability of the public and the dramatist's skill in avoiding resistances and offering fore-pleasures can alone determine the limits set upon the employment of abnormal characters on the stage.

[1][This play by Hermann Bahr, the Austrian novelist and playwright (1863–1934), was first produced at the end of 1905. Its plot turns upon the dual personality of its heroine, who is unable, in spite of every effort, to escape from an attachment (based on her physical feelings) to a man who has her in his power.—This paragraph was omitted from the 1942 translation.]

§ The Antithetical Meaning of Primal Words[1]

[155] In my *The Interpretation of Dreams* I made a statement about one of the findings of my analytic work which I did not then understand. I will repeat it here by way of preface to this review:

'The way in which dreams treat the category of contraries and contradictories is highly remarkable. It is simply disregarded. "No" seems not to exist so far as dreams are concerned. They show a particular preference for combining contraries into a unity or for representing them as one and the same thing. Dreams feel themselves at liberty, moreover, to represent any element by its wishful contrary; so that there is no way of deciding at a first glance whether any element that admits of a contrary is present in the dream-thoughts as a positive or as a negative.'[2]

The dream-interpreters of antiquity seem to have made the most extensive use of the notion that a thing in a dream can mean its opposite. This possibility has also occasionally been recognized by modern students of dreams, in so far as they concede at all that dreams have a meaning and can be interpreted.[3] Nor do I think

---

SOURCE: *Standard Ed.*, **11**, 155–61.

[1][In the editions previous to 1924, the title was printed in inverted commas, and there was a sub-title which ran as follows: 'A review of a pamphlet by Karl Abel (1884) bearing the same title.']

[2] *The Interpretation of Dreams* (1900*a*), *Standard Ed.*, **4**, 318.

[3]Cf. G. H. von Schubert (1814, Chapter II).

that I shall be contradicted if I assume that all who have followed me in interpreting dreams on scientific lines have found confirmation of the statement quoted above.

I did not succeed in understanding the dream-work's singular tendency to disregard negation and to employ the same means of representation for expressing contraries until I happened by chance to read a work by the philologist Karl Abel, which was published in 1884 as a separate pamphlet and included in the following year in the author's *Sprachwissenschaftliche Abhandlungen* [Philological Essays]. The subject is of sufficient interest to justify my quoting here the full text of the crucial passages in Abel's paper (omitting, however, most of the examples). We obtain from them the astonishing information that the behaviour of the dream-work which I have just described is identical with a peculiarity in the oldest languages known to us.   [156]

After stressing the antiquity of the Egyptian language which must have been developed a very long time before the first hieroglyphic inscriptions, Abel goes on (1884, 4):

'Now in the Egyptian language, this sole relic of a primitive world, there are a fair number of words with two meanings, one of which is the exact opposite of the other. Let us suppose, if such an obvious piece of nonsense can be imagined, that in German the word "strong" meant both "strong" and "weak"; that in Berlin the noun "light" was used to mean both "light" and "darkness"; that one Munich citizen called beer "beer", while another used the same word to speak of water: this is what the astonishing practice amounts to which the ancient Egyptians regularly followed in their language. How could anyone be blamed for shaking his head in disbelief? . . .' (Examples omitted.)

(Ibid., 7): 'In view of these and many similar cases of antithetical meaning (see the Appendix) it is beyond doubt that in one language at least there was a large number of words that denoted at once a thing and its opposite. However astonishing it may be, we are faced with the fact and have to reckon with it.'

The author goes on to reject an explanation of these circumstances which suggests that two words might happen by chance to have the same sound, and is equally firm in repudiating an attempt to refer it to the low state of mental development in Egypt:

(Ibid., 9): 'But Egypt was anything but a home of nonsense. On the contrary, it was one of the cradles of the development of human reason. . . . It recognized a pure and dignified morality and formulated a great part of the Ten Commandments at a time when the peoples in whose hands civilization rests to-day were in the habit of slaughtering human victims as a sacrifice to bloodthirsty idols. A people that kindled the torch of justice and culture in so dark an age cannot surely have been completely stupid in everyday speech and thought. . . . Men who were able to make glass and raise and [157] move huge blocks by machinery must at least have possessed sufficient sense not to regard a thing as being simultaneously both itself and its opposite. How are we then to reconcile this with the fact that the Egyptians allowed themselves such a strangely contradictory language? . . . that they used to give one and the same phonetic vehicle to the most mutually inimical thoughts, and used to bind together in a kind of indissoluble union things that were in the strongest opposition to each other?'

Before any explanation is attempted, mention must also be made of a further stage in this unintelligible behaviour of the Egyptian language. 'Of all the eccentricities of the Egyptian vocabulary perhaps the most extraordinary feature is that, quite apart from the words that combine antithetical meanings, it possesses other compound words in which two vocables of antithetical meanings are united so as to form a compound which bears the meaning of only one of its two constituents. Thus in this extraordinary language there are not only words meaning equally "strong" or "weak", and "command" or "obey"; but there are also compounds like "old-young", "far-near", "bind-sever", "outside-inside" . . . which, in spite of combining the extremes of difference, mean only "young", "near", "bind" and "inside" respectively . . . So that in these compound words contradictory concepts have been quite intentionally combined, not in order to produce a third concept, as occasionally happens in Chinese, but only in order to use the compound to express the meaning of one of its contradictory parts—a part which would have had the same meaning by itself . . .'

However, the riddle is easier to solve than it appears to be. Our concepts owe their existence to comparisons. 'If it were always light we should not be able to distinguish light from dark, and consequently we should not be able to have either the concept of light or the word for it . . .' 'It is clear that everything on this planet is relative and has an independent existence only in so far as it is differentiated in respect of its relations to other things . . .' 'Since every concept is in this way the twin of its contrary, how could it be first thought of and how could it be communicated to other people who were trying to conceive it, other than by being measured against its contrary . . .?' (Ibid., 15): 'Since the concept of strength could not be formed except as a contrary to weakness, the word de-   [158] noting "strong" contained a simultaneous recollection of "weak", as the thing by means of which it first came into existence. In reality this word denoted neither "strong" nor "weak", but the relation and difference between the two, which created both of them equally . . .' 'Man was not in fact able to acquire his oldest and simplest concepts except as contraries to their contraries, and only learnt by degrees to separate the two sides of an antithesis and think of one without conscious comparison with the other.'

Since language serves not only to express one's own thoughts but essentially to communicate them to others the question may be raised how it was that the 'primal Egyptian' made his neighbour understand 'which side of the twin concept he meant on any particular occasion'. In the written language this was done with the help of the so-called 'determinative' signs which, placed after the alphabetical ones, assign their meaning to them and are not themselves intended to be spoken. (Ibid., 18): 'If the Egyptian word "*ken*" is to mean "strong", its sound, which is written alphabetically, is followed by the picture of an upright armed man; if the same word has to express "weak", the letters which represent the sound are followed by the picture of a squatting, limp figure. The majority of other words with two meanings are similarly accompanied by explanatory pictures.' Abel thinks that in speech the desired meaning of the spoken word was indicated by gesture.

According to Abel it is in the 'oldest roots' that antithetical double meanings are found to occur. In the subsequent course of the language's development this ambiguity disappeared and, in Ancient Egyptian at any rate, all the intermediate stages can be followed, down to the unambiguousness of modern vocabularies. 'A word that originally bore two meanings separates in the later language into two words with single meanings, in a process whereby each of the two opposed meanings takes over a particular phonetic "reduction" (modification) of the original root.' Thus, for example, in hieroglyphics the word '*ken*', 'strong-weak', already divides into '*ken*', 'strong' and '*kan*', 'weak'. 'In other words, the concepts which could only be arrived at by means of an antithesis became in course of time sufficiently familiar to men's minds to [159] make an independent existence possible for each of their two parts and accordingly to enable a separate phonetic representative to be formed for each part.'

Proof of the existence of contradictory primal meanings, which is easily established in Egyptian, extends, according to Abel, to the Semitic and Indo-European languages as well. 'How far this may happen in other language-groups remains to be seen; for although antithesis must have been present originally to the thinking minds of every race, it need not necessarily have become recognizable or have been retained everywhere in the meanings of words.'

Abel further calls attention to the fact that the philosopher Bain, apparently without knowledge that the phenomenon actually existed, claimed this double meaning of words on purely theoretical grounds as a logical necessity. The passage in question[1] begins with these sentences:

'The essential relativity of all knowledge, thought or consciousness cannot but show itself in language. If everything that we can know is viewed as a transition from something else, every experience must have two sides; and either every name must have a double meaning, or else for every meaning there must be two names.'

From the 'Appendix of Examples of Egyptian, Indo-Germanic and Arabic Antithetical Meanings' I select a few instances which may impress even those of us who are not experts in philology. In

---

[1]Bain (1870, **1**, 54).

Latin '*altus*' means 'high' and 'deep', '*sacer*' 'sacred' and 'accursed';
here accordingly we have the complete antithesis in meaning
without any modification of the sound of the word. Phonetic
alteration to distinguish contraries is illustrated by examples like
'*clamare*' ('to cry')—'*clam*' ('softly', 'secretly'); '*siccus*' ('dry')—
'*succus*' ('juice'). In German '*Boden*' ['garret' or 'ground'] still
means the highest as well as the lowest thing in the house. Our '*bös*'
('bad') is matched by a word '*bass*' ('good'); in Old Saxon '*bat*'
('good') corresponds to the English 'bad', and the English 'to lock'
to the German '*Lücke*', '*Loch*' ['hole']. We can compare the German '*kleben*' ['to stick'] with the English 'to cleave' ([in the sense
of] 'to split'); the German words '*stumm*' ['dumb'] and '*Stimme*'
['voice'], and so on. In this way perhaps even the much derided   [160]
derivation *lucus a non lucendo*[1] would have some sense in it.

   In his essay on 'The Origin of Language' Abel (1885, 305) calls
attention to further traces of ancient difficulties in thinking. Even
to-day the Englishman in order to express '*ohne*' says 'without'
('*mitohne*' ['with-without'] in German), and the East Prussian does
the same. The word 'with' itself, which to-day corresponds to the
German '*mit*', originally meant 'without' as well as 'with', as can be
recognized from 'withdraw' and 'withhold'. The same transformation can be seen in the German '*wider*' ('against') and '*wieder*'
('together with').

   For comparison with the dream-work there is another extremely
strange characteristic of the ancient Egyptian language which is
significant. 'In Egyptian, words can—apparently, we will say to
begin with—*reverse their sound as well as their sense*. Let us suppose
that the German word "*gut*" ["good"] was Egyptian: it could then
mean "bad" as well as "good", and be pronounced "tug" as well as
"gut". Numerous examples of such reversals of sound, which are
too frequent to be explained as chance occurrences, can be produced from the Aryan and Semitic languages as well. Confining
ourselves in the first instance to Germanic languages we may note:
Topf [pot]—pot; boat—tub; wait—*täuwen* [tarry]; hurry—*Ruhe*

---

[1] ['*Lucus*' (Latin for 'a grove') is said to be derived from '*lucere*' ('to shine')
because it does not shine there. (Attributed to Quintilian.)]

[rest]; care—reck; *Balken* [beam]—*Klobe* [log], club. If we take the
other Indo-Germanic languages into consideration, the number of
relevant instances grows accordingly; for example, *capere* [Latin for
"take"]—*packen* [German for "seize"]; *ren* [Latin for "kidney"]—
Niere [German for "kidney"]; leaf—*folium* [Latin for "leaf"];
dum-a [Russian for "thought"], θυμός [Greek for "spirit", "courage"]—*mêdh, mûdha* [Sanscrit for "mind"], *Mut* [German for
"courage"]; *rauchen* [German for "to smoke"]—*Kur-ít* [Russian for
"to smoke"]; *kreischen* [German for "to shriek"]—to shriek, etc.'

Abel tries to explain the phenomenon of reversal of sound as a
doubling or reduplication of the root. Here we should find some
difficulty in following the philologist. We remember in this connection how fond children are of playing at reversing the sound of
[161]   words and how frequently the dream-work makes use of a reversal
of the representational material for various purposes. (Here it is no
longer letters but images whose order is reversed.) We should
therefore be more inclined to derive reversal of sound from a factor
of deeper origin.[1]

In the correspondence between the peculiarity of the dream-
work mentioned at the beginning of the paper and the practice
discovered by philology in the oldest languages, we may see a
confirmation of the view we have formed about the regressive,
archaic character of the expression of thoughts in dreams. And we
psychiatrists cannot escape the suspicion that we should be better
at understanding and translating the language of dreams if we
knew more about the development of language.[2]

[1]For the phenomenon of reversal of sound (metathesis), which is perhaps even
more intimately related to the dream-work than are contradictory meanings
(antithesis), compare also Meyer-Rinteln (1909).
[2]It is plausible to suppose, too, that the original antithetical meaning of words
exhibits the ready-made mechanism which is exploited for various purposes by
slips of the tongue that result in the opposite being said [of what was consciously
intended].

§ The Occurrence in Dreams of Material from Fairy Tales

[281]

IT is not surprising to find that psycho-analysis confirms our recognition of the important place which folk fairy tales have acquired in the mental life of our children. In a few people a recollection of their favourite fairy tales takes the place of memories of their own childhood; they have made the fairy tales into screen memories.

Elements and situations derived from fairy tales are also frequently to be found in dreams. In interpreting the passages in question the patient will produce the significant fairy tale as an association. In the present paper I shall give two instances of this very common occurrence. But it will not be possible to do more than hint at the relations between the fairy tales and the history of the dreamer's childhood and his neurosis, though this limitation will involve the risk of breaking links which were of the utmost importance to the analyst.

I

Here is a dream of a young married woman who had had a visit from her husband a few days before: *She was in a room that was entirely brown. A little door led to the top of a steep staircase, and up this staircase there came into the room a curious manikin—small, with*

SOURCE: *Standard Ed.*, **12**, 281–87.

white hair, a bald top to his head and a red nose. He danced round the room in front of her, carried on in the funniest way, and then went down the staircase again. He was dressed in a grey garment, through which every part of his figure was visible. (A correction was made subsequently: *He was wearing a long black coat and grey trousers.*)

The analysis was as follows. The description of the manikin's personal appearance fitted the dreamer's father-in-law without any alteration being necessary.[1] Immediately afterwards, however, she thought of the story of 'Rumpelstiltskin',[2] who danced around in the same funny way as the man in the dream and in so doing betrayed his name to the queen; but by that he lost his claim to the queen's first child, and in his fury tore himself in two.[3]

[282]

On the day before she had the dream she herself had been just as furious with her husband and had exclaimed: 'I could tear him in two.'

The brown room at first gave rise to difficulties. All that occurred to her was her parents' dining-room, which was panelled in that colour—in brown wood. She then told some stories of beds which were so uncomfortable for two people to sleep in. A few days before, when the subject of conversation had been beds in other countries, she had said something very *mal à propos*—quite innocently, as she maintained—and everyone in the room had roared with laughter.

The dream was now already intelligible. The brown wood room[4] was in the first place a bed, and through the connection with the dining-room it was a marriage bed.[5] She was therefore in her marriage bed. Her visitor should have been her young husband,

[1] Except for the detail that the manikin had his hair cut short, whereas her father-in-law wore his long.

[2] ['Rumpelstiltzchen.' Grimm, 1918, **1**, 250. (No. 55.)]

[3] [This, the climax of the story, is usually suppressed or softened in English translations.]

[4] Wood, as is well known, is frequently a female or maternal symbol: e.g. *materia, Madeira,* etc. [Cf. *The Interpretation of Dreams* (1900a), *Standard Ed.,* **5**, 355.]

[5] For bed and board stand for marriage. [Cf. the law-Latin phrase for a legal separation: '*separatio a mensa et toro*' ('separation from table and bed').]

who, after an absence of several months, had visited her to play his part in the double bed. But to begin with it was her husband's father, her father-in-law.

Behind this first interpretation we have a glimpse of deeper and purely sexual material. Here the room was the vagina. (The room was in her—this was reversed in the dream.) The little man who made grimaces and behaved so funnily was the penis. The narrow door and the steep stairs confirmed the view that the situation was a representation of intercourse. As a rule we are accustomed to find the penis symbolized by a child; but we shall find there was good reason for a father being introduced to represent the penis in this instance.

The solution of the remaining portion of the dream will entirely confirm us in this interpretation. The dreamer herself explained the transparent grey garment as a condom. We may gather that considerations of preventing conception and worries whether this visit of her husband's might not have sown the seed of a second child were among the instigating causes of the dream. [283]

The black coat. Coats of that kind suited her husband admirably. She wanted to persuade him always to wear them, instead of his usual clothes. Dressed in the black coat, therefore, her husband was as she liked to see him. *The black coat and the grey trousers.* At two different levels, one above the other, this had the same meaning: 'I should like you to be dressed like that. I like you like that.'

Rumpelstiltskin was connected with the contemporary thoughts underlying the dream—the day's residues—by a neat antithetic relation. In the fairy tale he comes in order to take away the queen's first child. In the dream the little man comes in the shape of a father, because he had presumably brought a second child. But Rumpelstiltskin also gave access to the deeper, infantile stratum of the dream-thoughts. The droll little fellow, whose very name is unknown, whose secret is so eagerly canvassed, who can perform such extraordinary tricks—in the fairy tale he turns straw into gold—the fury against him, or rather against his possessor, who is envied for possessing him (the girl's envy for the penis)—all of these were elements whose relation to the foundations of the patient's neurosis can, as I have said, barely be touched upon in this paper. The short-cut hair of the manikin in the dream was no doubt also connected with the subject of castration.

If we carefully observe from clear instances the way in which dreamers use fairy tales and the point at which they bring them in, we may perhaps also succeed in picking up some hints which will help in interpreting remaining obscurities in the fairy tales themselves.

II

A young man[1] told me the following dream. He had a chronological basis for his early memories in the circumstance that his parents moved from one country estate to another just before he was five years old; the dream, which he said was his earliest one, occurred while he was still upon the first estate.

'*I dreamt that it was night and that I was lying in my bed. (My bed stood with its foot towards the window: in front of the window there* [284] *was a row of old walnut trees. I know it was winter when I had the dream, and night-time.) Suddenly the window opened of its own accord, and I was terrified to see that some white wolves were sitting on the big walnut tree in front of the window. There were six or seven of them. The wolves were quite white, and looked more like foxes or sheep-dogs, for they had big tails like foxes and they had their ears pricked like dogs when they pay attention to something. In great terror, evidently of being eaten up by the wolves, I screamed* and woke up. My nurse hurried to my bed, to see what had happened to me. It took quite a long while before I was convinced that it had only been a dream; I had had such a clear and life-like picture of the window opening and the wolves sitting on the tree. At last I grew quieter, felt as though I had escaped from some danger, and went to sleep again.

'The only piece of action in the dream was the opening of the window; for the wolves sat quite still and without making any movement on the branches of the tree, to the right and left of the

[1][The 'Wolf Man'. See Editor's Note, p. 73.]

trunk, and looked at me. It seemed as though they had riveted their whole attention upon me.—I think this was my first anxiety-dream. I was three, four, or at most five years old at the time. From then until my eleventh or twelfth year I was always afraid of seeing something terrible in my dreams.'

He added a drawing of the tree with the wolves, which confirmed his description.[1] The analysis of the dream brought the following material to light.

He had always connected this dream with the recollection that during these years of his childhood he was most tremendously afraid of the picture of a wolf in a book of fairy tales. His elder sister, who was very much his superior, used to tease him by holding up this particular picture in front of him on some excuse or other, so that he was terrified and began to scream. In this picture the wolf was standing upright, striding out with one foot, with its claws stretched out and its ears pricked. He thought this picture must have been an illustration to the story of 'Little Red Riding-Hood'.[2]

Why were the wolves white? This made him think of the sheep, large flocks of which were kept in the neighbourhood of the estate. His father occasionally took him with him to visit these flocks, and every time this happened he felt very proud and blissful. Later on— [285] according to enquiries that were made it may easily have been shortly before the time of the dream—an epidemic broke out among the sheep. His father sent for a follower of Pasteur's, who inoculated the animals, but after the inoculation even more of them died than before.

How did the wolves come to be on the tree? This reminded him of a story that he had heard his grandfather tell. He could not remember whether it was before or after the dream, but its subject is a decisive argument in favour of the former view. The story ran as follows. A tailor was sitting at work in his room, when the window opened and a wolf leapt in. The tailor hit after him with his yard—

[1][This drawing is reproduced in *Standard Ed.*, **17**, 30.]
[2]['Rotkäpchen.' Grimm, 1918, **1**, 125. (No. 26.)]

no (he corrected himself), caught him by his tail and pulled it off, so that the wolf ran away in terror. Some time later the tailor went into the forest, and suddenly saw a pack of wolves coming towards him; so he climbed up a tree to escape from them. At first the wolves were in perplexity; but the maimed one, which was among them and wanted to revenge himself on the tailor, proposed that they should climb one upon another till the last one could reach him. He himself—he was a vigorous old fellow—would be the base of the pyramid. The wolves did as he suggested, but the tailor had recognized the visitor whom he had punished, and suddenly called out as he had before: 'Catch the grey one by his tail!' The tailless wolf, terrified by the recollection, ran away, and all the others tumbled down.

In this story the tree appears, upon which the wolves were sitting in the dream. But it also contains an unmistakable allusion to the castration complex. The *old* wolf was docked of his tail by the tailor. The fox-tails of the wolves in the dream were probably compensations for this taillessness.

Why were there six or seven wolves? There seemed to be no answer to this question, until I raised a doubt whether the picture that had frightened him could be connected with the story of 'Little Red Riding-Hood'. This fairy tale only offers an opportunity for two illustrations—Little Red Riding-Hood's meeting with the wolf in the wood, and the scene in which the wolf lies in bed in the grandmother's night-cap. There must therefore be some other fairy tale behind his recollection of the picture. He soon discovered that it could only be the story of 'The Wolf and the Seven Little Goats'.[1] Here the number seven occurs, and also the number six, for the wolf only ate up six of the little goats, while the seventh hid itself in the clock-case. The white, too, comes into this story, for the wolf had his paw made white at the baker's after the little goats had recognized him on his first visit by his grey paw. Moreover, the two fairy tales have much in common. In both there is the eating up, the cutting open of the belly, the taking out of the

[286]

[1] ['Der Wolf und die sieben Greisslein.' Grimm, 1918, **1**, 23. (No. 5.)]

people who have been eaten and their replacement by heavy stones, and finally in both of them the wicked wolf perishes. Besides all this, in the story of the little goats the tree appears. The wolf lay down under a tree after his meal and snored.

I shall have, for a special reason, to deal with this dream again elsewhere, and interpret it and consider its significance in greater detail. For it is the earliest anxiety dream that the dreamer remembered from his childhood, and its content, taken in connection with other dreams that followed it soon afterwards and with certain events in his earliest years, is of quite peculiar interest. We must confine ourselves here to the relation of the dream to the two fairy tales which have so much in common with each other, 'Little Red Riding-Hood' and 'The Wolf and the Seven Little Goats'. The effect produced by these stories was shown in the little dreamer by a regular animal phobia. This phobia was only distinguished from other similar cases by the fact that the anxiety-animal was not an object easily accessible to observation (such as a horse or a dog), but was known to him only from stories and picture-books.

I shall discuss on another occasion the explanation of these animal phobias and the significance attaching to them.[1] I will only remark in anticipation that this explanation is in complete harmony with the principal characteristic shown by the neurosis from which the present dreamer suffered later in his life. His fear of his father was the strongest motive for his falling ill, and his ambivalent attitude towards every father-surrogate was the dominating feature of his life as well as of his behaviour during the treatment.

If in my patient's case the wolf was merely a first father-surrogate, the question arises whether the hidden content in the fairy tales of the wolf that ate up the little goats and of 'Little Red Riding-Hood' may not simply be infantile fear of the father.[2] Moreover, my [287] patient's father had the characteristic, shown by so many people in relation to their children, of indulging in 'affectionate abuse'; and it

[1][This discussion will be found in the 'Wolf Man' case history (1918*b*).]
[2]Compare the similarity between these two fairy tales and the myth of Kronos, which has been pointed out by Rank (1912).

is possible that during the patient's earlier years his father (though he grew severe later on) may more than once, as he caressed the little boy or played with him, have threatened in fun to 'gobble him up'. One of my patients told me that her two children could never get to be fond of their grandfather, because in the course of his affectionate romping with them he used to frighten them by saying he would cut open their tummies.

§ The Theme of the Three Caskets

I

Two scenes from Shakespeare, one from a comedy and the other [291]
from a tragedy, have lately given me occasion for posing and
solving a small problem.

The first of these scenes is the suitors' choice between the three
caskets in *The Merchant of Venice*. The fair and wise Portia is bound
at her father's bidding to take as her husband only that one of her
suitors who chooses the right casket from among the three before
him. The three caskets are of gold, silver and lead: the right casket
is the one that contains her portrait. Two suitors have already
departed unsuccessful: they have chosen gold and silver. Bassanio,
the third, decides in favor of lead; thereby he wins the bride, whose
affection was already his before the trial of fortune. Each of the
suitors gives reasons for his choice in a speech in which he praises
the metal he prefers and depreciates the other two. The most
difficult task thus falls to the share of the fortunate third suitor;
what he finds to say in glorification of lead as against gold and silver
is little and has a forced ring. If in psycho-analytic practice we were
confronted with such a speech, we should suspect that there were
concealed motives behind the unsatisfying reasons produced.

SOURCE: *Standard Ed.*, **17**, 291–301.

Shakespeare did not himself invent this oracle of the choice of a
casket; he took it from a tale in the *Gesta Romanorum*,[1] in which a
girl has to make the same choice to win the Emperor's son.[2] Here
too the third metal, lead, is the bringer of fortune. It is not hard to
guess that we have here an ancient theme, which requires to be
interpreted, accounted for and traced back to its origin. A first
conjecture as to the meaning of this choice between gold, silver and
lead is quickly confirmed by a statement of Stucken's,[3] who has
made a study of the same material over a wide field. He writes: 'The
identity of Portia's three suitors is clear from their choice: the Prince
[292] of Morocco chooses the gold casket—he is the sun; the Prince
of Arragon chooses the silver casket—he is the moon; Bassanio
chooses the leaden casket—he is the star youth.' In support of this
explanation he cites an episode from the Estonian folk-epic 'Ka-
lewipoeg', in which the three suitors appear undisguisedly as the
sun, moon and star youths (the last being 'the Pole-star's eldest
boy') and once again the bride falls to the lot of the third.

Thus our little problem has led us to an astral myth! The only
pity is that with this explanation we are not at the end of the
matter. The question is not exhausted, for we do not share the
belief of some investigators that myths were read in the heavens
and brought down to earth; we are more inclined to judge with
Otto Rank[4] that they were projected on to the heavens after having
arisen elsewhere under purely human conditions. It is in this
human content that our interest lies.

Let us look once more at our material. In the Estonian epic, just
as in the tale from the *Gesta Romanorum*, the subject is a girl
choosing between three suitors; in the scene from *The Merchant of
Venice* the subject is apparently the same, but at the same time
something appears in it that is in the nature of an inversion of the
them: a *man* chooses between three—caskets. If what we were
concerned with were a dream, it would occur to us at once that

[1] [A mediaeval collection of stories of unknown authorship.]
[2] Brandes (1896).
[3] Stucken (1907, 655).
[4] Rank (1909, 8 ff.).

caskets are also women, symbols of what is essential in woman, and therefore of a woman herself—like coffers, boxes, cases, baskets, and so on.[1] If we boldly assume that there are symbolic substitutions of the same kind in myths as well, then the casket scene in *The Merchant of Venice* really becomes the inversion we suspected. With a wave of the wand, as though we were in a fairy tale, we have stripped the astral garment from our theme; and now we see that the theme is a human one, *a man's choice between three women.*

This same content, however, is to be found in another scene of Shakespeare's, in one of his most powerfully moving dramas; not the choice of a bride this time, yet linked by many hidden similarities to the choice of the casket in *The Merchant of Venice.* The old King Lear resolves to divide his kingdom while he is still alive among his three daughters, in proportion to the amount of love that each of them expresses for him. The two elder ones, Goneril and Regan, exhaust themselves in asseverations and laudations [293] of their love for him; the third, Cordelia, refuses to do so. He should have recognized the unassuming, speechless love of his third daughter and rewarded it, but he does not recognize it. He disowns Cordelia, and divides the kingdom between the other two, to his own and the general ruin. Is not this once more the scene of a choice between three women, of whom the youngest is the best, the most excellent one?

There will at once occur to us other scenes from myths, fairy tales and literature, with the same situation as their content. The shepherd Paris has to choose between three goddesses, of whom he declares the third to be the most beautiful. Cinderella, again, is a youngest daughter, who is preferred by the prince to her two elder sisters. Psyche, in Apuleius's story, is the youngest and fairest of three sisters. Psyche is, on the one hand, revered as Aphrodite in human form; on the other, she is treated by that goddess as Cinderella was treated by her stepmother and is set the task of sorting a heap of mixed seeds, which she accomplishes with the help of small creatures (doves in the case of Cinderella, ants in the case of

[1][See *The Interpretation of Dreams* (1900a), *Standard Ed.,* 5, 354.]

Psyche).[1] Anyone who cared to make a wider survey of the material would undoubtedly discover other versions of the same theme preserving the same essential features.

Let us be content with Cordelia, Aphrodite, Cinderella and Psyche. In all the stories the three women, of whom the third is the most excellent one, must surely be regarded as in some way alike if they are represented as sisters. (We must not be led astray by the fact that Lear's choice is between three *daughters*; this may mean nothing more than that he has to be represented as an old man. An old man cannot very well choose between three women in any other way. Thus they become his daughters.)

But who are these three sisters and why must the choice fall on the third? If we could answer this question, we should be in possession of the interpretation we are seeking. We have once already made use of an application of psycho-analytic technique, when we explained the three caskets symbolically as three women.

[294] If we have the courage to proceed in the same way, we shall be setting foot on a path which will lead us first to something unexpected and incomprehensible, but which will perhaps, by a devious route, bring us to a goal.

It must strike us that this excellent third woman has in several instances certain peculiar qualities besides her beauty. They are qualities that seem to be tending towards some kind of unity; we must certainly not expect to find them equally well marked in every example. Cordelia makes herself unrecognizable, inconspicuous like lead, she remains dumb, she 'loves and is silent'.[2] Cinderella hides so that she cannot be found. We may perhaps be allowed to equate concealment and dumbness. These would of course be only two instances out of the five we have picked out. But there is an intimation of the same thing to be found, curiously enough, in two other cases. We have decided to compare Cordelia, with her obstinate refusal, to lead. In Bassanio's short speech while he is choosing

[1] I have to thank Dr. Otto Rank for calling my attention to these similarities. [Cf. a reference to this in Chapter XII of *Group Psychology* (1921c), *Standard Ed.*, **18**, 136.]

[2] [From an aside of Cordelia's, Act I, Scene 1.]

the casket, he says of lead (without in any way leading up to the remark):

'Thy paleness[1] moves me more than eloquence.'

That is to say: 'Thy plainness moves me more than the blatant nature of the other two.' Gold and silver are 'loud'; lead is dumb—in fact like Cordelia, who 'loves and is silent'.[2]

In the ancient Greek accounts of the Judgement of Paris, nothing is said of any such reticence on the part of Aphrodite. Each of the three goddesses speaks to the youth and tries to win him by promises. But, oddly enough, in a quite modern handling of the same scene this characteristic of the third one which has struck us makes its appearance again. In the libretto of Offenbach's *La Belle Hélène*, Paris, after telling of the solicitations of the other two goddesses, describes Aphrodite's behaviour in this competition for the beauty-prize:

> La troisième, ah! la troisième . . .
> La troisième ne dit rien.
> Elle eut le prix tout de même . . .[3]

If we decide to regard the peculiarities of our 'third one' as concentrated in her 'dumbness', then psycho-analysis will tell us that in dreams dumbness is a common representation of death.[4]   [295]

More than ten years ago a highly intelligent man told me a dream which he wanted to use as evidence of the telepathic nature of dreams. In it he saw an absent friend from whom he had received

[1]'Plainness' according to another reading.
[2]In Schlegel's translation this allusion is quite lost; indeed, it is given the opposite meaning: 'Dein schlichtes Wesen spricht beredt mich an.' ['Thy plainness speaks to me with eloquence.']
[3][Literally: 'The third one, ah! the third one . . . the third one said nothing. She won the prize all the same.'—The quotation is from Act I, Scene 7, of Meilhac and Halévy's libretto. In the German version used by Freud 'the third one' '*blieb stumm*'—'remained dumb'.]
[4]In Stekel's *Sprache des Traumes*, too, dumbness is mentioned among the 'death' symbols (1911*a*, 351). [Cf. *The Interpretation of Dreams* (1900*a*), *Standard Ed.*, 5, 357.]

no news for a very long time, and reproached him energetically for his silence. The friend made no reply. It afterwards turned out that he had met his death by suicide at about the time of the dream. Let us leave the problem of telepathy on one side:[1] there seems, however, not to be any doubt that here the dumbness in the dream represented death. Hiding and being unfindable—a thing which confronts the prince in the fairly tale of Cinderella three times, is another unmistakable symbol of death in dreams; so, too, is a marked pallor, of which the 'paleness' of the lead in one reading of Shakespeare's text is a reminder.[2] It would be very much easier for us to transpose these interpretations from the language of dreams to the mode of expression used in the myth that is now under consideration if we could make it seem probable that dumbness must be interpreted as a sign of being dead in productions other than dreams.

At this point I will single out the ninth story in Grimm's *Fairy Tales*, which bears the title 'The Twelve Brothers'.[3] A king and a queen have twelve children, all boys. The king declares that if the thirteenth child is a girl, the boys will have to die. In expectation of her birth he has twelve coffins made. With their mother's help the twelve sons take refuge in a hidden wood, and swear death to any girl they may meet. A girl is born, grows up, and learns one day from her mother that she has had twelve brothers. She decides to seek them out, and in the wood she finds the youngest; he recognizes her, but is anxious to hide her on account of the brothers' oath. The sister says: 'I will gladly die, if by so doing I can save my twelve brothers.' The brothers welcome her affectionately, however, and she stays with them and looks after their house for them. In a little garden beside the house grow twelve lilies. The girl picks them and gives one to each brother. At that moment the brothers are changed into ravens, and disappear, together with the house and garden. (Ravens are spirit-birds; the killing of the twelve brothers by their sister is represented by the picking of

[296]

[1][Cf. Freud's later paper on 'Dreams and Telepathy' (1922a).]
[2]Stekel (1911a), loc. cit.
[3]['Die zwölf Brüder.' Grimm, 1918, 1, 42.]

the flowers, just as it is at the beginning of the story by the coffins and the disappearance of the brothers.) The girl, who is once more ready to save her brothers from death, is now told that as a condition she must be dumb for seven years, and not speak a single word. She submits to the test, which brings her herself into mortal danger. She herself, that is, dies for her brothers, as she promised to do before she met them. By remaining dumb she succeeds at last in setting the ravens free.

In the story of 'The Six Swans'[1] the brothers who are changed into birds are set free in exactly the same way—they are restored to life by their sister's dumbness. The girl has made a firm resolve to free her brothers, 'even if it should cost her her life'; and once again (being the wife of the king) she risks her own life because she refuses to give up her dumbness in order to defend herself against evil accusations.

It would certainly be possible to collect further evidence from fairy tales that dumbness is to be understood as representing death. These indications would lead us to conclude that the third one of the sisters between whom the choice is made is a dead woman. But she may be something else as well—namely, Death itself, the Goddess of Death. Thanks to a displacement that is far from infrequent, the qualities that a deity imparts to men are ascribed to the deity himself. Such a displacement will surprise us least of all in relation to the Goddess of Death, since in modern versions and representations, which these stories would thus be forestalling, Death itself is nothing other than a dead man.

But if the third of the sisters is the Goddess of Death, the sisters are known to us. They are the Fates, the Moerae, the Parcae or the Norns, the third of whom is called Atropos, the inexorable.

II

We will for the time being put aside the task of inserting the interpretation that we have found into our myth, and listen to

[1] ['Die sechs Schwäne.' Grimm, 1918, **1**, 217. (No. 49.)]

[297]   what the mythologists have to teach us about the role and origin of
the Fates.[1]

The earliest Greek mythology (in Homer) only knew a single
Μοῖρα, personifying inevitable fate. The further development of
this one Moera into a company of three (or less often two) sister-
goddesses probably came about on the basis of other divine figures
to which the Moerae were closely related—the Graces and the
Horae [the Seasons].

The Horae were originally goddesses of the waters of the sky,
dispensing rain and dew, and of the clouds from which rain falls;
and, since the clouds were conceived of as something that has been
spun, it came about that these goddesses were looked upon as
spinners, an attribute that then became attached to the Moerae. In
the sun-favoured Mediterranean lands it is the rain on which the
fertility of the soil depends, and thus the Horae became vegetation
goddesses. The beauty of flowers and the abundance of fruit was
their doing, and they were accredited with a wealth of agreeable
and charming traits. They became the divine representatives of the
Seasons, and it is possibly owing to this connection that there were
three of them, if the sacred nature of the number three is not a
sufficient explanation. For the peoples of antiquity at first distinguished only three seasons: winter, spring and summer. Autumn
was only added in late Graeco-Roman times, after which the Horae
were often represented in art as four in number.

The Horae retained their relation to time. Later they presided
over the times of day, as they did at first over the times of the year;
and at last their name came to be merely a designation of the hours
(*heure*, *ora*). The Norns of German mythology are akin to the
Horae and the Moerae and exhibit this time-signification in their
names.[2] It was inevitable, however, that a deeper view should come
to be taken of the essential nature of these deities, and that their
essence should be transposed on to the regularity with which the
seasons change. The Horae thus became the guardians of natural

---

[1] What follows is taken from Roscher's lexicon [1884–1937], under the relevant
headings.

[2] [Their names may be rendered: 'What was', 'What is', 'What shall be'.]

law and of the divine Order which causes the same thing to recur in Nature in an unalterable sequence.

This discovery of Nature reacted on the conception of human life. The nature-myth changed into a human myth: the weather-goddesses became goddesses of Fate. But this aspect of the Horae found expression only in the Moerae, who watch over the necessary ordering of human life as inexorably as do the Horae over the regular order of nature. The ineluctable severity of Law and its relation to death and dissolution, which had been avoided in the charming figures of the Horae, were now stamped upon the Moerae, as though men had only perceived the full seriousness of natural law when they had to submit their own selves to it. [298]

The names of the three spinners, too, have been significantly explained by mythologists. Lachesis, the name of the second, seems to denote 'the accidental that is included in the regularity of destiny'[1]—or, as we should say, 'experience'; just as Atropos stands for 'the ineluctable'—Death. Clotho would then be left to mean the innate disposition with its fateful implications.

But now it is time to return to the theme which we are trying to interpret—the theme of the choice between three sisters. We shall be deeply disappointed to discover how unintelligible the situations under review become and what contradictions of their apparent content result, if we apply to them the interpretation that we have found. On our supposition the third of the sisters is the Goddess of Death, Death itself. But in the Judgement of Paris she is the Goddess of Love, in the tale of Apuleius she is someone comparable to the goddess for her beauty, in *The Merchant of Venice* she is the fairest and wisest of women, in *King Lear* she is the one loyal daughter. We may ask whether there can be a more complete contradiction. Perhaps, improbable though it may seem, there is a still more complete one lying close at hand. Indeed, there certainly is; since, whenever our theme occurs, the choice between the women is free, and yet it falls on death. For, after all, no one chooses death, and it is only by a fatality that one falls a victim to it.

[1] Roscher [ibid.], quoting Preller, ed. Robert (1894).

However, contradictions of a certain kind—replacements by the precise opposite—offer no serious difficulty to the work of analytic interpretation. We shall not appeal here to the fact that contraries are so often represented by one and the same element in the modes of expression used by the unconscious, as for instance in dreams.[1] But we shall remember that there are motive forces in mental life which bring about replacement by the opposite in the form of what is known as reaction-formation; and it is precisely in the revelation of such hidden forces as these that we look for the reward of this enquiry. The Moerae were created as a result of a discovery that warned man that he too is a part of nature and therefore subject to the immutable law of death. Something in man was bound to struggle against this subjection, for it is only with extreme unwillingness that he gives up his claim to an exceptional position. Man, as we know, makes use of his imaginative activity in order to satisfy the wishes that reality does not satisfy. So his imagination rebelled against the recognition of the truth embodied in the myth of the Moerae, and constructed instead the myth derived from it, in which the Goddess of Death was replaced by the Goddess of Love and by what was equivalent to her in human shape. The third of the sisters was no longer Death; she was the fairest, best, most desirable and most lovable of women. Nor was this substitution in any way technically difficult: it was prepared for by an ancient ambivalence, it was carried out along a primaeval line of connection which could not long have been forgotten. The Goddess of Love herself, who now took the place of the Goddess of Death, had once been identical with her. Even the Greek Aphrodite had not wholly relinquished her connection with the underworld, although she had long surrendered her chthonic role to other divine figures, to Persephone, or to the tri-form Artemis-Hecate. The great Mother-goddesses of the oriental peoples, however, all seem to have been both creators and destroyers—both goddesses of life and fertility and goddesses of death. Thus the replacement by a wishful opposite in our theme harks back to a primaeval identity.

[1] [Cf. *The Interpretation of Dreams* (1900*a*), *Standard Ed.*, 4, 318.]

The same consideration answers the question how the feature of a choice came into the myth of the three sisters. Here again there has been a wishful reversal. Choice stands in the place of necessity, of destiny. In this way man overcomes death, which he has recognized intellectually. No greater triumph of wish-fulfilment is conceivable. A choice is made where in reality there is obedience to a compulsion; and what is chosen is not a figure of terror, but the fairest and most desirable of women.

On closer inspection we observe, to be sure, that the original myth is not so thoroughly distorted that traces of it do not show [300] through and betray its presence. The free choice between the three sisters is, properly speaking, no free choice, for it must necessarily fall on the third if every kind of evil is not to come about, as it does in *King Lear*. The fairest and best of women, who has taken the place of the Death-goddess, has kept certain characteristics that border on the uncanny, so that from them we have been able to guess at what lies beneath.[1]

So far we have been following out the myth and its transformation, and it is to be hoped that we have correctly indicated the hidden causes of the transformation. We may now turn our interest to the way in which the dramatist has made use of the theme. We get an impression that a reduction of the theme to the original myth is being carried out in his work, so that we once more have a sense of the moving significance which had been weakened by the distortion. It is by means of this reduction of the distortion, this

[1]The Psyche of Apuleius's story has kept many traits that remind us of her relation with death. Her wedding is celebrated like a funeral, she has to descend into the underworld, and afterwards she sinks into a death-like sleep (Otto Rank).—On the significance of Psyche as goddess of the spring and as 'Bride of Death', cf. Zinzow (1881).—In another of Grimm's Tales ('The Goose-girl at the Fountain' ['Die Gänsehirtin am Brunnen', 1918, 2, 300], No. 179) there is, as in 'Cinderella', an alternation between the beautiful and the ugly aspect of the third sister, in which one may no doubt see an indication of her double nature—before and after the substitution. This third daughter is repudiated by her father, after a test which is almost the same as the one in *King Lear*. Like her sisters, she has to declare how fond she is of their father, but can find no expression for her love but a comparison with salt. (Kindly communicated by Dr. Hanns Sachs.)

partial return to the original, that the dramatist achieves his more profound effect upon us.

To avoid misunderstandings, I should like to say that it is not my purpose to deny that King Lear's dramatic story is intended to inculcate two wise lessons: that one should not give up one's possessions and rights during one's lifetime, and that one must guard against accepting flattery at its face value. These and similar warning are undoubtedly brought out by the play; but it seems to me quite impossible to explain the overpowering effect of *King Lear* from the impression that such a train of thought would produce, or to suppose that the dramatist's personal motives did not go beyond the intention of teaching these lessons. It is suggested, too, that his [301] purpose was to present the tragedy of ingratitude, the sting of which he may well have felt in his own heart, and that the effect of the play rests on the purely formal element of its artistic presentation; but this cannot, so it seems to me, take the place of the understanding brought to us by the explanation we have reached of the theme of the choice between the three sisters.

Lear is an old man. It is for this reason, as we have already said, that the three sisters appear as his daughters. The relationship of a father to his children, which might be a fruitful source of many dramatic situations, is not turned to further account in the play. But Lear is not only an old man: he is a dying man. In this way the extraordinary premiss of the division of his inheritance loses all its strangeness. But the doomed man is not willing to renounce the love of women; he insists on hearing how much he is loved. Let us now recall the moving final scene, one of the culminating points of tragedy in modern drama. Lear carries Cordelia's dead body on to the stage. Cordelia is Death. If we reverse the situation it becomes intelligible and familiar to us. She is the Death-goddess who, like the Valkyrie in German mythology, carries away the dead hero from the battlefield. Eternal wisdom, clothed in the primaeval myth, bids the old man renounce love, choose death and make friends with the necessity of dying.

The dramatist brings us nearer to the ancient theme by representing the man who makes the choice between the three sisters as aged and dying. The regressive revision which he has thus applied to the myth, distorted as it was by wishful transformation, allows us enough glimpses of its original meaning to enable us perhaps to reach as well a superficial allegorical interpretation of the three female figures in the theme. We might argue that what is represented here are the three inevitable relations that a man has with a woman—the woman who bears him, the woman who is his mate and the woman who destroys him; or that they are the three forms taken by the figure of the mother in the course of a man's life—the mother herself, the beloved one who is chosen after her pattern, and lastly the Mother Earth who receives him once more. But it is in vain that an old man yearns for the love of woman as he had it first from his mother; the third of the Fates alone, the silent Goddess of Death, will take him into her arms.

§ The Moses of Michelangelo[1]

I MAY say at once that I am no connoisseur in art, but simply a layman. I have often observed that the subject-matter of works of art has a stronger attraction for me than their formal and technical qualities, though to the artist their value lies first and foremost in these latter. I am unable rightly to appreciate many of the methods used and the effects obtained in art. I state this so as to secure the reader's indulgence for the attempt I propose to make here.

Nevertheless, works of art do exercise a powerful effect on me, especially those of literature and sculpture, less often of painting. This has occasioned me, when I have been contemplating such things, to spend a long time before them trying to apprehend them in my own way, i.e. to explain to myself what their effect is due to. Wherever I cannot do this, as for instance with music, I am almost incapable of obtaining any pleasure. Some rationalistic, or perhaps analytic, turn of mind in me rebels against being moved by a thing without knowing why I am thus affected and what it is that affects me.

SOURCE: *Standard Ed.*, **13**, 211–38.
[1][The following footnote, obviously drafted by Freud himself, was attached to the title when the paper made its first, anonymous, appearance in *Imago*:

'Although this paper does not, strictly speaking, conform to the conditions under which contributions are accepted for publication in this Journal, the editors have decided to print it, since the author, who is personally known to them, moves in psycho-analytic circles, and since his mode of thought has in point of fact a certain resemblance to the methodology of psycho-analysis.']

This has brought me to recognize the apparently paradoxical fact that precisely some of the grandest and most overwhelming creations of art are still unsolved riddles to our understanding. We admire them, we feel overawed by them, but we are unable to say what they represent to us. I am not sufficiently well-read to know whether this fact has already been remarked upon; possibly, indeed, some writer on aesthetics has discovered that this state of intellec- [212] tual bewilderment is a necessary condition when a work of art is to achieve its greatest effects. It would be only with the greatest reluctance that I could bring myself to believe in any such necessity.

I do not mean that connoisseurs and lovers of art find no words with which to praise such objects to us. They are eloquent enough, it seems to me. But usually in the presence of a great work of art each says something different from the other; and none of them says anything that solves the problem for the unpretending admirer. In my opinion, what grips us so powerfully can only be the artist's *intention*, in so far as he has succeeded in expressing it in his work and in getting us to understand it. I realize that this cannot be merely a matter of *intellectual* comprehension; what he aims at is to awaken in us the same emotional attitude, the same mental constellation as that which in him produced the impetus to create. But why should the artist's intention not be capable of being communicated and comprehended in *words*, like any other fact of mental life? Perhaps where great works of art are concerned this would never be possible without the application of psycho-analysis. The product itself after all must admit of such an analysis, if it really is an effective expression of the intentions and emotional activities of the artist. To discover his intention, though, I must first find out the meaning and content of what is represented in his work; I must, in other words, be able to *interpret* it. It is possible, therefore, that a work of art of this kind needs interpretation, and that until I have accomplished that interpretation I cannot come to know why I have been so powerfully affected. I even venture to hope that the effect of the work will undergo no diminution after we have succeeded in thus analysing it.

Let us consider Shakespeare's masterpiece, *Hamlet*, a play now over three centuries old.[1] I have followed the literature of psycho-analysis closely, and I accept its claim that it was not until the material of the tragedy had been traced back by psycho-analysis to the Oedipus theme that the mystery of its effect was at last explained. [Cf. *The Interpretation of Dreams, Standard Ed.*, 4, 264–6.]

[213]   But before this was done, what a mass of differing and contradictory interpretative attempts, what a variety of opinions about the hero's character and the dramatist's intentions! Does Shakespeare claim our sympathies on behalf of a sick man, or of an ineffectual weakling, or of an idealist who is merely too good for the real world? And how many of these interpretations leave us cold!—so cold that they do nothing to explain the effect of the play and rather incline us to the view that its magical appeal rests solely upon the impressive thoughts in it and the splendour of its language. And yet, do not those very endeavours speak for the fact that we feel the need of discovering in it some source of power beyond them alone?

Another of these inscrutable and wonderful works of art is the marble statue of Moses, by Michelangelo, in the Church of S. Pietro in Vincoli in Rome. As we know, it was only a fragment of the gigantic tomb which the artist was to have erected for the powerful Pope Julius II.[2] It always delights me to read an appreciative sentence about this statue, such as that it is 'the crown of modern sculpture' (Grimm [1900, 189]). For no piece of statuary has ever made a stronger impression on me than this. How often have I mounted the steep steps from the unlovely Corso Cavour to the lonely piazza where the deserted church stands, and have essayed to support the angry scorn of the hero's glance! Sometimes I have crept cautiously out of the half-gloom of the interior as though I myself belonged to the mob upon whom his eye is turned—the mob which can hold fast no conviction, which has neither faith nor patience, and which rejoices when it has regained its illusory idols.

[1]Perhaps first performed in 1602.
[2]According to Henry Thode [1908, 194], the statue was made between the years 1512 and 1516.

But why do I call this statue inscrutable? There is not the slightest doubt that it represents Moses, the Law-giver of the Jews, holding the Tables of the Ten Commandments. That much is certain, but that is all. As recently as 1912 an art critic, Max Sauerlandt, has said, 'No other work of art in the world has been judged so diversely as the Moses with the head of Pan. The mere interpretation of the figure has given rise to completely opposed views. . . .' Basing myself on an essay published only five years ago,[1] I will first set out the doubts which are associated with this figure of   [214] Moses; and it will not be difficult to show that behind them lies concealed all that is most essential and valuable for the comprehension of this work of art.

I

The Moses of Michelangelo is represented as seated; his body faces forward, his head with its mighty beard looks to the left, his right foot rests on the ground and his left leg is raised so that only the toes touch the ground. His right arm links the Tables of the Law with a portion of his beard; his left arm lies in his lap. Were I to give a more detailed description of his attitude, I should have to anticipate what I want to say later on. The descriptions of the figure given by various writers are, by the way, curiously inapt. What has not been understood has been inaccurately perceived or reproduced. Grimm [1900, 189] says that the right hand, 'under whose arm the Tables rest, grasps his beard'. So also Lübke [1863, 666]: 'Profoundly shaken, he grasps with his right hand his magnificent, flowing beard . . .'; and Springer [1895, 33]: 'Moses presses one (the left) hand against his body, and thrusts the other, as though unconsciously, into the mighty locks of his beard.' Justi [1900, 326] thinks that the fingers of his (right) hand are playing with his beard, 'as an agitated man nowadays might play with his watch-chain.' Müntz [1895, 391*n*.], too, lays stress on this playing with the beard. Thode [1908, 205] speaks of the 'calm, firm posture of the right hand upon the Tables resting against his side'. He does not recognize any sign

[1]Thode (1908).

of excitement even in the right hand, as Justi and also Boito [1883] do. 'The hand remains grasping his beard, in the position it was in before the Titan turned his head to one side.' Jakob Burckhardt [1927, 634] complains that 'the celebrated left arm has no other function in reality than to press his beard to his body'.

If mere descriptions do not agree we shall not be surprised to find a divergence of view as to the meaning of various features of the statue. In my opinion we cannot better characterize the facial expression of Moses than in the words of Thode [1908, 205], who reads in it 'a mixture of wrath, pain and contempt',—'wrath in his [215] threatening contracted brows, pain in his glance, and contempt in his protruded under-lip and in the down-drawn corners of his mouth'. But other admirers must have seen with other eyes. Thus Dupaty says, 'His august brow seems to be but a transparent veil only half concealing his great mind'.[1] Lübke [1863, 666–7], on the other hand, declares that 'one would look in vain in that head for an expression of higher intelligence; his down-drawn brow speaks of nothing but a capacity for infinite wrath and an all-compelling energy'. Guillaume (1876 [96]) differs still more widely in his interpretation of the expression of the face. He finds no emotion in it, 'only a proud simplicity, an inspired dignity, a living faith. The eye of Moses looks into the future, he foresees the lasting survival of his people, the immutability of his law.' Similarly, to Müntz [1895, 391], 'the eyes of Moses rove far beyond the race of men. They are turned towards those mysteries which he alone has descried.' To Steinmann [1899, 169], indeed, this Moses is 'no longer the stern Lawgiver, no longer the terrible enemy of sin, armed with the wrath of Jehovah, but the royal priest, whom age may not approach, beneficent and prophetic, with the reflection of eternity upon his brow, taking his last farewell of his people'.

There have even been some for whom the Moses of Michelangelo had nothing at all to say, and who are honest enough to admit it. Thus a critic in the *Quarterly Review* of 1858 [**103**, 469]: 'There is an absence of meaning in the general conception, which precludes

[1]Quoted by Thode, ibid., 197.

the idea of a self-sufficing whole. . . .' And we are astonished to learn that there are yet others who find nothing to admire in the Moses, but who revolt against it and complain of the brutality of the figure and the animal cast of the head.

Has then the master-hand indeed traced such a vague or ambiguous script in the stone, that so many different readings of it are possible?

Another question, however, arises, which covers the first one. Did Michelangelo intend to create a 'timeless study of character and mood' in this Moses, or did he portray him at a particular moment of his life and, if so, at a highly significant one? The majority of judges have decided in the latter sense and are able to [216] tell us what episode in his life it is which the artist has immortalized in stone. It is the descent from Mount Sinai, where Moses has received the Tables from God, and it is the moment when he perceives that the people have meanwhile made themselves a Golden Calf and are dancing around it and rejoicing. This is the scene upon which his eyes are turned, this is the spectacle which calls out the feelings depicted in his countenance—feelings which in the next instant will launch his great frame into violent action. Michelangelo has chosen this last moment of hesitation, of calm before the storm, for his representation. In the next instant Moses will spring to his feet—his left foot is already raised from the ground—dash the Tables to the earth, and let loose his rage upon his faithless people.

Once more many individual differences of opinion exist among those who support this interpretation.

Burckhardt [1927, 634] writes: 'Moses seems to be shown at that moment at which he catches sight of the worship of the Golden Calf, and is springing to his feet. His form is animated by the inception of a mighty movement and the physical strength with which he is endowed causes us to await it with fear and trembling.'

Lübke [1863, 666] says: 'It is as if at this moment his flashing eye were perceiving the sin of the worship of the Golden Calf and a mighty inward movement were running through his whole frame. Profoundly shaken, he grasps with his right hand his magnificent, flowing beard, as though to master his actions for one instant longer, only for the explosion of his wrath to burst out with more shattering force the next.'

Springer [1895, 33] agrees with this view, but not without mentioning one misgiving, which will engage our attention later in this paper. He says, 'Burning with energy and zeal, it is with difficulty that the hero subdues his inward emotion. . . . We are thus involuntarily reminded of a dramatic situation and are brought to believe that Moses is represented at the moment at which he sees the people of Israel worshipping the Golden Calf and is about to start up in wrath. Such an impression, it is true, is not easy to reconcile with the artist's real intention, since the figure of Moses, like the other five seated figures on the upper part of the Papal

[217]   tomb, is meant primarily to have a decorative effect. But it testifies very convincingly to the vitality and individuality portrayed in the figure of Moses.'

One or two writers, without actually accepting the Golden Calf theory, do nevertheless agree on its main point, namely, that Moses is just about to spring to his feet and take action.

According to Grimm [1900, 189], 'The form' (of Moses) 'is filled with a majesty, a self-assurance, a feeling that all the thunders of heaven are at his command, and that yet he is holding himself in check before loosing them, waiting to see whether the foes whom he means to annihilate will dare to attack him. He sits there as if on the point of starting to his feet, his proud head carried high on his shoulders; the hand under whose arm the Tables rest grasps his beard, which falls in heavy waves over his breast, his nostrils distended and his lips shaped as though words were trembling upon them.'

Heath Wilson [1876, 450] declares that Moses' attention has been excited, and he is about to leap to his feet, but is still hesitating; and that his glance of mingled scorn and indignation is still capable of changing into one of compassion.

Wölfflin [1899, 72] speaks of 'inhibited movement'. The cause of this inhibition, he says, lies in the will of the man himself; it is the last moment of self-control before he lets himself go and leaps to his feet.

Justi [1900, 326–7] has gone the furthest of all in his interpretation of the statue as Moses in the act of perceiving the Golden Calf, and he has pointed out details hitherto unobserved in it and worked them into his hypothesis. He directs our attention to the position of the two Tables—an unusual one, for they are about to slip down on to the stone seat. 'He' (Moses) 'might therefore be looking in the direction from which the clamour was coming with an expression of evil foreboding, or it might be the actual sight of the abomination which has dealt him a stunning blow. Quivering with horror and pain he has sunk down.'[1] He has sojourned on the mountain forty days and nights and he is weary. A horror, a great [218] turn of fortune, a crime, even happiness itself, can be perceived in a single moment, but not grasped in its essence, its depths or its consequences. For an instant it seems to Moses that his work is destroyed and he despairs utterly of his people. In such moments the inner emotions betray themselves involuntarily in small movements. He lets the Tables slip from his right hand on to the stone seat; they have come to rest on their corner there and are pressed by his forearm against the side of his body. His hand, however, comes in contact with his breast and beard and thus, by the turning of the head to the spectator's right, it draws the beard to the left and breaks the symmetry of that masculine adornment. It looks as though his fingers were playing with his beard as an agitated man nowadays might play with his watch-chain. His left hand is buried in his garment over the lower part of his body—in the Old Testament the viscera are the seat of the emotions—but the left leg is already drawn back and the right put forward; in the next instant he will leap up, his mental energy will be transposed from feeling into action, his right arm will move, the Tables will fall to the

[1] It should be remarked that the careful arrangement of the mantle over the knees of the sitting figure invalidates this first part of Justi's view. On the contrary, this would lead us to suppose that Moses is represented as sitting there in calm repose until he is startled by some sudden perception.

ground, and the shameful trespass will be expiated in torrents of blood. . . .' 'This is not yet the moment of tension of an act. Pain of mind still dominates him and almost paralyses him.'

Knapp [1906, xxxii] takes the same view, except that he does not introduce the doubtful point at the beginning of the description,[1] and carries the idea of the slipping Tables further. 'He who just now was alone with his God is distracted by earthly sounds. He hears a noise; the noise of singing and dancing wakes him from his dream; he turns his eyes and his head in the direction of the clamour. In one instant fear, rage and unbridled passion traverse his huge frame. The Tables begin to slip down, and will fall to the ground and break when he leaps to his feet and hurls the angry thunder of his words into the midst of his backsliding people. . . . This is the moment of highest tension which is chosen. . . .' Knapp, therefore, emphasizes the element of preparation for action, and disagrees with the view that what is being represented is an initial inhibition due to an overmastering agitation.

[219]   It cannot be denied that there is something extraordinarily attractive about attempts at an interpretation of the kind made by Justi and Knapp. This is because they do not stop short at the general effect of the figure, but are based on separate features in it; these we usually fail to notice, being overcome by the total impression of the statue and as it were paralysed by it. The marked turn of the head and eyes to the left, whereas the body faces forwards, supports the view that the resting Moses has suddenly seen something on that side to rivet his attention. His lifted foot can hardly mean anything else but that he is preparing to spring up;[2] and the very unusual way in which the Tables are held (for they are most sacred objects and are not to be brought into the composition like any ordinary accessory) is fully accounted for if we suppose they have slipped down as a result of the agitation of their bearer and will fall to the ground. According to this view we should believe

[1][Cf. previous note.]

[2]Although the left foot of the reposeful seated figure of Giuliano in the Medici Chapel is similarly raised from the ground.

that the statue represents a special and important moment in the life of Moses, and we should be left in no doubt of what that moment is.

But two remarks of Thode's deprive us of the knowledge we thought to have gained. This critic says that to his eye the Tables are not slipping down but are 'firmly lodged'. He notes the 'calm, firm pose of the right hand upon the resting Tables'. If we look for ourselves we cannot but admit unreservedly that Thode is right. The Tables are firmly placed and in no danger of slipping. Moses' right hand supports them or is supported by them. This does not explain the position in which they are held, it is true, but that position cannot be used in favour of the interpretation of Justi and others. [Thode (1908), 205.]

The second observation is still more final. Thode reminds us that 'this statue was planned as one of six, and is intended to be seated. Both facts contradict the view that Michelangelo meant to record a particular historical moment. For, as regards the first consideration, the plan of representing a row of seated figures as types of human beings—as the *vita activa* and the *vita contemplativa*—excluded a representation of a particular historic episode. And, as regards the second, the representation of a seated posture— a posture necessitated by the artistic conception of the whole monument—contradicts the nature of that episode, namely, the descent of Moses from Mount Sinai into the camp.

[220]

If we accept Thode's objection we shall find that we can add to its weight. The figure of Moses was to have decorated the base of the tomb together with five other statues (or according to a later sketch, with three). Its immediate counterpart was to have been a figure of Paul. One other pair, representing the *vita activa* and the *vita contemplativa* in the shape of Leah and Rachel—standing, it is true—has been executed on the tomb as it still exists in its sadly aborted form. The Moses thus forms part of a whole and we cannot imagine that the figure was meant to arouse an expectation in the spectator that it was on the point of leaping up from its seat and rushing away to create a disturbance on its own account. If the other figures were not also represented as about to take violent action—and it seems very improbable that they were—then it would create a very bad impression for one of them to give us the illusion that it was going to leave its place and its companions, in fact to abandon its role in the general scheme. Such an intention would have a chaotic effect and we could not charge a great artist with it unless the facts drove us to it. A figure in the act of instant departure would be utterly at variance with the state of mind which the tomb is meant to induce in us.

The figure of Moses, therefore, cannot be supposed to be springing to his feet; he must be allowed to remain as he is in sublime repose like the other figures and like the proposed statue of the Pope (which was not, however, executed by Michelangelo himself). But then the statue we see before us cannot be that of a man filled with wrath, of Moses when he came down from Mount Sinai and found his people faithless and threw down the Holy Tables so that they were broken. And, indeed, I can recollect my own disillusionment when, during my first visits to San Pietro in Vincoli, I used to sit down in front of the statue in the expectation that I should now see how it would start up on its raised foot, dash the Tables of the Law to the ground and let fly its wrath. Nothing of the kind happened. Instead, the stone image became more and more transfixed, an almost oppressively solemn calm emanated from it, and I was obliged to realize that something was represented here [221] that could stay without change; that this Moses would remain sitting like this in his wrath for ever.

But if we have to abandon our interpretation of the statue as showing Moses just before his outburst of wrath at the sight of the Golden Calf, we have no alternative but to accept one of the hypotheses which regard it as a study of character. Thode's view seems to be the least arbitrary and to have the closest reference to the meaning of its movements. He says, 'Here, as always, he [Michelangelo] is concerned with representing a certain type of character. He creates the image of a passionate leader of mankind who, conscious of his divine mission as Lawgiver, meets the uncomprehending opposition of men. The only means of representing a man of action of this kind was to accentuate the power of his will, and this was done by a rendering of movement pervading the whole of his apparent quiet, as we see in the turn of his head, the tension of his muscles and the position of his left foot. These are the same distinguishing marks that we find again in the *vir activus* of the Medici Chapel in Florence. This general character of the figure is further heightened by laying stress on the conflict which is bound to arise between such a reforming genius and the rest of mankind. Emotions of anger, contempt and pain are typified in him. Without them it would not have been possible to portray the nature of a superman of this kind. Michelangelo has created, not a historical figure, but a character-type, embodying an inexhaustible inner force which tames the recalcitrant world; and he has given a form not only to the Biblical narrative of Moses, but to his own inner experiences, and to his impressions both of the individuality of Julius himself, and also, I believe, of the underlying springs of Savonarola's perpetual conflicts.' [1908, 206.]

This view may be brought into connection with Knackfuss's remark [1900, 69] that the great secret of the effect produced by the Moses lies in the artistic contrast between the inward fire and the outward calm of his bearing.

For myself, I see nothing to object to in Thode's explanation; but I feel the lack of something in it. Perhaps it is the need to discover a closer parallel between the state of mind of the hero as expressed in his attitude, and the contrast above-mentioned between his 'outward' calm and 'inward' emotion.

II

Long before I had any opportunity of hearing about psycho- [222] analysis, I learnt that a Russian art-connoisseur, Ivan Lermolieff,[1] had caused a revolution in the art galleries of Europe by questioning the authorship of many pictures, showing how to distinguish copies from originals with certainty, and constructing hypothetical

[1] His first essays were published in German between 1874 and 1876.

artists for those works whose former supposed authorship had been
discredited. He achieved this by insisting that attention should be
diverted from the general impression and main features of a picture, and by laying stress on the significance of minor details, of
things like the drawing of the fingernails, of the lobe of an ear, of
halos and such unconsidered trifles which the copyist neglects to
imitate and yet which every artist executes in his own characteristic
way. I was then greatly interested to learn that the Russian pseudo-
nym concealed the identity of an Italian physician called Morelli,
who died in 1891 with the rank of Senator of the Kingdom of Italy.
It seems to me that his method of inquiry is closely related to the
technique of psycho-analysis. It, too, is accustomed to divine secret
and concealed things from despised or unnoticed features, from the
rubbish-heap, as it were, of our observations.

Now in two places in the figure of Moses there are certain details
which have hitherto not only escaped notice but, in fact, have not
even been properly described. These are the attitude of his right
hand and the position of the two Tables of the Law. We may say
that this hand forms a very singular, unnatural link, and one which
calls for explanation, between the Tables and the wrathful hero's
beard. He has been described as running his fingers through his
beard and playing with its locks, while the outer edge of his hand
rests on the Tables. But this is plainly not so. It is worth while
examining more closely what those fingers of the right hand are
doing, and describing more minutely the mighty beard with which
they are in contact.

We now quite clearly perceive the following things: the thumb of
the hand is concealed and the index finger alone is in effective con-
[223]   tact with the beard. It is pressed so deeply against the soft masses
of hair that they bulge out beyond it both above and below, that is,
both towards the head and towards the abdomen. The other three
fingers are propped upon the wall of his chest and are bent at the
upper joints; they are barely touched by the extreme right-hand
lock of the beard which falls past them. They have, as it were, withdrawn from the beard. It is therefore not correct to say that the right
hand is playing with the beard or plunged in it; the simple truth is

that the index finger is laid over a part of the beard and makes a deep trough in it. It cannot be denied that to press one's beard with one finger is an extraordinary gesture and one not easy to understand.

The much-admired beard of Moses flows from his cheeks, chin and upper lip in a number of waving strands which are kept distinct from one another all the way down. One of the strands on his extreme right, growing from the cheek, falls down to the inward-pressing index finger, by which it is retained. We may assume that it resumes its course between that finger and the concealed thumb. The corresponding strand on his left side falls practically unimpeded far down over his breast. What has received the most unusual treatment is the thick mass of hair on the inside of this latter strand, the part between it and the middle line. It is not suffered to follow the turn of the head to the left; it is forced to roll over loosely and form part of a kind of scroll which lies across and over the strands on the inner right side of the beard. This is because it is held fast by the pressure of the right index finger, although it grows from the left side of the face and is, in fact, the main portion of the whole left side of the beard. Thus, the main mass of the beard is thrown to the right of the figure, whereas the head is sharply turned to the left. At the place where the right index finger is pressed in, a kind of whorl of hairs is formed; strands of hair coming from the left lie over strands coming from the right, both caught in by that despotic finger. It is only beyond this place that the masses of hair, deflected from their course, flow freely once more, and now they fall vertically until their ends are gathered up in Moses' left hand as it lies open on his lap.

I have no illusions as to the clarity of my description, and venture no opinion whether the sculptor really does invite us to solve the riddle of that knot in the beard of his statue. But apart [224] from this, the fact remains that the pressure of the *right* index finger affects mainly the strands of hair from the *left* side; and that this oblique hold prevents the beard from accompanying the turn of the head and eyes to the left. Now we may be allowed to ask what this arrangement means and to what motives it owes its existence. If it was indeed considerations of linear and spatial design which caused the sculptor to draw the downward-streaming wealth of hair across to the right of the figure which is looking to its left, how strangely unsuitable as a means does the pressure of a single finger appear to be! And what man who, for some reason or other, has drawn his beard over to the other side, would take it into his head to hold down the one half across the other by the pressure of one finger? Yet may not these minute particulars mean nothing in reality, and may we not be racking our brains about things which were of no moment to their creator?

But let us proceed on the assumption that even these details have significance. There is a solution which will remove our difficulties and afford a glimpse of a new meaning. If the *left* side of Moses' beard lies under the pressure of his *right* finger, we may perhaps take this pose as the last stage of some connection between his right hand and the left half of his beard, a connection which was a much more intimate one at some moment before that chosen for representation. Perhaps his hand had seized his beard with far more energy, had reached across to its left edge, and, in returning to that position in which the statue shows it, had been followed by a part of his beard which now testifies to the movement which has just taken place. The loop of the beard would thus be an indication of the path taken by this hand.

Thus we shall have inferred that there had been a retreating motion of the right hand. This one assumption necessarily brings others with it. In imagination we complete the scene of which this movement, established by the evidence of the beard, is a part; and we are brought back quite naturally to the hypothesis according to which the resting Moses is startled by the clamour of the people and the spectacle of the Golden Calf. He was sitting there calmly, we will suppose, his head with its flowing beard facing forward, and his hand in all probability not near it at all. Suddenly the clamour strikes his ear; he turns his head and eyes in the direction from which the disturbance comes, sees the scene and takes it in. Now wrath and indignation lay hold of him; and he would fain leap up and punish the wrong-doers, annihilate them. His rage, distant as yet from its object, is meanwhile directed in a gesture against his

[225]

own body. His impatient hand, ready to act, clutches at his beard which has moved with the turn of his head, and presses it between his thumb and palm in the iron grasp of his closing fingers. It is a gesture whose power and vehemence remind us of other creations of Michelangelo's. But now an alteration takes place, as yet we do not know how or why. The hand that had been put forward and had sunk into his beard is hastily withdrawn and unclasped, and the fingers let go their hold; but so deeply have they been plunged in that in their withdrawal they drag a great piece of the left side of the beard across to the right, and this piece remains lodged over the hair of the right under the weight of one finger, the longest and uppermost one of the hand. And this new position, which can only be understood with reference to the former one, is now retained.

It is time now to pause and reflect. We have assumed that the right hand was, to begin with, away from the beard; that then it reached across to the left of the figure in a moment of great emotional tension and seized the beard; and that it was finally drawn back again, taking a part of the beard with it. We have disposed of this right hand as though we had the free use of it. But may we do this? Is the hand indeed so free? Must it not hold or support the Tables? Are not such mimetic evolutions as these prohibited by its important function? And furthermore, what could have occasioned its withdrawal if the motive which made it leave its original position was such a strong one?

Here are indeed fresh difficulties. It is undeniable that the right hand is responsible for the Tables; and also that we have no motive to account for the withdrawal we have ascribed to it. But what if both difficulties could be solved together, and if then and then only they presented a clear and connected sequence of events? What if it is precisely something which is happening to the Tables that explains the movements of the hand?

If we look at the drawing in Fig. 4 we shall see that the Tables [226] present one or two notable features hitherto not deemed worthy of remark. It has been said that the right hand rests upon the Tables; or again that it supports them. And we can see at once that the two apposed, rectangular tablets stand on one corner. If we look closer

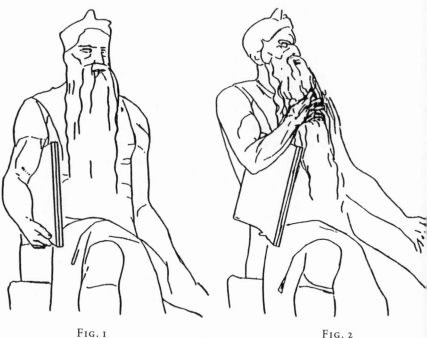

FIG. 1   FIG. 2

we shall notice that the lower edge is a different shape from the upper one, which is obliquely inclined forward. The upper edge is straight, whereas the lower one has a protuberance like a horn on the part nearest to us, and the Tables touch the stone seat precisely with this protuberance. What can be the meaning of this detail?[1] It can hardly be doubted that this projection is meant to mark the actual top side of the Tables, as regards the writing. It is only the top edge of rectangular tablets of this kind that is curved or [227] notched. Thus we see that the Tables are upside-down. This is a singular way to treat such sacred objects. They are stood on their heads and practically balanced on one corner. What consideration of form could have led Michelangelo to put them in such a position? Or was this detail as well of no importance to the artist?

[1]Which, by the way, is quite incorrectly reproduced in a large plaster cast in the collection of the Vienna Academy of Fine Arts.

FIG. 3   FIG. 4

We begin to suspect that the Tables too have arrived at their present position as the result of a previous movement; that this movement was a consequence of the change of place of the right hand that we have postulated, and in its turn compelled that hand to make its subsequent retreat. The movements of the hand and of the Tables can be co-ordinated in this way: at first the figure of Moses, while it was still sitting quietly, carried the Tables perpendicularly under its right arm. Its right hand grasped their lower edge and found a hold in the projection on their front part. (The fact that this made them easier to carry sufficiently accounts for the upside-down position in which the Tables were held.) Then came the moment when Moses' calm was broken by the disturbance. He [228] turned his head in its direction, and when he saw the spectacle he lifted his foot preparatory to starting up, let go the Tables with his hand and plunged it to the left and upwards into his beard, as

though to turn his violence against his own body. The Tables were
now consigned to the pressure of his arm, which had to squeeze
them against his side. But this support was not sufficient and the
Tables began to slip in a forward and downward direction. The
upper edge, which had been held horizontally, now began to face
forwards and downwards; and the lower edge, deprived of its stay,
was nearing the stone seat with its front corner. Another instant
and the Tables would have pivoted upon this new point of support,
have hit the ground with the upper edge foremost, and been
shattered to pieces. It is *to prevent this* that the right hand retreated,
let go the beard, a part of which was drawn back with it unintentionally, came against the upper edge of the Tables in time and held
them near the hind corner, which had now come uppermost. Thus
the singularly constrained air of the whole—beard, hand and tilted
Tables—can be traced to that one passionate movement of the
hand and its natural consequences. If we wish to reverse the effects
of those stormy movements, we must raise the upper front corner
of the Tables and push it back, thus lifting their lower front corner
(the one with the protuberance) from the stone seat; and then
lower the right hand and bring it under the now horizontal lower
edge of the Tables.

I have procured from the hand of an artist three drawings to
illustrate my meaning. Fig. 3 reproduces the statue as it actually is;
Figs. 1 and 2 represent the preceding stages according to my
hypothesis—the first that of calm, the second that of highest
tension, in which the figure is preparing to spring up and has
abandoned its hold of the Tables, so that these are beginning to slip
down. Now it is remarkable how the two postures in the imaginary
drawings vindicate the incorrect descriptions of earlier writers.
Condivi, a contemporary of Michelangelo's, says: 'Moses, the cap-
tain and leader of the Hebrews, is seated in the attitude of a
contemplative sage, holding the Tables of the Law under his right
arm, and leaning his chin on his left hand(!), as one who is weary
[229]   and full of care.' No such attitude is to be seen in Michelangelo's
statue, but it describes almost exactly the view on which the first
drawing is based. Lübke writes, together with other critics: 'Pro-

foundly shaken, he grasps with his right hand his magnificent, flowing beard.' This is incorrect if we look at the reproduction of the actual statue, but it is true of the second sketch (Fig. 2). Justi and Knapp have observed, as we have seen, that the Tables are about to slip down and are in danger of being broken. Thode set them right and showed that the Tables were securely held by the right hand; yet they would have been correct if they had been describing not the statue itself but the middle stage of our reconstructed action. It almost seems as if they had emancipated themselves from the visual image of the statue and had unconsciously begun an analysis of the motive forces behind it, and that that analysis had led them to make the same claim as we have done more consciously and more explicitly.

III

We may now, I believe, permit ourselves to reap the fruits of our endeavours. We have seen how many of those who have felt the influence of this statue have been impelled to interpret it as representing Moses agitated by the spectacle of his people fallen from grace and dancing round an idol. But this interpretation had to be given up, for it made us expect to see him spring up in the next moment, break the Tables and accomplish the work of vengeance. Such a conception, however, would fail to harmonize with the design of making this figure, together with three (or five) more seated figures, a part of the tomb of Julius II. We may now take up again the abandoned interpretation, for the Moses we have reconstructed will neither leap up nor cast the Tables from him. What we see before us is not the inception of a violent action but the remains of a movement that has already taken place. In his first transport of fury, Moses desired to act, to spring up and take vengeance and forget the Tables; but he has overcome the temptation, and he will now remain seated and still, in his frozen wrath and in his pain mingled with contempt. Nor will he throw away the Tables so that they will break on the stones, for it is on their especial account that he has controlled his anger; it was to preserve them that he kept his

[230]   passion in check. In giving way to his rage and indignation, he had
to neglect the Tables, and the hand which upheld them was
withdrawn. They began to slide down and were in danger of being
broken. This brought him to himself. He remembered his mission
and for its sake renounced an indulgence of his feelings. His hand
returned and saved the unsupported Tables before they had actually fallen to the ground. In this attitude he remained immobilized,
and in this attitude Michelangelo has portrayed him as the guardian of the tomb.[1]

As our eyes travel down it the figure exhibits three distinct
emotional strata. The lines of the face reflect the feelings which
have won the ascendancy; the middle of the figure shows the traces
of suppressed movement; and the foot still retains the attitude of
the projected action. It is as though the controlling influence had
proceeded downwards from above. No mention has been made so
far of the left arm, and it seems to claim a share in our interpretation. The hand is laid in the lap in a mild gesture and holds as
though in a caress the end of the flowing beard. It seems as if it is
meant to counteract the violence with which the other hand had
misused the beard a few moments ago.

But here it will be objected that after all this is not the Moses of
the Bible. For that Moses did actually fall into a fit of rage and did
throw away the Tables and break them. This Moses must be a quite
different man, a new Moses of the artist's conception; so that
Michelangelo must have had the presumption to emend the sacred
text and to falsify the character of that holy man. Can we think him
capable of a boldness which might almost be said to approach an
act of blasphemy?

The passage in the Holy Scriptures which describes Moses' ac-

---

[1][It has been suggested by Ernest Jones that Freud may have been partly drawn
into making this analysis of the feelings depicted in Michelangelo's statue by his
own attitude towards the dissident movements of Adler and Jung, which had so
much occupied his mind during the period immediately preceding his composition of this paper.—Freud's interest in the *historical* figure of Moses was, of course,
shown in his last published work, *Moses and Monotheism* (1939*a*).]

tion at the scene of the Golden Calf is as follows:[1] (Exodus xxxii. 7) [231]
'And the Lord said unto Moses, Go, get thee down; for thy people,
which thou broughtest out of the land of Egypt, have corrupted
themselves: (8) They have turned aside quickly out of the way
which I commanded them: they have made them a molten calf,
and have worshipped it, and have sacrificed thereunto, and said,
These be thy gods, O Israel, which brought thee up out of the land
of Egypt. (9) And the Lord said unto Moses, I have seen this
people, and, behold, it is a stiff-necked people: (10) Now therefore
let me alone, that my wrath may wax hot against them, and that I
may consume them; and I will make of thee a great nation. (11) And
Moses besought the Lord his God, and said, Lord, why doth thy
wrath wax hot against thy people, which thou hast brought forth
out of the land of Egypt with great power, and with a mighty
hand? . . .

'(14) And the Lord repented of the evil which he thought to do
unto his people. (15) And Moses turned, and went down from the
mount, and the two tables of the testimony were in his hand:
the tables were written on both their sides; on the one side and on
the other were they written. (16) And the tables were the work of
God, and the writing was the writing of God, graven upon the
tables. (17) And when Joshua heard the noise of the people as they
shouted, he said unto Moses, There is a noise of war in the camp.
(18) And he said, It is not the voice of them that shout for mastery,
neither is it the voice of them that cry for being overcome; but the
noise of them that sing do I hear. (19) And it came to pass, as soon
as he came nigh unto the camp, that he saw the calf, and the
dancing: and Moses' anger waxed hot, and he cast the tables out of
his hands, and brake them beneath the mount. (20) And he took
the calf which they had made, and burnt it in the fire, and ground
it to powder, and strawed it upon the water, and made the children
of Israel drink of it. . . .

[1][In the original, Freud apologizes for his 'anachronistic use of Luther's
translation'. What follows is from the Authorized Version.]

'(30) And it came to pass on the morrow, that Moses said unto the people, Ye have sinned a great sin: and now I will go up unto the Lord; peradventure I shall make an atonement for your sin. (31) And Moses returned unto the Lord, and said, Oh! this people have sinned a great sin, and have made them gods of gold! (32) Yet now, if thou wilt forgive their sin—; and if not, blot me, I pray thee, out
[232]   of thy book which thou has written. (33) And the Lord said unto Moses, Whosoever hath sinned against me, him will I blot out of my book. (34) Therefore now go, lead the people unto the place of which I have spoken unto thee. Behold, mine Angel shall go before thee: nevertheless, in the day when I visit, I will visit their sin upon them. (35) And the Lord plagued the people, because they made the calf which Aaron made.'

It is impossible to read the above passage in the light of modern criticism of the Bible without finding evidence that it has been clumsily put together from various sources. In verse 8 the Lord Himself tells Moses that his people have fallen away and made themselves an idol; and Moses intercedes for the wrongdoers. And yet he speaks to Joshua as though he knew nothing of this (18), and is suddenly aroused to wrath as he sees the scene of the worshipping of the Golden Calf (19). In verse 14 he has already gained a pardon from God for his erring people, yet in verse 31 he returns to the mountains to implore this forgiveness, tells God about his people's sin and is assured of the postponement of the punishment. Verse 35 speaks of a visitation of his people by the Lord about which nothing more is told us; whereas the verses 20–30 describe the punishment which Moses himself dealt out. It is well known that the historical parts of the Bible, dealing with the Exodus, are crowded with still more glaring incongruities and contradictions.

The age of the Renaissance had naturally no such critical attitude towards the text of the Bible, but had to accept it as a consistent whole, with the result that the passage in question was not a very good subject for representation. According to the Scriptures Moses was already instructed about the idolatry of his people and had ranged himself on the side of mildness and forgiveness; nevertheless, when he saw the Golden Calf and the dancing crowd, he was overcome by a sudden frenzy of rage. It would therefore not surprise us to find that the artist, in depicting the reaction of his hero to that painful surprise, had deviated from the text from inner motives. Moreover, such deviations from the scriptural text on a much slighter pretext were by no means unusual or disallowed to artists. A celebrated picture by Parmigiano possessed by his native town depicts Moses sitting on the top of a mountain and dashing the Tables to the ground, although the Bible expressly says that he broke them 'beneath the mount'. Even the representation of a seated Moses finds no support in the text and seems rather to bear out those critics who maintain that Michelangelo's statue is not meant to record any particular moment in the prophet's life.　[233]

More important than his infidelity to the text of the Scriptures is the alteration which Michelangelo has, in our supposition, made in the character of Moses. The Moses of legend and tradition had a hasty temper and was subject to fits of passion. It was in a transport of divine wrath of this kind that he slew an Egyptian who was maltreating an Israelite, and had to flee out of the land into the wilderness; and it was in a similar passion that he broke the Tables of the Law, inscribed by God Himself. Tradition, in recording such a characteristic, is unbiased, and preserves the impression of a great personality who once lived. But Michelangelo has placed a different Moses on the tomb of the Pope, one superior to the historical or traditional Moses. He has modified the theme of the broken Tables; he does not let Moses break them in his wrath, but makes him be influenced by the danger that they will be broken and makes him calm that wrath, or at any rate prevent it from becoming an act. In this way he has added something new and more than human to the figure of Moses; so that the giant frame with its tremendous physical power becomes only a concrete expression of the highest mental achievement that is possible in a man, that of struggling successfully against an inward passion for the sake of a cause to which he has devoted himself.

We have now completed our interpretation of Michelangelo's

statue, though it can still be asked what motives prompted the sculptor to select the figure of Moses, and a so greatly altered Moses, as an adornment for the tomb of Julius II. In the opinion of many these motives are to be found in the character of the Pope and in Michelangelo's relations with him. Julius II was akin to Michelangelo in this, that he attempted to realize great and mighty ends, and especially designs on a grand scale. He was a man of action and he had a definite purpose, which was to unite Italy under the Papal supremacy. He desired to bring about single-handed what was not to happen for several centuries, and then only [234] through the conjunction of many alien forces; and he worked alone, with impatience, in the short span of sovereignty allowed him, and used violent means. He could appreciate Michelangelo as a man of his own kind, but he often made him smart under his sudden anger and his utter lack of consideration for others. The artist felt the same violent force of will in himself, and, as the more introspective thinker, may have had a premonition of the failure to which they were both doomed. And so he carved his Moses on the Pope's tomb, not without a reproach against the dead pontiff, as a warning to himself, thus, in self-criticism, rising superior to his own nature.

IV

In 1863 an Englishman, Watkiss Lloyd, devoted a little book to the Moses of Michelangelo. I succeeded in getting hold of this short essay of forty-six pages, and read it with mixed feelings. I once more had an opportunity of experiencing in myself what unworthy and puerile motives enter into our thoughts and acts even in a serious cause. My first feeling was one of regret that the author should have anticipated so much of my thought, which seemed precious to me because it was the result of my own efforts; and it was only in the second instance that I was able to get pleasure from its unexpected confirmation of my opinion. Our views, however, diverse on one very important point.

Lloyd remarks in the first place that the usual descriptions of the figure are incorrect, and that Moses is not in the act of rising[1]—that the right hand is not grasping the beard, but that the index-finger alone is resting upon it.[2] Lloyd also recognizes, and this is much more important, that the attitude portrayed can only be explained by postulating a foregoing one, which is not represented, and that the drawing of the left lock of the beard across to the right signifies that the right hand and the left side of the beard have at a previous stage been in closer and more natural contact. But he suggests another way of reconstructing the earlier contact which must necessarily be assumed. According to him, it was not the hand which had been plunged into the beard, but the beard which had been where the hand now is. We must, he says, imagine that just before the sudden interruption the head of the statue was turned far round to its right over the hand which, then as now, was holding the Tables of the Law. The pressure (of the Tables) against the palm of the hand caused the fingers to open naturally beneath the flowing locks of the beard, and the sudden turn of the head to the other side resulted in a part of the beard being detained for an instant by the motionless hand and forming the loop of hair which is to be looked on as a mark of the course it has taken—its 'wake', to use Lloyd's own word.

In rejecting the other possibility, that of the right hand having previously been in contact with the left side of the beard, Lloyd has allowed himself to be influenced by a consideration which shows how near he came to our interpretation. He says that it was not possible for the prophet, even in very great agitation, to have put out his hand to draw his beard across to the right. For in that case his fingers would have been in an entirely different position; and, moreover, such a movement would have allowed the Tables to slip

[235]

---

[1]'But he is not rising or preparing to rise; the bust is fully upright, not thrown forward for the alteration of balance preparatory for such a movement. . . .' (Lloyd, 1863, 10).

[2]'Such a description is altogether erroneous; the fillets of the beard are detained by the right hand but they are not held, nor grasped, enclosed or taken hold of. They are even detained but momentarily—momentarily engaged, they are on the point of being free for disengagement' (ibid., 11).

down, since they are only supported by the pressure of the right arm—unless, in Moses' endeavour to save them at the last moment, we think of them as being 'clutched by a gesture so awkward that to imagine it is profanation'.

It is easy to see what the writer has overlooked. He has correctly interpreted the anomalies of the beard as indicating a preceding movement, but he has omitted to apply the same explanation to the no less unnatural details in the position of the Tables. He examines only the data connected with the beard and not those connected with the Tables, whose position he assumes to be the original one. In this way he closes the door to a conception like ours which, by examining certain insignificant details, has arrived at an unexpected interpretation of the meaning and aim of the figure as a whole.

[236]   But what if both of us have strayed on to a wrong path? What if we have taken too serious and profound a view of details which were nothing to the artist, details which he had introduced quite arbitrarily or for some purely formal reasons with no hidden intention behind? What if we have shared the fate of so many interpreters who have thought they saw quite clearly things which the artist did not intend either consciously or unconsciously? I cannot tell. I cannot say whether it is reasonable to credit Michelangelo—an artist in whose works there is so much thought striving for expression—with such an elementary want of precision, and especially whether this can be assumed in regard to the striking and singular features of the statue under discussion. And finally we may be allowed to point out, in all modesty, that the artist is no less responsible than his interpreters for the obscurity which surrounds his work. In his creations Michelangelo has often enough gone to the utmost limit of what is expressible in art; and perhaps in his statue of Moses he has not completely succeeded, if his purpose was to make the passage of a violent gust of passion visible in the signs left behind it in the ensuing calm.

Postscript
(1927)

Several years after the publication of my paper on the Moses of Michelangelo, which appeared anonymously in *Imago* in 1914, Dr. Ernest Jones very kindly sent me a copy of the April number of the *Burlington Magazine* of 1921 (Vol. XXXVIII), which could not fail to turn my interest once more to the interpretation of the statue which I had originally suggested. This number contains (pp. 157–66) a short article by H. P. Mitchell on two bronzes of the twelfth century, now in the Ashmolean Museum at Oxford, which are attributed to an outstanding artist of that day, Nicholas of Verdun. We possess other works by the same hand in Tournay, Arras and Klosterneuburg, near Vienna; his masterpiece is considered to be the Shrine of the Three Kings in Cologne.

One of the two statuettes described by Mitchell, which is just over 9 inches high, is identifiable beyond all doubt as a Moses, because of the two Tables of the Law which he holds in his hand. This Moses, too, is represented as seated, enveloped in a flowing robe. His face is expressive of strong passion, mixed, perhaps, with grief; and his hand grasps his long beard and presses its strands between palm and thumb as in a vice. He is, that is to say, making the very gesture which I postulated in Fig. 2 of my former paper as a preliminary stage of the attitude into which Michelangelo has cast him.

A glance at the accompanying illustration [in the original, a statuette of Moses attributed to Nicholas of Verdun] will show the main difference between the two compositions, which are separated from each other by an interval of more than three centuries. The Moses of the Lorraine artist is holding the Tables by their top edge with his left hand, resting them on his knee. If we were to transfer them to the other side of his body and put them under his right arm we should have established the preliminary posture of Michelangelo's Moses. If my view of the thrusting of the hand into the beard is right, then the Moses of the year 1180 shows us an instant during his storm of feeling, whilst the statue in S. Pietro in Vincoli depicts the calm when the storm is over.

In my opinion this new piece of evidence increases the probability that the interpretation which I attempted in 1914 was a correct one. Perhaps some connoisseur of art will be able to bridge the gulf in time between the Moses of Nicholas of Verdun and the Moses of the Master of the Italian Renaissance by telling us where examples of representations of Moses belonging to the intervening period are to be found.

§ Some Character-Types Met with in Psycho-analytic Work

[311]

WHEN a doctor carries out the psycho-analytic treatment of a neurotic, his interest is by no means directed in the first instance to the patient's character. He would much rather know what the symptoms mean, what instinctual impulses are concealed behind them and are satisfied by them, and what course was followed by the mysterious path that has led from the instinctual wishes to the symptoms. But the technique which he is obliged to follow soon compels him to direct his immediate curiosity towards other objectives. He observes that his investigation is threatened by resistances set up against him by the patient, and these resistances he may justly count as part of the latter's character. This now acquires the first claim on his interest.

What opposes the doctor's efforts is not always those traits of character which the patient recognizes in himself and which are attributed to him by people round him. Peculiarities in him which he had seemed to possess only to a modest degree are often brought to light in surprisingly increased intensity, or attitudes reveal themselves in him which had not been betrayed in other relations of life. The pages which follow will be devoted to describing and tracing back a few of these surprising traits of character.

SOURCE: *Standard Ed.*, **14**, 311–33.

I
The 'Exceptions'

PSYCHO-ANALYTIC work is continually confronted with the task of inducing the patient to renounce an immediate and directly attainable yield of pleasure. He is not asked to renounce all pleasure; that could not, perhaps, be expected of any human being, and even religion is obliged to support its demand that earthly pleasure shall be set aside by promising that it will provide instead an incomparably greater amount of superior pleasure in another [312] world. No, the patient is only asked to renounce such satisfactions as will inevitably have detrimental consequences. His privation is only to be temporary; he has only to learn to exchange an immediate yield of pleasure for a better assured, even though a postponed one. Or, in other words, under the doctor's guidance he is asked to make the advance from the pleasure principle to the reality principle by which the mature human being is distinguished from the child. In this educative process, the doctor's clearer insight can hardly be said to play a decisive part; as a rule, he can only tell his patient what the latter's own reason can tell him. But it is not the same to know a thing in one's own mind and to hear it from someone outside. The doctor plays the part of this effective outsider; he makes use of the influence which one human being exercises over another. Or—recalling that it is the habit of psychoanalysis to replace what is derivative and etiolated by what is original and basic—let us say that the doctor, in his educative work, makes use of one of the components of love. In this work of after-education, he is probably doing no more than repeat the process which made education of any kind possible in the first instance. Side by side with the exigencies of life, love is the great educator; and it is by the love of those nearest him that the incomplete human being is induced to respect the decrees of necessity and to spare himself the punishment that follows any infringement of them.

When in this way one asks the patient to make a provisional

renunciation of some pleasurable satisfaction, to make a sacrifice, to show his readiness to accept some temporary suffering for the sake of a better end, or even merely to make up his mind to submit to a necessity which applies to everyone, one comes upon individuals who resist such an appeal on a special ground. They say that they have renounced enough and suffered enough, and have a claim to be spared any further demands; they will submit no longer to any disagreeable necessity, for they are *exceptions* and, moreover, intend to remain so. In one such patient this claim was magnified into a conviction that a special providence watched over him, which would protect him from any painful sacrifices of the sort. The doctor's arguments will achieve nothing against an inner confidence which expresses itself as strongly as this; even *his* influence, indeed, is powerless at first, and it becomes clear to him that he must discover the sources from which this damaging prepossession is being fed.

Now it is no doubt true that everyone would like to consider [313] himself an 'exception' and claim privileges over others. But precisely because of this there must be a particular reason, and one not universally present, if someone actually proclaims himself an exception and behaves as such. This reason may be of more than one kind; in the cases I investigated I succeeded in discovering a common peculiarity in the earlier experiences of these patients' lives. Their neuroses were connected with some experience or suffering to which they had been subjected in their earliest childhood, one in respect of which they knew themselves to be guiltless, and which they could look upon as an unjust disadvantage imposed upon them. The privileges that they claimed as a result of this injustice, and the rebelliousness it engendered, had contributed not a little to intensifying the conflicts leading to the outbreak of their neurosis. In one of these patients, a woman, the attitude towards life which I am discussing came to a head when she learnt that a painful organic trouble, which had hindered her from attaining her aims in life, was of congenital origin. So long as she looked upon this trouble as an accidental and late acquisition, she bore it patiently; as soon as she found that it was part of an innate inheritance, she became rebellious. The young man who believed that he was watched over by a special providence had in his infancy been the victim of an accidental infection from his wet-nurse, and had spent his whole later life making claims for compensation, an accident pension, as it were, without having any idea on what he based those claims. In his case the analysis, which constructed this event out of obscure mnemic residues and interpretations of the symptoms, was confirmed objectively by information from his family.

For reasons which will be easily understood I cannot communicate very much about these or other case histories. Nor do I propose to go into the obvious analogy between deformities of character resulting from protracted sickliness in childhood and the behaviour of whole nations whose past history has been full of suffering. Instead, however, I will take the opportunity of pointing to a figure created by the greatest of poets—a figure in whose character the claim to be an exception is closely bound up with and is motivated by the circumstance of congenital disadvantage.

[314] In the opening soliloquy to Shakespeare's *Richard III*, Gloucester, who subsequently becomes King, says:

> But I, that am not shaped for sportive tricks,
> Nor made to court an amorous looking-glass;
> I that am rudely stamp'd, and want love's majesty
> To strut before a wanton ambling nymph;
> I, that am curtail'd of this fair proportion,
> Cheated of feature by dissembling Nature,
> Deform'd, unfinish'd, sent before my time
> Into this breathing world, scarce half made up,
> And that so lamely and unfashionable,
> That dogs bark at me as I halt by them;
>
> * * * * *
>
> And therefore, since I cannot prove a lover,
> To entertain these fair well-spoken days,
> I am determined to prove a villain,
> And hate the idle pleasures of these days.

At a first glance this tirade may perhaps seem unrelated to our present theme. Richard seems to say nothing more than: 'I find these idle times tedious, and I want to enjoy myself. As I cannot play the lover on account of my deformity, I will play the villain; I will intrigue, murder and do anything else I please.' Such a frivolous motivation could not but stifle any stirring of sympathy in the audience, if it were not a screen for something much more serious. Otherwise the play would be psychologically impossible, for the writer must know how to furnish us with a secret background of sympathy for his hero, if we are to admire his boldness and adroitness without inward protest; and such sympathy can only be based on understanding or on a sense of a possible inner fellow-feeling for him.

I think, therefore, that Richard's soliloquy does not say everything; it merely gives a hint, and leaves us to fill in what it hints at. When we do so, however, the appearance of frivolity vanishes, the bitterness and minuteness with which Richard has depicted his deformity make their full effect, and we clearly perceive the fellow-feeling which compels our sympathy even with a villain like him. What the soliloquy thus means is: 'Nature has done me a grievous wrong in denying me the beauty of form which wins human love. Life owes me reparation for this, and I will see that I get it. I have a right to be an exception, to disregard the scruples by which others let themselves be held back. I may do wrong myself, since wrong [315] has been done to me.' And now we feel that we ourselves might become like Richard, that on a small scale, indeed, we are already like him. Richard is an enormous magnification of something we find in ourselves as well. We all think we have reason to reproach Nature and our destiny for congenital and infantile disadvantages; we all demand reparation for early wounds to our narcissism, our self-love. Why did not Nature give us the golden curls of Balder or the strength of Siegfried or the lofty brow of genius or the noble profile of aristocracy? Why were we born in a middle-class home instead of in a royal palace? We could carry off beauty and distinction quite as well as any of those whom we are now obliged to envy for these qualities.

It is, however, a subtle economy of art in the poet that he does not permit his hero to give open and complete expression to all his secret motives. By this means he obliges us to supplement them; he engages our intellectual activity, diverts it from critical reflection and keeps us firmly identified with his hero. A bungler in his place would give conscious expression to all that he wishes to reveal to us, and would then find himself confronted by our cool, untrammelled intelligence, which would preclude any deepening of the illusion.

Before leaving the 'exceptions', however, we may point out that the claim of women to privileges and to exemption from so many of the importunities of life rests upon the same foundation. As we learn from psycho-analytic work, women regard themselves as having been damaged in infancy, as having been undeservedly cut short of something and unfairly treated; and the embitterment of so many daughters against their mother derives, ultimately, from the reproach against her of having brought them into the world as women instead of as men.

II
Those Wrecked by Success

PSYCHO-ANALYTIC work has furnished us with the thesis that

PSYCHO-ANALYTIC work has furnished us with the thesis that [316]
people fall ill of a neurosis as a result of *frustration*.[1] What is meant
is the frustration of the satisfaction of their libidinal wishes, and
some digression is necessary in order to make the thesis intelligible.
For a neurosis to be generated there must be a conflict between a
person's libidinal wishes and the part of his personality we call his
ego, which is the expression of his instinct of self-preservation and
which also includes his *ideals* of his personality. A pathogenic
conflict of this kind takes place only when the libido tries to follow
paths and aims which the ego has long since overcome and condemned and has therefore prohibited for ever; and this the libido
only does if it is deprived of the possibility of an ideal ego-syntonic
satisfaction. Hence privation, frustration of a real satisfaction, is
the first condition for the generation of a neurosis, although,
indeed, it is far from being the only one.

So much the more surprising, and indeed bewildering, must it
appear when as a doctor one makes the discovery that people
occasionally fall ill precisely when a deeply-rooted and long-
cherished wish has come to fulfilment. It seems then as though they
were not able to tolerate their happiness; for there can be no
question that there is a causal connection between their success and
their falling ill.

I had an opportunity of obtaining an insight into a woman's
history, which I propose to describe as typical of these tragic
occurrences. She was of good birth and well brought-up, but as
quite a young girl she could not restrain her zest for life; she ran
away from home and roved about the world in search of adven-
tures, till she made the acquaintance of an artist who could appreciate her feminine charms but could also divine, in spite of what she
had fallen to, the finer qualities she possessed. He took her to live
with him, and she proved a faithful companion to him, and seemed

[1][See 'Types of Onset of Neurosis' (1912c).]

157

only to need social rehabilitation to achieve complete happiness. After many years of life together, he succeeded in getting his family reconciled to her, and was then prepared to make her his legal wife. At that moment she began to go to pieces. She neglected the house of which she was now about to become the rightful mistress, imagined herself persecuted by his relatives, who wanted to take her into the family, debarred her lover, through her senseless jealousy, from all social intercourse, hindered him in his artist's work, and soon succumbed to an incurable mental illness.

On another occasion I came across the case of a most respectable man who, himself an academic teacher, had for many years cherished the natural wish to succeed the master who had initiated him into his own studies. When this older man retired, and his colleagues informed him that it was he who was chosen as successor, he began to hesitate, depreciated his merits, declared himself unworthy to fill the position designed for him, and fell into a melancholia which unfitted him for all activity for some years.

Different as these two cases are in other respects, they yet agree in this one point: the illness followed close upon the fulfilment of a wish and put an end to all enjoyment of it.

The contradiction between such experiences and the rule that what induces illness is frustration is not insoluble. It disappears if we make a distinction between an *external* and an *internal* frustration. If the object in which the libido can find its satisfaction is withheld *in reality*, this is an external frustration. In itself it is inoperative, not pathogenic, until an internal frustration is joined to it. This latter must proceed from the ego, and must dispute the access by the libido to other objects, which it now seeks to get hold of. Only then does a conflict arise, and the possibility of a neurotic illness, i.e. of a substitutive satisfaction reached circuitously by way of the repressed unconscious. Internal frustration is potentially present, therefore, in every case, only it does not come into operation until external, real frustration has prepared the ground for it. In those exceptional cases in which people are made ill by success, the internal frustration has operated by itself; indeed it has only made its appearance after an external frustration has been replaced by fulfilment of a wish. At first sight there is something strange about this; but on closer consideration we shall reflect that it is not at all unusual for the ego to tolerate a wish as harmless so long as it exists in phantasy alone and seems remote from fulfilment, [318] whereas the ego will defend itself hotly against such a wish as soon as it approaches fulfilment and threatens to become a reality. The distinction between this and familiar situations in neurosis-formation is merely that ordinarily it is internal intensifications of the libidinal cathexis that turn the phantasy, which has hitherto been thought little of and tolerated, into a dreaded opponent; while in these cases of ours the signal for the outbreak of conflict is given by a real external change.

Analytic work has no difficulty in showing us that it is forces of conscience which forbid the subject to gain the long hoped-for advantage from the fortunate change in reality. It is a difficult task, however, to discover the essence and origin of these judging and punishing trends, which so often surprise us by their existence where we do not expect to find them. For the usual reasons I shall not discuss what we know or conjecture on the point in relation to cases of clinical observation, but in relation to figures which great writers have created from the wealth of their knowledge of the mind.

We may take as an example of a person who collapses on reaching success, after striving for it with single-minded energy, the figure of Shakespeare's Lady Macbeth. Beforehand there is no hesitation, no sign of any internal conflict in her, no endeavour but that of overcoming the scruples of her ambitious and yet tender-minded husband. She is ready to sacrifice even her womanliness to her murderous intention, without reflecting on the decisive part which this womanliness must play when the question afterwards arises of preserving the aim of her ambition, which has been attained through a crime.

Come, you spirits
That tend on mortal thoughts, unsex me here

> . . . Come to my woman's breasts,
> And take my milk for gall, you murdering ministers!
>
> (Act I, Sc. 5.)

> . . . I have given suck, and know
> How tender 'tis to love the babe that milks me:
> I would, while it was smiling in my face,
> Have pluck'd my nipple from his boneless gums,
> And dashed the brains out, had I so sworn as you
> Have done to this.
>
> (Act I, Sc. 7.)

[319]   One solitary faint stirring of reluctance comes over her before the deed:

> . . . Had he not resembled
> My father as he slept, I had done it . . .
>
> (Act II, Sc. 2.)

Then, when she has become Queen through the murder of Duncan, she betrays for a moment something like disappointment, something like disillusionment. We cannot tell why.

> . . . Nought's had, all's spent,
> Where our desire is got without content:
> 'Tis safer to be that which we destroy,
> Than by destruction dwell in doubtful joy.
>
> (Act III, Sc. 2.)

Nevertheless, she holds out. In the banqueting scene which follows on these words, she alone keeps her head, cloaks her husband's state of confusion and finds a pretext for dismissing the guests. And then she disappears from view. We next see her in the sleep-walking scene in the last Act, fixated to the impressions of the night of the murder. Once again, as then, she seeks to put heart into her husband:

> 'Fie, my lord, fie! a soldier, and afeard? What need we fear who knows it, when none can call our power to account?'
>
> (Act V, Sc. 1.)

She hears the knocking at the door, which terrified her husband after the deed. But at the same time she strives to 'undo the deed which cannot be undone'. She washes her hands, which are blood-stained and smell of blood, and is conscious of the futility of the attempt. She who had seemed so remorseless seems to have been borne down by remorse. When she dies, Macbeth, who meanwhile has become as inexorable as she had been in the beginning, can only find a brief epitaph for her:

> She should have died hereafter;
> There would have been a time for such a word.
>
> (Act V, Sc. 5.)

And now we ask ourselves what it was that broke this character which had seemed forged from the toughest metal? Is it only disillusionment—the different aspect shown by the accomplished deed[1]—and are we to infer that even in Lady Macbeth an originally gentle and womanly nature had been worked up to a concentration and high tension which could not endure for long, or ought we to seek for signs of a deeper motivation which will make this collapse more humanly intelligible to us? [320]

It seems to me impossible to come to any decision. Shakespeare's *Macbeth* is a *pièce d'occasion*, written for the accession of James, who had hitherto been King of Scotland. The plot was ready-made, and had been handled by other contemporary writers, whose work Shakespeare probably made use of in his customary manner. It offered remarkable analogies to the actual situation. The 'virginal' Elizabeth, of whom it was rumoured that she had never been capable of child-bearing and who had once described herself as 'a barren stock',[2] in an anguished outcry at the news of James's birth, was obliged by this very childlessness of hers to make the Scottish

[1] [An allusion to a line in Schiller's *Die Braut von Messina*, III, 5.]
[2] Cf. *Macbeth*, Act III, Sc. 1:

> Upon my head they placed a fruitless crown,
> And put a barren septre in my gripe,
> Thence to be wrenched with an unlineal hand,
> No son of mine succeeding . . .

king her successor. And he was the son of the Mary Stuart whose
execution she, even though reluctantly, had ordered, and who, in
spite of the clouding of their relations by political concerns, was
nevertheless of her blood and might be called her guest.

The accession of James I was like a demonstration of the curse of
unfruitfulness and the blessings of continuous generation. And the
action of Shakespeare's *Macbeth* is based on this same contrast.[1]

The Weird Sisters assured Macbeth that he himself should be
king, but to Banquo they promised that his children should succeed to the crown. Macbeth is incensed by this decree of destiny.
He is not content with the satisfaction of his own ambition. He
wants to found a dynasty—not to have murdered for the benefit of
strangers. This point is overlooked if Shakespeare's play is regarded
only as a tragedy of ambition. It is clear that Macbeth cannot live
for ever, and thus there is but one way for him to invalidate the part
of the prophecy which opposes him—namely, to have children
himself who can succeed him. And he seems to expect them from
his indomitable wife:

> Bring forth men-children only!
> For thy undaunted mettle should compose
> Nothing but males . . . .
>
> (Act I, Sc. 7.)

And equally it is clear that if he is deceived in this expectation he
must submit to destiny; otherwise his actions lose all purpose and
are transformed into the blind fury of one doomed to destruction,
who is resolved to destroy beforehand all that he can reach. We
watch Macbeth pass through this development, and at the height
of the tragedy we hear Macduff's shattering cry, which has so often
been recognized to be ambiguous and which may perhaps contain
the key to the change in Macbeth:

> He has no children!
>
> (Act IV, Sc. 3.)

[1][Freud had already suggested this in the first edition of *The Interpretation of
Dreams* (1900*a*), *Standard Ed.*, 4, 266.]

[321]

There is no doubt that this means: 'Only because he is himself childless could he murder my children.' But more may be implied in it, and above all it might lay bare the deepest motive which not only forces Macbeth to go far beyond his own nature, but also touches the hard character of his wife at its only weak point. If one surveys the whole play from the summit marked by these words of Macduff's, one sees that it is sown with references to the father-children relation. The murder of the kindly Duncan is little else than parricide; in Banquo's case, Macbeth kills the father while the son escapes him; and in Macduff's, he kills the children because the father has fled from him. A bloody child, and then a crowned one, are shown him by the witches in the apparition scene; the armed head which is seen earlier is no doubt Macbeth himself. But in the background rises the sinister form of the avenger, Macduff, who is himself an exception to the laws of generation, since he was not born of his mother but ripp'd from her womb.

It would be a perfect example of poetic justice in the manner of the talion if the childlessness of Macbeth and the barrenness of his Lady were the punishment for their crimes against the sanctity of generation—if Macbeth could not become a father because he had robbed children of their father and a father of his children, and if Lady Macbeth suffered the unsexing she had demanded of the spirits of murder. I believe Lady Macbeth's illness, the transforma- [322] tion of her callousness into penitence, could be explained directly as a reaction to her childlessness, by which she is convinced of her impotence against the decrees of nature, and at the same time reminded that it is through her own fault if her crime has been robbed of the better part of its fruits.

In Holinshed's *Chronicle* (1577), from which Shakespeare took the plot of *Macbeth*, Lady Macbeth is only once mentioned as the ambitious wife who instigates her husband to murder in order that she may herself become queen. There is no mention of her subse- quent fate and of the development of her character. On the other hand, it would seem that the change of Macbeth's character into a bloodthirsty tyrant is ascribed to the same motives as we have suggested here. For in Holinshed *ten years* pass between the murder of Duncan, through which Macbeth becomes king, and his further misdeeds; and in these ten years he is shown as a stern but just ruler. It is not until after this lapse of time that the change begins in him, under the influence of the tormenting fear that the prophecy to Banquo may be fulfilled just as the prophecy of his own destiny has been. Only then does he contrive the murder of Banquo, and, as in Shakespeare, is driven from one crime to another. It is not expressly stated in Holinshed that it was his childlessness which urged him to these courses, but enough time and room is given for that plausible motive. Not so in Shakespeare. Events crowd upon us in the tragedy with breathless haste so that, to judge by the statements made by the characters in it, the course of its action covers about *one week*.[1] This acceleration takes the ground from under all our constructions of the motives for the change in the characters of Macbeth and his wife. There is no time for a long-drawn-out disappointment of their hopes of offspring to break the woman down and drive the man to defiant rage; and the contradiction remains that though so many subtle interrelations in the plot, and between it and its occasion, point to a common origin of them in the theme of childlessness, nevertheless the economy of time in the tragedy expressly precludes a development of character from any motives but those inherent in the action itself.

[323]   What, however, these motives can have been which in so short a space of time could turn the hesitating, ambitious man into an unbridled tyrant, and his steely-hearted instigator into a sick woman gnawed by remorse, it is, in my view, impossible to guess. We must, I think, give up any hope of penetrating the triple layer of obscurity into which the bad preservation of the text, the unknown intention of the dramatist, and the hidden purport of the legend have become condensed. But I should not subscribe to the objection that investigations like these are idle in the face of the powerful effect which the tragedy has upon the spectator. The dramatist can indeed, during the representation, overwhelm us by his art and paralyse our powers of reflection; but he cannot prevent us from

[1]Darmesteter (1881, lxxv).

attempting subsequently to grasp its effect by studying its psychological mechanism. Nor does the contention that a dramatist is at liberty to shorten at will the natural chronology of the events he brings before us, if by the sacrifice of common probability he can enhance the dramatic effect, seem to me relevant in this instance. For such a sacrifice is justified only when it merely interferes with probability,[1] and not when it breaks the causal connection; moreover, the dramatic effect would hardly have suffered if the passage of time had been left indeterminate, instead of being expressly limited to a few days.

One is so unwilling to dismiss a problem like that of *Macbeth* as insoluble that I will venture to bring up a fresh point, which may offer another way out of the difficulty. Ludwig Jekels, in a recent Shakespearean study,[2] thinks he has discovered a particular technique of the poet's, and this might apply to *Macbeth*. He believes that Shakespeare often splits a character up into two personages, which, taken separately, are not completely understandable and do not become so until they are brought together once more into a unity. This might be so with Macbeth and Lady Macbeth. In that case it would of course be pointless to regard her as an independent character and seek to discover the motives for her change, without considering the Macbeth who completes her. I shall not follow this clue any further, but I should, nevertheless, like to point out something which strikingly confirms this view: the germs of fear [324] which break out in Macbeth on the night of the murder do not develop further in *him* but in *her*.[3] It is he who has the hallucination of the dagger before the crime; but it is she who afterwards falls ill of a mental disorder. It is he who after the murder hears the cry in the house: 'Sleep no more! Macbeth does murder sleep . . .' and

[1] As in Richard III's wooing of Anne beside the bier of the King whom he has murdered.
[2] [This does not appear to have been published. In a later paper on *Macbeth* Jekels (1917) barely refers to this theory, apart from quoting the present paragraph. In a still later paper, on 'The Psychology of Comedy', Jekels (1926) returns to the subject, but again very briefly.]
[3] Cf. Darmesteter (1881, lxxv).

so 'Macbeth shall sleep no more'; but we never hear that *he* slept no more, while the Queen, as we see, rises from her bed and, talking in her sleep, betrays her guilt. It is he who stands helpless with bloody hands, lamenting that 'all great Neptune's ocean' will not wash them clean, while she comforts him: 'A little water clears us of this deed'; but later it is she who washes her hands for a quarter of an hour and cannot get rid of the bloodstains: 'All the perfumes of Arabia will not sweeten this little hand.' Thus what he feared in his pangs of conscience is fulfilled in her; she becomes all remorse and he all defiance. Together they exhaust the possibilities of reaction to the crime, like two disunited parts of a single psychical individuality, and it may be that they are both copied from a single prototype.

If we have been unable to give any answer to the question why Lady Macbeth should collapse after her success, we may perhaps have a better chance when we turn to the creation of another great dramatist, who loves to pursue problems of psychological responsibility with unrelenting rigour.

Rebecca Gamvik, the daughter of a midwife, has been brought up by her adopted father, Dr. West, to be a freethinker and to despise the restrictions which a morality founded on religious belief seeks to impose on the desires of life. After the doctor's death she finds a position at Rosmersholm, the home for many generations of an ancient family whose members know nothing of laughter and have sacrificed joy to a rigid fulfilment of duty. Its occupants are Johannes Rosmer, a former pastor, and his invalid wife, the childless Beata. Overcome by 'a wild, uncontrollable passion'[1] for the love of the high-born Rosmer, Rebecca resolves to remove the wife who stands in her way, and to this end makes use of her 'fearless, free' will, which is restrained by no scruples. She contrives [325] that Beata shall read a medical book in which the aim of marriage is represented to be the begetting of offspring, so that the poor woman begins to doubt whether her own marriage is justifiable.

[1][The quotations are based on William Archer's English translation.]

Rebecca then hints that Rosmer, whose studies and ideas she shares, is about to abandon the old faith and join the 'party of enlightenment'; and after she has thus shaken the wife's confidence in her husband's moral integrity, gives her finally to understand that she, Rebecca, will soon leave the house in order to conceal the consequences of her illicit intercourse with Rosmer. The criminal scheme succeeds. The poor wife, who has passed for depressed and irresponsible, throws herself from the path beside the mill into the mill-race, possessed by the sense of her own worthlessness and wishing no longer to stand between her beloved husband and his happiness.

For more than a year Rebecca and Rosmer have been living alone at Rosmersholm in a relationship which he wishes to regard as a purely intellectual and ideal friendship. But when this relationship begins to be darkened from outside by the first shadow of gossip, and at the same time tormenting doubts arise in Rosmer about the motives for which his wife put an end to herself, he begs Rebecca to become his second wife, so that they may counter the unhappy past with a new living reality (Act II). For an instant she exclaims with joy at his proposal, but immediately afterwards declares that it can never be, and that if he urges her further she will 'go the way Beata went'. Rosmer cannot understand this rejection; and still less can we, who know more of Rebecca's actions and designs. All we can be certain of is that her 'no' is meant in earnest.

How could it come about that the adventuress with the 'fearless, free will', who forged her way ruthlessly to her desired goal, should now refuse to pluck the fruit of success when it is offered to her? She herself gives us the explanation in the fourth Act: '*This* is the terrible part of it: that now, when all life's happiness is within my grasp—my heart is changed and my own past cuts me off from it.' That is to say, she has in the meantime become a different being; her conscience has awakened, she has acquired a sense of guilt which debars her from enjoyment.

And what has awakened her conscience? Let us listen to her herself, and then consider whether we can believe her entirely. 'It is the Rosmer view of life—or your view of life at any rate—that has

[326] infected my will. . . . And made it sick. Enslaved it to laws that had no power over me before. You—life with you—has ennobled my mind.'

This influence, we are further to understand, has only become effective since she has been able to live alone with Rosmer: 'In quiet—in solitude—when you showed me all your thoughts without reserve—every tender and delicate feeling, just as it came to you—*then* the great change came over me.'

Shortly before this she has lamented the other aspect of the change: 'Because Rosmersholm has sapped my strength. My old fearless will has had its wings clipped here. It is crippled! The time is past when I had courage for anything in the world. I have lost the power of action, Rosmer.'

Rebecca makes this declaration after she had revealed herself as a criminal in a voluntary confession to Rosmer and Rector Kroll, the brother of the woman she has got rid of. Ibsen has made it clear by small touches of masterly subtlety that Rebecca does not actually tell lies, but is never entirely straightforward. Just as, in spite of all her freedom from prejudices, she has understated her age by a year, so her confession to the two men is incomplete, and as a result of Kroll's insistence it is supplemented on some important points. Hence it is open to us to suppose that her explanation of her renunciation exposes one motive only to conceal another.

Certainly, we have no reason to disbelieve her when she declares that the atmosphere of Rosmersholm and her association with the high-minded Rosmer have ennobled—and crippled—her. She is here expressing what she knows and has felt. But this is not necessarily all that has happened in her, nor need she have understood all that has happened. Rosmer's influence may only have been a cloak, which concealed another influence that was operative, and a remarkable indication points in this other direction.

Even after her confession, Rosmer, in their last conversation which brings the play to an end, again beseeches her to be his wife. He forgives her the crime she has committed for love of him. And now she does not answer, as she should, that no forgiveness can rid her of the feeling of guilt she has incurred from her malignant

deception of poor Beata; but she charges herself with another
reproach which affects us as coming strangely from this freethink-
ing woman, and is far from deserving the importance which Rebecca attaches to it: 'Dear—never speak of this again! It is impossible! For you must know, Rosmer, I have a—a past behind me.' She
means, of course, that she has had sexual relations with another
man; and we do not fail to observe that these relations, which
occurred at a time when she was free and accountable to nobody,
seem to her a greater hindrance to the union with Rosmer than her
truly criminal behaviour to his wife.

Rosmer refuses to hear anything about this past. We can guess
what it was, though everything that refers to it in the play is, so to
speak, subterranean and has to be pieced together from hints. But
nevertheless they are hints inserted with such art that it is impossible to misunderstand them.

Between Rebecca's first refusal and her confession something
occurs which has a decisive influence on her future destiny. Rector
Kroll arrives one day at the house on purpose to humiliate Rebecca
by telling her that he knows she is an illegitimate child, the
daughter of the very Dr. West who adopted her after her mother's
death. Hate has sharpened his perceptions, yet he does not suppose
that this is any news to her. 'I really did not suppose you were
ignorant of this, otherwise it would have been very odd that you
should have let Dr. West adopt you . . .' 'And then he takes you into
his house—as soon as your mother dies. He treats you harshly. And
yet you stay with him. You know that he won't leave you a half-
penny—as a matter of fact you got only a case of books—and yet
you stay on; you bear with him; you nurse him to the last.' . . . 'I
attribute your care for him to the natural filial instinct of a daughter. Indeed, I believe your whole conduct is a natural result of your
origin.'

But Kroll is mistaken. Rebecca had no idea at all that she could
be Dr. West's daughter. When Kroll began with dark hints at her
past, she must have thought he was referring to something else.
After she has gathered what he means, she can still retain her
composure for a while, for she is able to suppose that her enemy is

[327]

basing his calculations on her age, which she had given falsely on an earlier visit of his. But Kroll demolishes this objection by saying: 'Well, so be it, but my calculation may be right, none the less; for Dr. West was up there on a short visit the year before he got the appointment.' After this new information, she loses her self-possession. 'It is not true!' She walks about wringing her hands. 'It

[328] is impossible. You want to cheat me into believing it. This can never, never be true. It cannot be true. Never in this world!—' Her agitation is so extreme that Kroll cannot attribute it to his information alone.

'KROLL: But, my dear Miss West—why in Heaven's name are you so terribly excited? You quite frighten me. What am I to think—to believe—?

'REBECCA: Nothing. You are to think and believe nothing.

'KROLL: Then you must really tell me how you can take this affair—this possibility—so terribly to heart.

'REBECCA (*controlling herself*): It is perfectly simple, Rector Kroll. I have no wish to be taken for an illegitimate child.'

The enigma of Rebecca's behaviour is susceptible of only one solution. The news that Dr. West was her father is the heaviest blow that can befall her, for she was not only his adopted daughter, but had been his mistress. When Kroll began to speak, she thought that he was hinting at these relations, the truth of which she would probably have admitted and justified by her emancipated ideas. But this was far from the Rector's intention; he knew nothing of the love-affair with Dr. West, just as she knew nothing of Dr. West's being her father. She *cannot* have had anything else in her mind but this love-affair when she accounted for her final rejection of Rosmer on the ground that she had a past which made her unworthy to be his wife. And probably, if Rosmer had consented to hear of that past, she would have confessed half her secret only and have kept silence on the more serious part of it.

But now we understand, of course, that this past must seem to her the more serious obstacle to their union—the more serious crime.

After she has learnt that she has been the mistress of her own father, she surrenders herself wholly to her now overmastering sense of guilt. She makes the confession to Rosmer and Kroll which stamps her as a murderess; she rejects for ever the happiness to which she has paved the way by crime, and prepares for departure. But the true motive of her sense of guilt, which results in her being wrecked by success, remains a secret. As we have seen, it is something quite other than the atmosphere of Rosmersholm and the refining influence of Rosmer.

At this point no one who has followed us will fail to bring forward an objection which may justify some doubts. Rebecca's first refusal of Rosmer occurs before Kroll's second visit, and therefore before his exposure of her illegitimate origin and at a time when she as yet knows nothing of her incest—if we have rightly understood the dramatist. Yet this first refusal is energetic and seriously meant. The sense of guilt which bids her renounce the fruit of her actions is thus effective before she knows anything of her cardinal crime; and if we grant so much, we ought perhaps entirely to set aside her incest as a source of that sense of guilt. [329]

So far we have treated Rebecca West as if she were a living person and not a creation of Ibsen's imagination, which is always directed by the most critical intelligence. We may therefore attempt to maintain the same position in dealing with the objection that has been raised. The objection is valid: before the knowledge of her incest, conscience was already in part awakened in Rebecca; and there is nothing to prevent our making the influence which is acknowledged and blamed by Rebecca herself responsible for this change. But this does not exempt us from recognizing the second motive. Rebecca's behaviour when she hears what Kroll has to tell her, the confession which is her immediate reaction, leave no doubt that then only does the stronger and decisive motive for renunciation begin to take effect. It is in fact a case of multiple motivation, in which a deeper motive comes into view behind the more superficial one. Laws of poetic economy necessitate this way of presenting the situation, for this deeper motive could not be explicitly enunciated. It had to remain concealed, kept from the easy perception of the spectator or the reader; otherwise serious resistances, based on the most distressing emotions, would have arisen, which might have imperilled the effect of the drama.

We have, however, a right to demand that the explicit motive shall not be without an internal connection with the concealed one, but shall appear as a mitigation of, and a derivation from, the latter. And if we may rely on the fact that the dramatist's conscious creative combination arose logically from unconscious premisses, we may now make an attempt to show that he has fulfilled this demand. Rebecca's feeling of guilt has its source in the reproach of incest, even before Kroll, with analytical perspicacity, has made her conscious of it. If we reconstruct her past, expanding and filling in the author's hints, we may feel sure that she cannot have been [330] without some inkling of the intimate relation between her mother and Dr. West. It must have made a great impression on her when she became her mother's successor with this man. She stood under the domination of the Oedipus complex, even though she did not know that this universal phantasy had in her case become a reality. When she came to Rosmersholm, the inner force of this first experience drove her into bringing about, by vigorous action, the same situation which had been realized in the original instance through no doing of hers—into getting rid of the wife and mother, so that she might take her place with the husband and father. She describes with a convincing insistence how, against her will, she was obliged to proceed, step by step, to the removal of Beata.

'You think then that I was cool and calculating and self-possessed all the time! I was not the same woman then that I am now, as I stand here telling it all. Besides, there are two sorts of will in us, I believe! I wanted Beata away, by one means or another; but I never really believed that it would come to pass. As I felt my way forward, at each step I ventured, I seemed to hear something within me cry out: No farther! Not a step farther! And yet I *could* not stop. I *had* to venture the least little bit farther. And only one hair's-breadth more. And then one more—and always one more. And then it happened.—That is the way such things come about.'

That is not an embellishment, but an authentic description. Everything that happened to her at Rosmersholm, her falling in love with Rosmer and her hostility to his wife, was from the first a consequence of the Oedipus complex—an inevitable replica of her relations with her mother and Dr. West.

And so the sense of guilt which first causes her to reject Rosmer's proposal is at bottom no different from the greater one which drives her to her confession after Kroll has opened her eyes. But just as under the influence of Dr. West she had become a freethinker and despiser of religious morality, so she is transformed by her love for Rosmer into a being of conscience and nobility. This much of the mental processes within her she herself understands, and so she is justified in describing Rosmer's influence as the motive for her change—the motive that had become accessible to her.

The practising psycho-analytic physician knows how frequently, or how invariably, a girl who enters a household as servant, companion or governess, will consciously or unconsciously weave a day-dream, which derives from the Oedipus complex, of the mistress of the house disappearing and the master taking the newcomer as his wife in her place.[1] *Rosmersholm* is the greatest work of art of the class that treats of this common phantasy in girls. What makes it into a tragic drama is the extra circumstance that the heroine's day-dream had been preceded in her childhood by a precisely corresponding reality.[2] [331]

After this long digression into literature, let us return to clinical experience—but only to establish in a few words the complete agreement between them. Psycho-analytic work teaches that the forces of conscience which induce illness in consequence of success, instead of, as normally, in consequence of frustration, are closely connected with the Oedipus complex, the relation to father and mother—as perhaps, indeed, is our sense of guilt in general.[3]

[1][Cf. the case of Miss Lucy R. in the *Studies on Hysteria* (1895*d*), *Standard Ed.*, **2**, 116 ff.]

[2]The presence of the theme of incest in *Rosmersholm* has already been demonstrated by the same arguments as mine in Otto Rank's extremely comprehensive *Das Inzest-Motiv in Dichtung und Sage* (1912, [404–5]).

[3][Some twenty years later, in his Open Letter to Romain Rolland describing his first visit to the Acropolis at Athens (1936*a*) Freud compared the feeling of something being 'too good to be true' with the situation analysed in the present paper.]

III
Criminals from a Sense of Guilt

[332] IN telling me about their early youth, particularly before puberty, people who have afterwards often become very respectable have informed me of forbidden actions which they committed at that time—such as thefts, frauds and even arson. I was in the habit of dismissing these statements with the comment that we are familiar with the weakness of moral inhibitions at that period of life, and I made no attempt to find a place for them in any more significant context. But eventually I was led to make a more thorough study of such incidents by some glaring and more accessible cases in which the misdeeds were committed while the patients were actually under my treatment, and were no longer so youthful. Analytic work then brought the surprising discovery that such deeds were done principally because they were forbidden, and because their execution was accompanied by mental relief for their doer. He was suffering from an oppressive feeling of guilt, of which he did not know the origin, and after he had committed a misdeed this oppression was mitigated. His sense of guilt was at least attached to something.

Paradoxical as it may sound, I must maintain that the sense of guilt was present before the misdeed, that it did not arise from it, but conversely—the misdeed arose from the sense of guilt. These people might justly be described as criminals from a sense of guilt. The pre-existence of the guilty feeling had of course been demonstrated by a whole set of other manifestations and effects.

But scientific work is not satisfied with the establishment of a curious fact. There are two further questions to answer: what is the origin of this obscure sense of guilt before the deed, and is it probable that this kind of causation plays any considerable part in human crime?

An examination of the first question held out the promise of bringing us information about the source of mankind's sense of guilt in general. The invariable outcome of analytic work was to show that this obscure sense of guilt derived from the Oedipus [333] complex and was a reaction to the two great criminal intentions of

174

killing the father and having sexual relations with the mother. In comparison with these two, the crimes committed in order to fix the sense of guilt to something came as a relief to the sufferers. We must remember in this connection that parricide and incest with the mother are the two great human crimes, the only ones which, as such, are pursued and abhorred in primitive communities. And we must remember, too, how close other investigations have brought us to the hypothesis that the conscience of mankind, which now appears as an inherited mental force, was acquired in connection with the Oedipus complex.

In order to answer the second question we must go beyond the scope of psycho-analytic work. With children it is easy to observe that they are often 'naughty' on purpose to provoke punishment, and are quiet and contented after they have been punished. Later analytic investigation can often put us on the track of the guilty feeling which induced them to seek punishment. Among adult criminals we must no doubt except those who commit crimes without any sense of guilt, who have either developed no moral inhibitions or who, in their conflict with society, consider themselves justified in their action. But as regards the majority of other criminals, those for whom punitive measures are really designed, such a motivation for crime might very well be taken into consideration; it might throw light on some obscure points in the psychology of the criminal, and furnish punishment with a new psychological basis.

A friend has since called my attention to the fact that the 'criminal from a sense of guilt' was known to Nietzsche too. The pre-existence of the feeling of guilt, and the utilization of a deed in order to rationalize this feeling, glimmer before us in Zarathustra's sayings[1] 'On the Pale Criminal'. Let us leave it to future research to decide how many criminals are to be reckoned among these 'pale' ones.

[1] [In the editions before 1924, 'obscure sayings'.—A hint at the idea of the sense of guilt being a motive for misdeeds is already to be found in the case history of 'Little Hans' (1909*b*), *Standard Ed.*, **10**, 42, as well as in that of the 'Wolf Man' (1918*b*), *Standard Ed.*, **17**, 28, which, though published later than the present paper, was in fact mostly written in the year before it. In this latter passage the complicating factor of masochism is introduced.]

§ On Transience

NOT long ago I went on a summer walk through a smiling countryside in the company of a taciturn friend and of a young but already famous poet.[1] The poet admired the beauty of the scene around us but felt no joy in it. He was disturbed by the thought that all this beauty was fated to extinction, that it would vanish when winter came, like all human beauty and all the beauty and splendour that men have created or may create. All that he would otherwise have loved and admired seemed to him to be shorn of its worth by the transience which was its doom.

The proneness to decay of all that is beautiful and perfect can, as we know, give rise to two different impulses in the mind. The one leads to the aching despondency felt by the young poet, while the other leads to rebellion against the fact asserted. No! it is impossible that all this loveliness of Nature and Art, of the world of our sensations and of the world outside, will really fade away into nothing. It would be too senseless and too presumptuous to believe it. Somehow or other this loveliness must be able to persist and to escape all the powers of destruction.

But this demand for immortality is a product of our wishes too unmistakable to lay claim to reality: what is painful may none the

SOURCE: *Standard Ed.*, **14**, 305–7.
[1][Freud spent part of August, 1913, in the Dolomites, but the identity of his companions cannot be established.]

less be true. I could not see my way to dispute the transience of all things, nor could I insist upon an exception in favour of what is beautiful and perfect. But I did dispute the pessimistic poet's view that the transience of what is beautiful involves any loss in its worth.

On the contrary, an increase! Transience value is scarcity value in time. Limitation in the possibility of an enjoyment raises the value of the enjoyment. It was incomprehensible, I declared, that the thought of the transience of beauty should interfere with our joy in it. As regards the beauty of Nature, each time it is destroyed by winter it comes again next year, so that in relation to the length of our lives it can in fact be regarded as eternal. The beauty of the human form and face vanish for ever in the course of our own lives, [306] but their evanescence only lends them a fresh charm. A flower that blossoms only for a single night does not seem to us on that account less lovely. Nor can I understand any better why the beauty and perfection of a work of art or of an intellectual achievement should lose its worth because of its temporal limitation. A time may indeed come when the pictures and statues which we admire to-day will crumble to dust, or a race of men may follow us who no longer understand the works of our poets and thinkers, or a geological epoch may even arrive when all animate life upon the earth ceases; but since the value of all this beauty and perfection is determined only by its significance for our own emotional lives, it has no need to survive us and is therefore independent of absolute duration.

These considerations appeared to me incontestable; but I noticed that I had made no impression either upon the poet or upon my friend. My failure led me to infer that some powerful emotional factor was at work which was disturbing their judgement, and I believed later that I had discovered what it was. What spoilt their enjoyment of beauty must have been a revolt in their minds against mourning. The idea that all this beauty was transient was giving these two sensitive minds a foretaste of mourning over its decease; and, since the mind instinctively recoils from anything that is painful, they felt their enjoyment of beauty interfered with by thoughts of its transience.

Mourning over the loss of something that we have loved or admired seems so natural to the layman that he regards it as self-evident. But to psychologists mourning is a great riddle, one of those phenomena which cannot themselves be explained but to which other obscurities can be traced back. We possess, as it seems, a certain amount of capacity for love—what we call libido—which in the earliest stages of development is directed towards our own ego. Later, though still at a very early time, this libido is diverted from the ego on to objects, which are thus in a sense taken into our ego. If the objects are destroyed or if they are lost to us, our capacity for love (our libido) is once more liberated; and it can then either take other objects instead or can temporarily return to the ego. But why it is that this detachment of libido from its objects should be such a painful process is a mystery to us and we have not hitherto been able to frame any hypothesis to account for it. We only see that libido clings to its objects and will not renounce those that are lost even when a substitute lies ready to hand. Such then is mourning.

[307]

My conversation with the poet took place in the summer before the war. A year later the war broke out and robbed the world of its beauties. It destroyed not only the beauty of the countrysides through which it passed and the works of art which it met with on its path but it also shattered our pride in the achievements of our civilization, our admiration for many philosophers and artists and our hopes of a final triumph over the differences between nations and races. It tarnished the lofty impartiality of our science, it revealed our instincts in all their nakedness and let loose the evil spirits within us which we thought had been tamed for ever by centuries of continuous education by the noblest minds. It made our country small again and made the rest of the world far remote. It robbed us of very much that we had loved, and showed us how ephemeral were many things that we had regarded as changeless.

We cannot be surprised that our libido, thus bereft of so many of its objects, has clung with all the greater intensity to what is left to us, that our love of our country, our affection for those nearest us and our pride in what is common to us have suddenly grown stronger. But have those other possessions, which we have now lost, really ceased to have any worth for us because they have proved so perishable and so unresistant? To many of us this seems to be, but once more wrongly, in my view. I believe that those who think thus, and seem ready to make a permanent renunciation because what was precious has proved not to be lasting, are simply in a state of mourning for what is lost. Mourning, as we know, however painful it may be, comes to a spontaneous end. When it has renounced everything that has been lost, then it has consumed itself, and our libido is once more free (in so far as we are still young and active) to replace the lost objects by fresh ones equally or still more precious. It is to be hoped that the same will be true of the losses caused by this war. When once the mourning is over, it will be found that our high opinion of the riches of civilization has lost nothing from our discovery of their fragility. We shall build up again all that war has destroyed, and perhaps on firmer ground and more lastingly than before.

§ A Mythological Parallel to a Visual Obsession

[337] IN a patient of about twenty-one years of age the products of unconscious mental activity became conscious not only in obsessive thoughts but also in obsessive images. The two could accompany each other or appear independently. At one particular time, whenever he saw his father entering the room, there came into his mind in close connection an obsessive word and an obsessive image. The word was '*Vaterarsch*' ['father-arse']; the accompanying image presented his father as the naked lower part of a body, provided with arms and legs, but without the head or upper part. The genitals were not indicated, and the facial features were painted on the abdomen.

It will help to explain this more than usually absurd symptom if I mention that the patient, who was a man of fully developed intellect and high moral ideals, manifested a very lively anal erotism in the most various ways until after his tenth year. After this had been got over, his sexual life was once again forced back to the preliminary anal stage by his later struggle against genital erotism. He loved and respected his father greatly, and also feared him not a little; judged by his own high standards in regard to asceticism and the suppression of the instincts, however, his father seemed to him a person who stood for debauchery and the pursuit of enjoyment in material things.

SOURCE: *Standard Ed.*, **14**, 337–38.

'Father-arse' was soon explained as a jocular Teutonizing of the honorific title of 'patriarch'.[1] The obsessive image is an obvious caricature. It recalls other representations which, with a derogatory end in view, replace a whole person by one of his organs, e.g. his genitals; it reminds us, too, of unconscious phantasies which lead to the identification of the genitals with the whole person, and also of joking figures of speech, such as 'I am all ears'. [338]

The placing of the facial features on the abdomen of the carica-ture struck me at first as very strange. But I soon remembered having seen the same thing in French caricatures.[2] Chance then brought to my notice an antique representation, which tallied exactly with my patient's obsessive image.

According to the Greek legend, Demeter came to Eleusis in search of her daughter after she had been abducted, and was given lodging by Dysaules and his wife Baubo; but in her great sorrow she refused to touch food or drink. Thereupon her hostess Baubo made her laugh by suddenly lifting up her dress and exposing her body. A discussion of this anecdote, which was probably intended to explain a magic ceremonial which was no longer understood, is to be found in the fourth volume of Salomon Reinach's work, *Cultes, Mythes, et Religions,* 1912 [115]. In the same passage the author mentions that during the excavations at Priene in Asia Minor some terracottas were found which represented Baubo. They show the body of a woman without a head or chest and with a face drawn on the abdomen: the lifted dress frames this face like a crown of hair (ibid., 117).

---

[1][The two words sound more alike in German than in English. 'Patriarch' is spelt the same in both languages, but pronounced differently.]

[2]Cf. 'L'impudique Albion', a caricature of England drawn in 1901 by Jean Véber, reproduced in Fuchs, 1908 [384].

§ A Childhood Recollection from *Dichtung und Wahrheit*

[147] 'IF we try to recollect what happened to us in the earliest years of childhood, we often find that we confuse what we have heard from others with what is really a possession of our own derived from what we ourselves have witnessed.' This remark is found on one of the first pages of Goethe's account of his life [*Dichtung und Wahrheit*], which he began to write at the age of sixty. It is preceded only by some information about his birth, which 'took place on August 28, 1749, at midday on the stroke of twelve'. The stars were in a favourable conjunction and may well have been the cause of his survival, for at his entry into the world he was 'as though dead', and it was only after great efforts that he was brought to life. There follows on this a short description of the house and of the place in it where the children—he and his younger sister—best liked to play. After this, however, Goethe relates in fact only one single event which can be assigned to the 'earliest years of childhood' (the years up to four?) and of which he seems to have preserved a recollection of his own.

The account of it runs as follows: 'And three brothers (von Ochsenstein by name) who lived over the way became very fond of me; they were orphan sons of the late magistrate, and they took an interest in me and used to tease me in all sorts of ways.'

SOURCE: *Standard Ed.*, **17**, 147–56.

'My people used to like to tell of all kinds of pranks in which these men, otherwise of a serious and retiring disposition, used to encourage me. I will quote only one of these exploits. The crockery-fair was just over, and not only had the kitchen been fitted up from it with what would be needed for some time to come, but miniature utensils of the same sort had been bought for us children to play with. One fine afternoon, when all was quiet in the house, I was playing with my dishes and pots in the hall' (a place which had already been described, opening on to the street) 'and, since this seemed to lead to nothing, I threw a plate into the street, and was overjoyed to see it go to bits so merrily. The von Ochsensteins, who saw how delighted I was and how joyfully I clapped my little hands, called out "Do it again!" I did not hesitate to sling out a pot on to [148] the paving-stones, and then, as they kept crying "Another!", one after another all my little dishes, cooking-pots and pans. My neighbours continued to show their approval and I was highly delighted to be amusing them. But my stock was all used up, and still they cried "Another!" So I ran off straight into the kitchen and fetched the earthenware plates, which made an even finer show as they smashed to bits. And thus I ran backwards and forwards, bringing one plate after another, as I could reach them in turn from the dresser; and, as they were not content with that, I hurled every piece of crockery I could get hold of to the same destruction. Only later did someone come and interfere and put a stop to it all. The damage was done, and to make up for so much broken earthenware there was at least an amusing story, which the rascals who had been its instigators enjoyed to the end of their lives.'

In pre-analytic days it was possible to read this without finding occasion to pause and without feeling surprised, but later on the analytic conscience became active. We had formed definite opinions and expectations about the memories of earliest childhood, and would have liked to claim universal validity for them. It should not be a matter of indifference or entirely without meaning which detail of a child's life had escaped the general oblivion. It might on the contrary be conjectured that what had remained in memory was the most significant element in that whole period of life, whether it had possessed such an importance at the time, or whether it had gained subsequent importance from the influence of later events.

The high value of such childish recollections was, it is true, obvious only in a few cases. Generally they seemed indifferent, worthless even, and it remained at first incomprehensible why just these memories should have resisted amnesia; nor could the person who had preserved them for long years as part of his own store of memories see more in them than any stranger to whom he might relate them. Before their significance could be appreciated, a certain work of interpretation was necessary. This interpretation either showed that their content required to be replaced by some other content, or revealed that they were related to some other unmistakably important experiences and had appeared in their place as what are known as 'screen memories'.[1]

[149]   In every psycho-analytic investigation of a life-history it is always possible to explain the meaning of the earliest childhood memories along these lines. Indeed, it usually happens that the very recollection to which the patient gives precedence, which he relates first, with which he introduces the story of his life, proves to be the most important, the very one that holds the key to the secret pages of his mind.[2] But the little childish episode related in *Dichtung und Wahrheit* does not rise to our expectations. The ways and means that with our patients lead to interpretation are of course not available to us here; the episode does not seem in itself to admit of any traceable connection with important impressions at a later date. A mischievous trick with damaging effects on the household economy, carried out under the spur of outside encouragement, is certainly no fitting head-piece for all that Goethe has to tell us of his richly filled life. An impression of utter innocence and irrelevance clings to this childless memory, and it might be taken as a warning not to stretch the claims of psycho-analysis too far nor to apply it in unsuitable places.

[1][See Chapter IV of *The Psychopathology of Everyday Life* (1901*b*).]
[2][Cf. a footnote of Freud's near the beginning of his case history of the 'Rat Man' (1909*d*), *Standard Ed.*, **10**, 160.]

The little problem, therefore, had long since slipped out of my mind, when one day chance brought me a patient in whom a similar childhood memory appeared in a clearer connection. He was a man of twenty-seven, highly educated and gifted, whose life at that time was entirely filled with a conflict with his mother that affected all his interests, and from the effects of which his capacity for love and his ability to lead an independent existence had suffered greatly. This conflict went far back into his childhood; certainly to his fourth year. Before that he had been a very weakly child, always ailing, and yet that sickly period was glorified into a paradise in his memory; for then he had had exclusive, uninterrupted possession of his mother's affection. When he was not yet four, a brother, who is still living, was born, and in his reaction to that disturbing event he became transformed into an obstinate, unmanageable boy, who perpetually provoked his mother's severity. Moreover, he never regained the right path.

When he came to me for treatment—by no means the least reason for his coming was that his mother, a religious bigot, had a horror of psycho-analysis—his jealousy of the younger brother [150] (which had once actually been manifested as a murderous attack on the infant in its cradle) had long been forgotten. He now treated his brother with great consideration; but certain curious fortuitous actions of his (which involved sudden and severe injuries to favourite animals, like his sporting dog or birds which he had carefully reared,) were probably to be understood as echoes of these hostile impulses against the little brother.

Now this patient related that, at about the time of the attack on the baby he so much hated, he had thrown all the crockery he could lay hands on out of the window of their country house into the road—the very same thing that Goethe relates of his childhood in *Dichtung und Wahrheit*! I may remark that my patient was of foreign nationality and was not acquainted with German literature; he had never read Goethe's autobiography.

This communication naturally suggested to me that an attempt might be made to explain Goethe's childish memory on the lines forced upon us by my patient's story. But could the necessary conditions for this explanation be shown to exist in the poet's childhood? Goethe himself, it is true, makes the instigation of the von Ochsenstein brothers responsible for his childish prank. But from his own narrative it can be seen that these grown-up neighbours merely encouraged him to go on with what he was doing. The beginning was on his own initiative, and the reason he gives for this beginning—'since this (the game) seemed to lead to nothing'—is surely, without any forcing of its meaning, a confession that at the time of writing it down and probably for many years previously he was not aware of any adequate motive for his behaviour.

It is well known that Johann Wolfgang and his sister Cornelia were the eldest survivors of a considerable family of very weakly children. Dr. Hanns Sachs has been so kind as to supply me with the following details concerning these brothers and sisters of Goethe's, who died in childhood:

(*a*) Hermann Jakob, baptized Monday, November 27, 1752; reached the age of six years and six weeks; buried January 13, 1759.

(*b*) Katharina Elisabetha, baptized Monday, September 9, 1754; buried Thursday, December 22, 1755. (One year and four months old).

[151]   (*c*) Johanna Maria, baptized Tuesday, March 29, 1757, and buried Saturday, August 11, 1759. (Two years and four months old). (This was doubtless the very pretty and attractive little girl celebrated by her brother.)

(*d*) Georg Adolph, baptized Sunday, June 15, 1760; buried, eight months old, Wednesday, February 18, 1761.

Goethe's next youngest sister, Cornelia Friederica Christiana, was born on December 7, 1750, when he was fifteen months old. This slight difference in age almost excludes the possibility of her having been an object of jealousy. It is known that, when their passions awake, children never develop such violent reactions against the brothers and sisters they find already in existence, but direct their hostility against the newcomers. Nor is the scene we are endeavouring to interpret reconcilable with Goethe's tender age at the time of, or shortly after, Cornelia's birth.

At the time of the birth of the first little brother, Hermann Jakob, Johann Wolfgang was three and a quarter years old. Nearly two years later, when he was about five years old, the second sister was born. Both ages come under consideration in dating the episode of the throwing out of the crockery. The earlier is perhaps to be preferred; and it would best agree with the case of my patient, who was about three and a quarter years old at the birth of his brother.

Moreover, Goethe's brother Hermann Jakob, to whom we are thus led in our attempt at interpretation, did not make so brief a stay in the family nursery as the children born afterwards. One might feel some surprise that the autobiography does not contain a word of remembrance of him.[1] He was over six, and Johann Wolfgang was nearly ten, when he died. Dr. Hitschmann, who was kind enough to place his notes on this subject at my disposal, says:

'*Goethe, too, as a little boy saw a younger brother die without regret.* At least, according to Bettina Brentano his mother gave the following account: "It struck her as very extraordinary that he shed no tears at the death of his younger brother Jakob who was his   [152] playfellow; he seemed on the contrary to feel annoyance at the grief of his parents and sisters. When, later on, his mother asked the young rebel if he had not been fond of his brother, he ran into his room and brought out from under the bed a heap of papers on which lessons and little stories were written, saying that he had done all this to teach his brother." So it seems all the same that the elder brother enjoyed playing father to the younger and showing him his superiority.'

The opinion might thus be formed that the throwing of crockery out of the window was a symbolic action, or, to put it more

[1](*Footnote added* 1924:) I take this opportunity of withdrawing an incorrect statement which should not have been made. In a later passage in this first volume the younger brother *is* mentioned and described. It occurs in connection with memories of the serious illnesses of childhood, from which this brother also suffered 'not a little'. 'He was a delicate child, quiet and self-willed, and we never had much to do with each other. Besides, he hardly survived the years of infancy.'

correctly, a *magic* action, by which the child (Goethe as well as my patient) gave violent expression to his wish to get rid of a disturbing intruder. There is no need to dispute a child's enjoyment of smashing things; if an action is pleasurable in itself, that is not a hindrance but rather an inducement to repeat it in obedience to other purposes as well. It is unlikely, however, that it could have been the pleasure in the crash and the breaking which ensured the childish prank a lasting place in adult memory. Nor is there any objection to complicating the motivation of the action by adding a further factor. A child who breaks crockery knows quite well that he is doing something naughty for which grown-ups will scold him, and if he is not restrained by that knowledge, he probably has a grudge against his parents that he wants to satisfy; he wants to show naughtiness.

The pleasure in breaking and in broken things would be satisfied, too, if the child simply threw the breakable object on the ground. The hurling them out of the window into the street would still remain unexplained. This 'out!' seems to be an essential part of the magic action and to arise directly from its hidden meaning. The new baby must be got rid of—through the window, perhaps became he came in through the window. The whole action would thus be equivalent to the verbal response, already familiar to us, of a child who was told that the stork had brought a little brother. 'The stork can take him away again!' was his verdict.[1]

All the same, we are not blind to the objections—apart from any internal uncertainties—against basing the interpretation of a childhood act on a single parallel. For this reason I had for years kept [153] back my theory about the little scene in *Dichtung und Wahrheit*. Then one day I had a patient who began his analysis with the following remarks, which I set down word for word: 'I am the eldest of a family of eight or nine children.[2] One of my earliest

---

[1][See *The Interpretation of Dreams* (1900a), Chapter V (D), *Standard Ed.*, 4, 251.]

[2]A momentary error of a striking character. It was probably induced by the influence of the intention, which was already showing itself, to get rid of a brother. (Cf. Ferenczi, 1912, 'On Transitory Symptoms during Analysis'.)

recollections is of my father sitting on the bed in his night-shirt, and telling me laughingly that I had a new brother. I was then three and three-quarters years old; that is the difference in age between me and my next younger brother. I know, too, that a short time after (or was it a year before?)[1] I threw a lot of things, brushes—or was it only one brush?—shoes and other things, out of the window into the street. I have a still earlier recollection. When I was two years old, I spent a night with my parents in a hotel bedroom at Linz on the way to the Salzkammergut. I was so restless in the night and made such a noise that my father had to beat me.'

After hearing this statement I threw all doubts to the winds. When in analysis two things are brought out one immediately after the other, as though in one breath, we have to interpret this proximity as a connection of thought. It was, therefore, as if the patient had said, '*Because* I found that I had got a new brother, I shortly afterwards threw these things into the street.' The act of flinging the brushes, shoes and so on, out of the window must be recognized as a reaction to the birth of the brother. Nor is it a matter for regret that in this instance the objects thrown out were not crockery but other things, probably anything the child could reach at the moment.—The hurling out (through the window into the street) thus proves to be the essential thing in the act, while the pleasure in the smashing and the noise, and the class of object on which 'execution is done', are variable and unessential points.

Naturally, the principle of there being a connection of thought must be applied as well to the patient's third childish recollection, which is the earliest, though it was put at the end of the short series. This can easily be done. Evidently the two-year-old child was so restless because he could not bear his parents being in bed together. [154] On the journey it was no doubt impossible to avoid the child being a witness of this. The feelings which were aroused at that time in the jealous little boy left him with an embitterment against women

[1] This doubt, attaching to the essential point of the communication for purposes of resistance, was shortly afterwards withdrawn by the patient of his own accord.

which persisted and permanently interfered with the development of his capacity for love.

After making these two observations I expressed the opinion at a meeting of the Vienna Psycho-Analytical Society that occurrences of the same kind might be not infrequent among young children; in response, Frau Dr. von Hug-Hellmuth placed two further observations at my disposal, which I append here.

I

'At the age of about three and a half, little Erich quite suddenly acquired the habit of throwing everything he did not like out of the window. He also did it, however, with things that were not in his way and did not concern him. On his father's birthday—he was three years and four and a half months old—he snatched a heavy rolling-pin from the kitchen, dragged it into the living-room and threw it out of the window of the third-floor flat into the street. Some days later he sent after it the kitchen-pestle, and then a pair of heavy mountaineering boots of his father's, which he had first to take out of the cupboard.[1]

'At that time his mother had a miscarriage, in the seventh or eighth month of pregnancy, and after that the child was "sweet and quiet and so good that he seemed quite changed". In the fifth or sixth month he repeatedly said to his mother, "Mummy, I'll jump on your tummy"—or, "I'll push your tummy in." And shortly before the miscarriage, in October, he said, "If I must have a brother, at least I don't want him till after Christmas."'

II

'A young lady of nineteen told me spontaneously that her earliest recollection was as follows: "I see myself, frightfully naughty, sitting under the table in the dining-room, ready to creep out. My cup of coffee is standing on the table—I can still see the pattern on the china quite plainly—and Granny comes into the room just as I am going to throw it out of the window.

[155]

---

[1] 'He always chose heavy objects.'

' "For the fact was that no one had been bothering about me, and in the meantime a skin had formed on the coffee, which was always perfectly dreadful to me and still is.

' "On that day my brother, who is two and a half years younger than I am, was born, and so no one had had any time to spare for me.

' "They always tell me that I was insupportable on that day: at dinner I threw my father's favourite glass on the floor, I dirtied my frock several times, and was in the worst temper from morning to night. In my rage I tore a bath-doll to pieces." '

These two cases scarcely call for a commentary. They establish without further analytic effort that the bitterness children feel about the expected or actual appearance of a rival·finds expression in throwing objects out of the window and in other acts of naughtiness and destructiveness. In the first case the 'heavy objects' probably symbolized the mother herself, against whom the child's anger was directed so long as the new baby had not yet appeared. The three-and-a-half-year-old boy knew about his mother's pregnancy and had no doubt that she had got the baby in her body. 'Little Hans'[1] and his special dread of heavily loaded carts may be recalled here.[2] In the second case the very youthful age of the child, two and a half years, is noteworthy.

If we now return to Goethe's childhood memory and put in the place it occupies in *Dichtung und Wahrheit* what we believe we have obtained through observations of other children, a perfectly valid [156]

[1] Cf. 'Analysis of a Phobia in a Five-Year-Old Boy', (1909*b*) [*Standard Ed.*, **10**, 91 and 128].

[2] Further confirmation of this pregnancy-symbolism was given me some time ago by a lady of over fifty. She had often been told that as a little child, when she could hardly talk, she used to drag her father to the window in great agitation whenever a heavy furniture-van was passing along the street. In view of other recollections of the houses they had lived in, it became possible to establish that she was then younger than two and three quarter years. At about that time the brother next to her was born, and in consequence of this addition to the family a move was made. At about the same time, she often had an alarming feeling before going to sleep of something uncannily large, that came up to her, and 'her hands got so thick'.

train of thought emerges which we should not otherwise have discovered. It would run thus: 'I was a child of fortune: destiny preserved my life, although I came into the world as though dead. Even more, destiny removed my brother, so that I did not have to share my mother's love with him.' The train of thought [in *Dichtung und Wahrheit*] then goes on to someone else who died in those early days—the grandmother who lived like a quiet friendly spirit in another part of the house.

I have, however, already remarked elsewhere[1] that if a man has been his mother's undisputed darling he retains throughout life the triumphant feeling, the confidence in success, which not seldom brings actual success along with it. And Goethe might well have given some such heading to his autobiography as: 'My strength has its roots in my relation to my mother.'

[1][In a footnote added in 1911 to Chapter VI (E) of *The Interpretation of Dreams* (1900*a*), *Standard Ed.*, 5, 398*n*.]

§ The 'Uncanny'

I

IT is only rarely that a psycho-analyst feels impelled to investigate the subject of aesthetics, even when aesthetics is understood to mean not merely the theory of beauty but the theory of the qualities of feeling. He works in other strata of mental life and has little to do with the subdued emotional impulses which, inhibited in their aims and dependent on a host of concurrent factors, usually furnish the material for the study of aesthetics. But it does occasionally happen that he has to interest himself in some particular province of that subject; and this province usually proves to be a rather remote one, and one which has been neglected in the specialist literature of aesthetics.

The subject of the 'uncanny'[1] is a province of this kind. It is undoubtedly related to what is frightening—to what arouses dread and horror; equally certainly, too, the word is not always used in a clearly definable sense, so that it tends to coincide with what excites fear in general. Yet we may expect that a special core of feeling is present which justifies the use of a special conceptual term. One is

SOURCE: *Standard Ed.*, **17**, 219–56.
[1][The German word, translated throughout this paper by the English 'uncanny', is '*unheimlich*', literally 'unhomely'. The English term is not, of course, an exact equivalent of the German one.]

193

curious to know what this common core is which allows us to distinguish as 'uncanny' certain things which lie within the field of what is frightening.

As good as nothing is to be found upon this subject in comprehensive treatises on aesthetics, which in general prefer to concern themselves with what is beautiful, attractive and sublime—that is, with feelings of a positive nature—and with the circumstances and the objects that call them forth, rather than with the opposite feelings of repulsion and distress. I know of only one attempt in medico-psychological literature, a fertile but not exhaustive paper by Jentsch (1906). But I must confess that I have not made a very thorough examination of the literature, especially the foreign literature, relating to this present modest contribution of mine, for [220] reasons which, as may easily be guessed, lie in the times in which we live;[1] so that my paper is presented to the reader without any claim to priority.

In his study of the 'uncanny' Jentsch quite rightly lays stress on the obstacle presented by the fact that people vary so very greatly in their sensitivity to this quality of feeling. The writer of the present contribution, indeed, must himself plead guilty to a special obtuseness in the matter, where extreme delicacy of perception would be more in place. It is long since he has experienced or heard of anything which has given him an uncanny impression, and he must start by translating himself into that state of feeling, by awakening in himself the possibility of experiencing it. Still, such difficulties make themselves powerfully felt in many other branches of aesthetics; we need not on that account despair of finding instances in which the quality in question will be unhesitatingly recognized by most people.

Two courses are open to us at the outset. Either we can find out what meaning has come to be attached to the word 'uncanny' in the course of its history; or we can collect all those properties of persons, things, sense-impressions, experiences and situations which arouse in us the feeling of uncanniness, and then infer the un-

[1][An allusion to the first World War only just concluded.]

known nature of the uncanny from what all these examples have in common. I will say at once that both courses lead to the same result: the uncanny is that class of the frightening which leads back to what is known of old and long familiar. How this is possible, in what circumstances the familiar can become uncanny and frightening, I shall show in what follows. Let me also add that my investigation was actually begun by collecting a number of individual cases, and was only later confirmed by an examination of linguistic usage. In this discussion, however, I shall follow the reverse course.

The German word '*unheimlich*' is obviously the opposite of '*heimlich*' ['homely'], '*heimisch*' ['native']—the opposite of what is familiar; and we are tempted to conclude that what is 'uncanny' is frightening precisely because it is *not* known and familiar. Naturally not everything that is new and unfamiliar is frightening, however; the relation is not capable of inversion. We can only say [221] that what is novel can easily become frightening and uncanny; some new things are frightening but not by any means all. Something has to be added to what is novel and unfamiliar in order to make it uncanny.

On the whole, Jentsch did not get beyond this relation of the uncanny to the novel and unfamiliar. He ascribes the essential factor in the production of the feeling of uncanniness to intellectual uncertainty; so that the uncanny would always, as it were, be something one does not know one's way about in. The better oriented in his environment a person is, the less readily will he get the impression of something uncanny in regard to the objects and events in it.

It is not difficult to see that this definition is incomplete, and we will therefore try to proceed beyond the equation 'uncanny' = 'unfamiliar'. We will first turn to other languages. But the dictionaries that we consult tell us nothing new, perhaps only because we ourselves speak a language that is foreign. Indeed, we get an impression that many languages are without a word for this particular shade of what is frightening.

I should like to express my indebtedness to Dr. Theodor Reik for the following excerpts:—

LATIN: (K. E. Georges, *Deutschlateinisches Wörterbuch*, 1898). An uncanny place: *locus suspectus*; at an uncanny time of night: *intempesta nocte.*

GREEK: (Rost's and Schenkl's Lexikons). ξένος (i.e. strange, foreign).

ENGLISH: (from the dictionaries of Lucas, Bellows, Flügel and Muret-Sanders). Uncomfortable, uneasy, gloomy, dismal, uncanny, ghastly; (of a house) haunted; (of a man) a repulsive fellow.

FRENCH: (Sachs-Villatte). *Inquiétant, sinistre, lugubre, mal à son aise.*

SPANISH: (Tollhausen, 1889). *Sospechoso, de mal agüero, lúgubre, siniestro.*

The Italian and Portuguese languages seem to content themselves with words which we should describe as circumlocutions. In Arabic and Hebrew 'uncanny' means the same as 'daemonic', 'gruesome'.

Let us therefore return to the German language. In Daniel Sanders's *Wörterbuch der Deutschen Sprache* (1860, I, 729), the [222] following entry, which I here reproduce in full, is to be found under the word '*heimlich*'. I have laid stress on one or two passages by italicizing them.[1]

Heimlich, adj., subst. *Heimlichkeit* (pl. *Heimlichkeiten*): I. Also *heimelich, heimelig*, belonging to the house, not strange, familiar, tame, intimate, friendly, etc.

(*a*) (Obsolete) belonging to the house or the family, or regarded as so belonging (cf. Latin *familiaris*, familiar): *Die Heimlichen*, the members of the household; *Der heimliche Rat* (Gen. xli, 45; 2 Sam. xxiii. 23; 1 Chron. xii. 25; Wisd. viii. 4), now more usually *Geheimer Rat* [Privy Councillor].

(*b*) Of animals: tame, companionable to man. As opposed to

---

[1] [In the translation which follows in the text above, a few details, mainly giving the sources of the quotations, have been omitted. For purposes of reference, we reprint in an Appendix the entire extract from Sanders's Dictionary exactly as it is given in German in Freud's original paper except that a few minor misprints have been put right. (Cf. p. 253.)]

wild, e.g. 'Animals which are neither wild nor *heimlich*', etc. 'Wild animals . . . that are trained to be *heimlich* and accustomed to men.' 'If these young creatures are brought up from early days among men they become quite *heimlich*, friendly' etc.—So also: 'It (the lamb) is so *heimlich* and eats out of my hand.' 'Nevertheless, the stork is a beautiful, *heimelich* bird.'

(*c*) Intimate, friendlily comfortable; the enjoyment of quiet content, etc., arousing a sense of agreeable restfulness and security as in one within the four walls of his house.[1] 'Is it still *heimlich* to you in your country where strangers are felling your woods?' 'She did not feel too *heimlich* with him.' 'Along a high, *heimlich*, shady path . . ., beside a purling, gushing and babbling woodland brook.' 'To destroy the *Heimlichkeit* of the home.' 'I could not readily find another spot so intimate and *heimlich* as this.' 'We pictured it so comfortable, so nice, so cosy and *heimlich*.' 'In quiet *Heimlichkeit*, surrounded by close walls.' 'A careful housewife, who knows how to make a pleasing *Heimlichkeit* (*Häuslichkeit* [domesticity]) out of the smallest means.' 'The man who till recently had been so strange to him now seemed to him all the more *heimlich*.' 'The protestant land-owners do not feel . . . *heimlich* among their catholic inferiors.' 'When it grows *heimlich* and still, and the evening quiet alone watches over your cell.' 'Quiet, lovely and *heimlich*, no place more fitted for their rest.' 'He did not feel at all *heimlich* about it.'— Also, [in compounds] 'The place was so peaceful, so lonely, so shadily-*heimlich*.' 'The in- and outflowing waves of the current, dreamy and lullaby-*heimlich*.' Cf. in especial *Unheimlich* [see below]. Among Swabian Swiss authors in especial, often as a trisyllable: 'How *heimelich* it seemed to Ivo again of an evening, when he was at home.' 'It was so *heimelig* in the house.' 'The warm room and the *heimelig* afternoon.' 'When a man feels in his heart that he is so small and the Lord so great—that is what is truly *heimelig*.' 'Little by little they grew at ease and *heimelig* among themselves.' 'Friendly *Heimeligkeit*.' 'I shall be nowhere more *heimelich* than I

[223]

---

[1][It may be remarked that the English 'canny', in addition to its more usual meaning of 'shrewd', can mean 'pleasant', 'cosy'.]

am here.' 'That which comes from afar ... assuredly does not live quite *heimelig* (*heimatlich* [at home], *freundnachbarlich* [in a neighbourly way]) among the people.' 'The cottage where he had once sat so often among his own people, so *heimelig*, so happy.' 'The sentinel's horn sounds so *heimelig* from the towers, and his voice invites so hospitably.' 'You go to sleep there so soft and warm, so wonderfully *heim'lig*.' — *This form of the word deserves to become general in order to protect this perfectly good sense of the word from becoming obsolete through an easy confusion with* II [see below]. Cf: ' "*The Zecks* [a family name] *are all 'heimlich'.*" (in sense II) "*Heimlich'? ... What do you understand by 'heimlich'?" "Well, ... they are like a buried spring or a dried-up pond. One cannot walk over it without always having the feeling that water might come up there again." "Oh, we call it 'unheimlich'; you call it 'heimlich'. Well, what makes you think that there is something secret and untrustworthy about this family?"* ' (Gutzkow).

(*d*) Especially in Silesia: gay, cheerful; also of the weather.

II. Concealed, kept from sight, so that others do not get to know of or about it, withheld from others. To do something *heimlich*, i.e. behind someone's back; to steal away *heimlich*; *heimlich* meetings and appointments; to look on with *heimlich* pleasure at someone's discomfiture; to sigh or weep *heimlich*; to behave *heimlich*, as though there was something to conceal; *heimlich* love-affair, love, sin; *heimlich* places (which good manners oblige us to conceal) (1 Sam. v. 6). 'The *heimlich* chamber' (privy) (2 Kings x. 27.). Also, 'the *heimlich* chair'. 'To throw into pits or *Heimlichkeiten*'. — 'Led the steeds *heimlich* before Laomedon.' — 'As secretive, *heimlich*, deceitful and malicious towards cruel masters ... as frank, open, sympathetic and helpful towards a friend in misfortune.' 'You have still to learn what is *heimlich* holiest to me.' 'The *heimlich* art' (magic). 'Where public ventilation has to stop, there *heimlich* machinations begin.' 'Freedom is the whispered watchword of *heimlich* conspirators and the loud battle-cry of professed revolutionaries.' 'A holy, *heimlich* effect.' 'I have roots that are most *heimlich*, I am grown in the deep earth.' 'My *heimlich* pranks.' 'If he is not given it openly and scrupulously he may seize it *heimlich* and

[224]

unscrupulously.' 'He had achromatic telescopes constructed *heim-lich* and secretly.' 'Henceforth I desire that there should be nothing *heimlich* any longer between us.'—To discover, disclose, betray someone's *Heimlichkeiten*; 'to concoct *Heimlichkeiten* behind my back'. 'In my time we studied *Heimlichkeit*.' 'The hand of under-standing can alone undo the powerless spell of the *Heimlichkeit* (of hidden gold).' 'Say, where is the place of concealment . . . in what place of hidden *Heimlichkeit*?' 'Bees, who make the lock of *Heim-lichkeiten*' (i.e. sealing-wax). 'Learned in strange *Heimlichkeiten*' (magic arts).

For compounds see above, Ic. Note especially the negative '*un-*': eerie, weird, arousing gruesome fear: 'Seeming quite *unheimlich* and ghostly to him.' 'The *unheimlich*, fearful hours of night.' 'I had already long since felt an *unheimlich*, even gruesome feeling.' 'Now I am beginning to have an *unheimlich* feeling.' . . . 'Feels an *unheimlich* horror.' '*Unheimlich* and motionless like a stone image.' 'The *unheimlich* mist called hill-fog.' 'These pale youths are *un-heimlich* and are brewing heaven knows what mischief.' ' "*Un-heimlich*" is the name for everything that ought to have remained . . . secret and hidden but has come to light*' (Schelling).—'To veil the divine, to surround it with a certain *Unheimlichkeit*.'—*Unheimlich* is not often used as opposite to meaning II (above).

What interests us most in this long extract is to find that among its different shades of meaning the word '*heimlich*' exhibits one which is identical with its opposite, '*unheimlich*'. What is *heimlich* thus comes to be *unheimlich*. (Cf. the quotation from Gutzkow: 'We call it "*unheimlich*"; you call it "*heimlich*".') In general we are reminded that the word '*heimlich*' is not unambiguous, but be-longs to two sets of ideas, which, without being contradictory, are yet very different: on the one hand it means what is familiar and agreeable, and on the other, what is concealed and kept out of sight.[1] '*Unheimlich*' is customarily used, we are told, as the con-

[225]

---

[1][According to the Oxford English Dictionary, a similar ambiguity attaches to the English 'canny', which may mean not only 'cosy' but also 'endowed with occult or magical powers'.]

trary only of the first signification of '*heimlich*', and not of the second. Sanders tells us nothing concerning a possible genetic connection between these two meanings of *heimlich*. On the other hand, we notice that Schelling says something which throws quite a new light on the concept of the *Unheimlich*, for which we were certainly not prepared. According to him, everything is *unheimlich* that ought to have remained secret and hidden but has come to light.

Some of the doubts that have thus arisen are removed if we consult Grimm's dictionary. (1877, 4, Part 2, 873 ff.)

We read:

Heimlich; adj. and adv. *vernaculus, occultus*; MHG. heimelîch, heimlîch.

(P. 874.) In a slightly different sense: 'I feel *heimlich*, well, free from fear.' . . .

[3] (*b*) *Heimlich* is also used of a place free from ghostly influences . . . familiar, friendly, intimate.

(P. 875: *ß*) Familiar, amicable, unreserved.

4. *From the idea of 'homelike', 'belonging to the house', the further idea is developed of something withdrawn from the eyes of strangers, something concealed, secret; and this idea is expanded in many ways* . . .

(P. 876.) 'On the left bank of the lake there lies a meadow *heimlich* in the wood.' (Schiller, *Wilhelm Tell*, I. 4.) . . . Poetic licence, rarely so used in modern speech . . . *Heimlich* is used in conjunction with a verb expressing the act of concealing: 'In the secret of his tabernacle he shall hide me *heimlich*.' (Ps. xxvii. 5.) . . . *Heimlich* parts of the human body, *pudenda* . . . 'the men that died not were smitten on their *heimlich* parts.' (1 Samuel v. 12.) . . .

(*c*) Officials who give important advice which has to be kept secret in matters of state are called *heimlich* councillors; the adjective, according to modern usage, has been replaced by *geheim* [secret] . . . 'Pharaoh called Joseph's name "him to whom secrets are revealed"' (*heimlich* councillor). (Gen. xli. 45.)

[226]   (P. 878.) 6. *Heimlich*, as used of knowledge—mystic, allegorical: a *heimlich* meaning, *mysticus, divinus, occultus, figuratus*.

(P. 878.) *Heimlich* in a different sense, as withdrawn from knowl-edge, unconscious . . . *Heimlich* also has the meaning of that which is obscure, inaccessible to knowledge . . . 'Do you not see? They do not trust us; they fear the *heimlich* face of the Duke of Friedland.' (Schiller, *Wallensteins Lager*, Scene 2.)

9. *The notion of something hidden and dangerous, which is expressed in the last paragraph, is still further developed, so that 'heimlich' comes to have the meaning usually ascribed to 'unheimlich'*. Thus: 'At times I feel like a man who walks in the night and believes in ghosts; every corner is *heimlich* and full of terrors for him'. (Klinger, *Theater*, 3. 298.)

Thus *heimlich* is a word the meaning of which develops in the direction of ambivalence, until it finally coincides with its opposite, *unheimlich*. *Unheimlich* is in some way or other a sub-species of *heimlich*. Let us bear this discovery in mind, though we cannot yet rightly understand it, alongside of Schelling's[1] definition of the *Unheimlich*. If we go on to examine individual instances of uncan-niness, these hints will become intelligible to us.

II

When we proceed to review the things, persons, impressions, events and situations which are able to arouse in us a feeling of the uncanny in a particularly forcible and definite form, the first requirement is obviously to select a suitable example to start on. Jentsch has taken as a very good instance 'doubts whether an apparently animate being is really alive; or conversely, whether a lifeless object might not be in fact animate'; and he refers in this connection to the impression made by wax-work figures, inge-niously constructed dolls and automata. To these he adds the uncanny effect of epileptic fits, and of manifestations of insanity, because these excite in the spectator the impression of automatic,

[1][In the original version of the paper (1919) only, the name 'Schleiermacher' was printed here, evidently in error.]

mechanical processes at work behind the ordinary appearance of
mental activity. Without entirely accepting this author's view, we
will take it as a starting-point for our own investigation because in
[227]   what follows he reminds us of a writer who has succeeded in
producing uncanny effects better than anyone else.

Jentsch writes: 'In telling a story, one of the most successful
devices for easily creating uncanny effects is to leave the reader in
uncertainty whether a particular figure in the story is a human
being or an automaton, and to do it in such a way that his attention
is not focused directly upon his uncertainty, so that he may not be
led to go into the matter and clear it up immediately. That, as we
have said, would quickly dissipate the peculiar emotional effect of
the thing. E. T. A. Hoffmann has repeatedly employed this psychological artifice with success in his fantastic narratives.'

This observation, undoubtedly a correct one, refers primarily to
the story of 'The Sand-Man' in Hoffmann's *Nachtstücken*,[1] which
contains the original of Olympia, the doll that appears in the first
act of Offenbach's opera, *Tales of Hoffmann*. But I cannot think—
and I hope most readers of the story will agree with me—that the
theme of the doll Olympia, who is to all appearances a living being,
is by any means the only, or indeed the most important, element
that must be held responsible for the quite unparalleled atmosphere of uncanniness evoked by the story. Nor is this atmosphere
heightened by the fact that the author himself treats the episode of
Olympia with a faint touch of satire and uses it to poke fun at the
young man's idealization of his mistress. The main theme of the
story is, on the contrary, something different, something which
gives it its name, and which is always re-introduced at critical
moments: it is the theme of the 'Sand-Man' who tears out children's eyes.

This fantastic tale opens with the childhood recollections of the
student Nathaniel. In spite of his present happiness, he cannot

---

[1]Hoffmann's *Sämtliche Werke*, Grisebach Edition, 3. [A translation of 'The
Sand-Man' is included in *Eight Tales of Hoffmann*, translated by J. M. Cohen,
London, Pan Books, 1952.]

banish the memories associated with the mysterious and terrifying death of his beloved father. On certain evenings his mother used to send the children to bed early, warning them that 'the Sand-Man was coming'; and, sure enough, Nathaniel would not fail to hear the heavy tread of a visitor, with whom his father would then be occupied for the evening. When questioned about the Sand-Man, his mother, it is true, denied that such a person existed except as a figure of speech; but his nurse could give him more definite information: 'He's a wicked man who comes when children won't go to bed, and throws handfuls of sand in their eyes so that they jump out of their heads all bleeding. Then he puts the eyes in a sack and carries them off to the half-moon to feed his children. They sit up there in their nest, and their beaks are hooked like owls' beaks, and they use them to peck up naughty boys' and girls' eyes with.' [228]

Although little Nathaniel was sensible and old enough not to credit the figure of the Sand-Man with such gruesome attributes, yet the dread of him became fixed in his heart. He determined to find out what the Sand-Man looked like; and one evening, when the Sand-Man was expected again, he hid in his father's study. He recognized the visitor as the lawyer Coppelius, a repulsive person whom the children were frightened of when he occasionally came to a meal; and he now identified this Coppelius with the dreaded Sand-Man. As regards the rest of the scene, Hoffmann already leaves us in doubt whether what we are witnessing is the first delirium of the panic-stricken boy, or a succession of events which are to be regarded in the story as being real. His father and the guest are at work at a brazier with glowing flames. The little eavesdropper hears Coppelius call out: 'Eyes here! Eyes here!' and betrays himself by screaming aloud. Coppelius seizes him and is on the point of dropping bits of red-hot coal from the fire into his eyes, and then of throwing them into the brazier, but his father begs him off and saves his eyes. After this the boy falls into a deep swoon; and a long illness brings his experience to an end. Those who decide in favour of the rationalistic interpretation of the Sand-Man will not fail to recognize in the child's phantasy the persisting influence of his nurse's story. The bits of sand that are to be thrown into the child's eyes turn into bits of red-hot coal from the flames; and in both cases they are intended to make his eyes jump out. In the course of another visit of the Sand-Man's, a year later, his father is killed in his study by an explosion. The lawyer Coppelius disappears from the place without leaving a trace behind.

Nathaniel, now a student, believes that he has recognized this phantom of horror from his childhood in an itinerant optician, an Italian called Giuseppe Coppola, who at his university town, offers [229] him weather-glasses for sale. When Nathaniel refuses, the man goes on: 'Not weather-glasses? not weather-glasses? also got fine eyes, fine eyes!' The student's terror is allayed when he finds that the proffered eyes are only harmless spectacles, and he buys a pocket spy-glass from Coppola. With its aid he looks across into Professor Spalanzani's house opposite and there spies Spalanzani's beautiful, but strangely silent and motionless daughter, Olympia. He soon falls in love with her so violently that, because of her, he quite forgets the clever and sensible girl to whom he is betrothed. But Olympia is an automaton whose clock-work has been made by Spalanzani, and whose eyes have been put in by Coppola, the Sand-Man. The student surprises the two Masters quarrelling over their handiwork. The optician carries off the wooden eyeless doll; and the mechanician, Spalanzani, picks up Olympia's bleeding eyes from the ground and throws them at Nathaniel's breast, saying that Coppola had stolen them from the student. Nathaniel succumbs to a fresh attack of madness, and in his delirium his recollection of his father's death is mingled with this new experience. 'Hurry up! hurry up! ring of fire!' he cries. 'Spin about, ring of fire—Hurrah! Hurry up, wooden doll! lovely wooden doll, spin about—.' He then falls upon the professor, Olympia's 'father', and tries to strangle him.

Rallying from a long and serious illness, Nathaniel seems at last to have recovered. He intends to marry his betrothed, with whom he has become reconciled. One day he and she are walking through the city market-place, over which the high tower of the Town Hall throws its huge shadow. On the girl's suggestion, they climb the tower, leaving her brother, who is walking with them, down below.

From the top, Clara's attention is drawn to a curious object moving along the street. Nathaniel looks at this thing through Coppola's spy-glass, which he finds in his pocket, and falls into a new attack of madness. Shouting 'Spin about, wooden doll!' he tries to throw the girl into the gulf below. Her brother, brought to her side by her cries, rescues her and hastens down with her to safety. On the tower above, the madman rushes round, shrieking 'Ring of fire, spin about!'—and we know the origin of the words. Among the people who begin to gather below there comes forward the figure of the lawyer Coppelius, who has suddenly returned. We may suppose that it was his approach, seen through the spy-glass, which threw Nathaniel into his fit of madness. As the onlookers prepare to go up [230] and overpower the madman, Coppelius laughs and says: 'Wait a bit; he'll come down of himself.' Nathaniel suddenly stands still, catches sight of Coppelius, and with a wild shriek 'Yes! "Fine eyes— fine eyes"!' flings himself over the parapet. While he lies on the paving-stones with a shattered skull the Sand-Man vanishes in the throng.

This short summary leaves no doubt, I think, that the feeling of something uncanny is directly attached to the figure of the Sand-Man, that is, to the idea of being robbed of one's eyes, and that Jentsch's point of an intellectual uncertainty has nothing to do with the effect. Uncertainty whether an object is living or inanimate, which admittedly applied to the doll Olympia, is quite irrelevant in connection with this other, more striking instance of uncanniness. It is true that the writer creates a kind of uncertainty in us in the beginning by not letting us know, no doubt purposely, whether he is taking us into the real world or into a purely fantastic one of his own creation. He has, of course, a right to do either; and if he chooses to stage his action in a world peopled with spirits, demons and ghosts, as Shakespeare does in *Hamlet*, in *Macbeth* and, in a different sense, in *The Tempest* and *A Midsummer-Night's Dream*, we must bow to his decision and treat his setting as though it were real for as long as we put ourselves into his hands. But this uncertainty disappears in the course of Hoffmann's story, and we perceive that he intends to make us, too, look through the demon optician's spectacles or spy-glass—perhaps, indeed, that the author in his very own person once peered through such an instrument. For the conclusion of the story makes it quite clear that Coppola the optician really *is* the lawyer Coppelius[1] and also, therefore, the Sand-Man.

There is no question therefore, of any intellectual uncertainty here: we know now that we are not supposed to be looking on at the products of a madman's imagination, behind which we, with the superiority of rational minds, are able to detect the sober truth; and yet this knowledge does not lessen the impression of uncanni-

[231]   ness in the least degree. The theory of intellectual uncertainty is thus incapable of explaining that impression.

We know from psycho-analytic experience, however, that the fear of damaging or losing one's eyes is a terrible one in children. Many adults retain their apprehensiveness in this respect, and no physical injury is so much dreaded by them as an injury to the eye. We are accustomed to say, too, that we will treasure a thing as the apple of our eye. A study of dreams, phantasies and myths has taught us that anxiety about one's eyes, the fear of going blind, is often enough a substitute for the dread of being castrated. The self-blinding of the mythical criminal, Oedipus, was simply a mitigated form of the punishment of castration—the only punishment that was adequate for him by the *lex talionis*. We may try on rationalistic grounds to deny that fears about the eye are derived from the fear of castration, and may argue that it is very natural that so precious an organ as the eye should be guarded by a proportionate dread. Indeed, we might go further and say that the fear of castration itself contains no other significance and no deeper secret than a justifiable dread of this rational kind. But this view does not account adequately for the substitutive relation between the eye and the male organ which is seen to exist in dreams and myths and phan-

---

[1]Frau Dr. Rank has pointed out the association of the name with '*coppella*' = crucible, connecting it with the chemical operations that caused the father's death; and also with '*coppo*' = eye-socket. [Except in the first (1919) edition this footnote was attached, it seems erroneously, to the first occurrence of the name Coppelius on this page.]

tasies; nor can it dispel the impression that the threat of being castrated in especial excites a peculiarly violent and obscure emotion, and that this emotion is what first gives the idea of losing other organs its intense colouring. All further doubts are removed when we learn the details of their 'castration complex' from the analysis of neurotic patients, and realize its immense importance in their mental life.

Moreover, I would not recommend any opponent of the psychoanalytic view to select this particular story of the Sand-Man with which to support his argument that anxiety about the eyes has nothing to do with the castration complex. For why does Hoffmann bring the anxiety about eyes into such intimate connection with the father's death? And why does the Sand-Man always appear as a disturber of love? He separates the unfortunate Nathaniel from his betrothed and from her brother, his best friend; he destroys the second object of his love, Olympia, the lovely doll; and he drives him into suicide at the moment when he has won back his Clara and is about to be happily united to her. Elements in the story like [232] these, and many others, seem arbitrary and meaningless so long as we deny all connection between fears about the eye and castration; but they become intelligible as soon as we replace the Sand-Man by the dreaded father at whose hands castration is expected.[1]

[1]In fact, Hoffmann's imaginative treatment of his material has not made such wild confusion of its elements that we cannot reconstruct their original arrangement. In the story of Nathaniel's childhood, the figures of his father and Coppelius represent the two opposites into which the father-imago is split by his ambivalence; whereas the one threatens to blind him—that is, to castrate him—, the other, the 'good' father, intercedes for his sight. The part of the complex which is most strongly repressed, the death-wish against the 'bad' father, finds expression in the death of the 'good' father, and Coppelius is made answerable for it. This pair of fathers is represented later, in his student days, by Professor Spalanzani and Coppola the optician. The Professor is in himself a member of the father-series, and Coppola is recognized as identical with Coppelius the lawyer. Just as they used before to work together over the secret brazier, so now they have jointly created the doll Olympia; the Professor is even called the father of Olympia. This double occurrence of activity in common betrays them as divisions of the father-imago: both the mechanician and the optician were the father of Nathaniel (and of Olympia as well). In the frightening scene in

[233]   We shall venture, therefore, to refer the uncanny effect of the
Sand-Man to the anxiety belonging to the castration complex of
childhood. But having reached the idea that we can make an
infantile factor such as this responsible for feelings of uncanniness,
we are encouraged to see whether we can apply it to other instances
of the uncanny. We find in the story of the Sand-Man the other
theme on which Jentsch lays stress, of a doll which appears to be
alive. Jentsch believes that a particularly favourable condition for
awakening uncanny feelings is created when there is intellectual
uncertainty whether an object is alive or not, and when an inanimate object becomes too much like an animate one. Now, dolls are
of course rather closely connected with childhood life. We remember that in their early games children do not distinguish at all
sharply between living and inanimate objects, and that they are

---

childhood, Coppelius, after sparing Nathaniel's eyes, had screwed off his arms
and legs as an experiment; that is, he had worked on him as a mechanician would
on a doll. This singular feature, which seems quite outside the picture of the
Sand-Man, introduces a new castration equivalent; but it also points to the inner
identity of Coppelius with his later counterpart, Spalanzani the mechanician,
and prepares us for the interpretation of Olympia. This automatic doll can be
nothing else than a materialization of Nathaniel's feminine attitude towards his
father in his infancy. Her fathers, Spalanzani and Coppola, are, after all, nothing
but new editions, reincarnations of Nathaniel's pair of fathers. Spalanzani's
otherwise incomprehensible statement that the optician has stolen Nathaniel's
eyes (see above, [p. 229]), so as to set them in the doll, now becomes significant as
supplying evidence of the identity of Olympia and Nathaniel. Olympia is, as it
were, a dissociated complex of Nathaniel's which confronts him as a person, and
Nathaniel's enslavement to this complex is expressed in his senseless obsessive
love for Olympia. We may with justice call love of this kind narcissistic, and we
can understand why someone who has fallen victim to it should relinquish the
real, external object of his love. The psychological truth of the situation in which
the young man, fixated upon his father by his castration complex, becomes
incapable of loving a woman, is amply proved by numerous analyses of patients
whose story, though less fantastic, is hardly less tragic than that of the student
Nathaniel.
    Hoffmann was the child of an unhappy marriage. When he was three years
old, his father left his small family, and was never united to them again.
According to Grisebach, in his biographical introduction to Hoffmann's works,
the writer's relation to his father was always a most sensitive subject with him.

especially fond of treating their dolls like live people. In fact, I have occasionally heard a woman patient declare that even at the age of eight she had still been convinced that her dolls would be certain to come to life if she were to look at them in a particular, extremely concentrated, way. So that here, too, it is not difficult to discover a factor from childhood. But, curiously enough, while the Sand-Man story deals with the arousing of an early childhood fear, the idea of a 'living doll' excites no fear at all; children have no fear of their dolls coming to life, they may even desire it. The source of uncanny feelings would not, therefore, be an infantile fear in this case, but rather an infantile wish or even merely an infantile belief. There seems to be a contradiction here; but perhaps it is only a complication, which may be helpful to us later on.

Hoffmann is the unrivalled master of the uncanny in literature. His novel, *Die Elixire des Teufels* [*The Devil's Elixir*], contains a whole mass of themes to which one is tempted to ascribe the uncanny effect of the narrative;[1] but it is too obscure and intricate a story for us to venture upon a summary of it. Towards the end of the book the reader is told the facts, hitherto concealed from him, from which the action springs; with the result, not that he is at last enlightened, but that he falls into a state of complete bewilderment. The author has piled up too much material of the same kind. In consequence one's grasp of the story as a whole suffers, though [234]

[1][Under the rubric 'Varia' in one of the issues of the *Internationale Zeitschrift für Psychoanalyse* for 1919 (5, 308), the year in which the present paper was first published, there appears over the initials 'S.F.' a short note which it is not unreasonable to attribute to Freud. Its insertion here, though strictly speaking irrelevant, may perhaps be excused. The note is headed: 'E. T. A. Hoffmann on the Function of Consciousness' and it proceeds: 'In *Die Elixire des Teufels* (Part II, p. 210, in Hesse's edition)—a novel rich in masterly descriptions of pathological mental states—Schönfeld comforts the hero, whose consciousness is temporarily disturbed, with the following words: "And what do you get out of it? I mean out of the particular mental function which we call consciousness, and which is nothing but the confounded activity of a damned toll-collector—excise-man—deputy-chief customs officer, who has set up his infamous bureau in our top storey and who exclaims, whenever any goods try to get out: 'Hi! hi! exports are prohibited . . . they must stay here . . . here, in this country. . . .'" ']

not the impression it makes. We must content ourselves with selecting those themes of uncanniness which are most prominent, and with seeing whether they too can fairly be traced back to infantile sources. These themes are all concerned with the phenomenon of the 'double', which appears in every shape and in every degree of development. Thus we have characters who are to be considered identical because they look alike. This relation is accentuated by mental processes leaping from one of these characters to another—by what we should call telepathy—, so that the one possesses knowledge, feelings and experience in common with the other. Or it is marked by the fact that the subject identifies himself with someone else, so that he is in doubt as to which his self is, or substitutes the extraneous self for his own. In other words, there is a doubling, dividing and interchanging of the self. And finally there is the constant recurrence of the same thing[1]—the repetition of the same features or character-traits or vicissitudes, of the same crimes, or even the same names through several consecutive generations.

[235]   The theme of the 'double' has been very thoroughly treated by Otto Rank (1914). He has gone into the connections which the 'double' has with reflections in mirrors, with shadows, with guardian spirits, with the belief in the soul and with the fear of death; but he also lets in a flood of light on the surprising evolution of the idea. For the 'double' was originally an insurance against the destruction of the ego, an 'energetic denial of the power of death', as Rank says; and probably the 'immortal' soul was the first 'double' of the body. This invention of doubling as a preservation against extinction has its counterpart in the language of dreams, which is fond of representing castration by a doubling or multiplication of a genital symbol.[2] The same desire led the Ancient Egyptians to develop the art of making images of the dead in lasting materials.

---

[1][This phrase seems to be an echo from Nietzsche (e.g. from the last part of *Also Sprach Zarathustra*). In Chapter III of *Beyond the Pleasure Principle* (1920g), *Standard Ed.*, **18**, 22, Freud puts a similar phrase 'the perpetual recurrence of the same thing' into inverted commas.]

[2][Cf. *The Interpretation of Dreams*, *Standard Ed.*, **5**, 357.]

Such ideas, however, have sprung from the soil of unbounded self-love, from the primary narcissism which dominates the mind of the child and of primitive man. But when this stage has been surmounted, the 'double' reverses its aspect. From having been an assurance of immortality, it becomes the uncanny harbinger of death.

The idea of the 'double' does not necessarily disappear with the passing of primary narcissism, for it can receive fresh meaning from the later stages of the ego's development. A special agency is slowly formed there, which is able to stand over against the rest of the ego, which has the function of observing and criticizing the self and of exercising a censorship within the mind, and which we become aware of as our 'conscience'. In the pathological case of delusions of being watched, this mental agency becomes isolated, dissociated from the ego, and discernible to the physician's eye. The fact that an agency of this kind exists, which is able to treat the rest of the ego like an object—the fact, that is, that man is capable of self-observation—renders it possible to invest the old idea of a 'double' with a new meaning and to ascribe a number of things to it—above all, those things which seem to self-criticism to belong to the old surmounted narcissism of earlier times.[1]

But it is not only this latter material, offensive as it is to the criticism of the ego, which may be incorporated in the idea of a double. There are also all the unfulfilled but possible futures to which we still like to cling in phantasy, all the strivings of the ego

[236]

---

[1] I believe that when poets complain that two souls dwell in the human breast, and when popular psychologists talk of the splitting of people's egos, what they are thinking of is this division (in the sphere of ego-psychology) between the critical agency and the rest of the ego, and not the antithesis discovered by psycho-analysis between the ego and what is unconscious and repressed. It is true that the distinction between these two antitheses is to some extent effaced by the circumstance that foremost among the things that are rejected by the criticism of the ego are derivatives of the repressed.—[Freud had already discussed this critical agency at length in Section III of his paper on narcissism (1914c), and it was soon to be further expanded into the 'ego-ideal' and 'super-ego' in Chapter XI of his *Group Psychology* (1921c) and Chapter III of *The Ego and the Id* (1923b) respectively.]

which adverse external circumstances have crushed, and all our suppressed acts of volition which nourish in us the illusion of Free Will.[1] [Cf. Freud, 1901*b*, Chapter XII (B).]

But after having thus considered the *manifest* motivation of the figure of a 'double', we have to admit that none of this helps us to understand the extraordinarily strong feeling of something uncanny that pervades the conception; and our knowledge of pathological mental processes enables us to add that nothing in this more superficial material could account for the urge towards defence which has caused the ego to project that material outward as something foreign to itself. When all is said and done, the quality of uncanniness can only come from the fact of the 'double' being a creation dating back to a very early mental stage, long since surmounted—a stage, incidentally, at which it wore a more friendly aspect. The 'double' has become a thing of terror, just as, after the collapse of their religion, the gods turned into demons.[2]

The other forms of ego-disturbance exploited by Hoffmann can easily be estimated along the same lines as the theme of the 'double'. They are a harking-back to particular phases in the evolution of the self-regarding feeling, a regression to a time when the ego had not yet marked itself off sharply from the external world and from other people. I believe that these factors are partly responsible for the impression of uncanniness, although it is not easy to isolate and determine exactly their share of it.

[237] The factor of the repetition of the same thing will perhaps not appeal to everyone as a source of uncanny feeling. From what I have observed, this phenomenon does undoubtedly, subject to certain conditions and combined with certain circumstances, arouse an uncanny feeling, which, furthermore, recalls the sense of helplessness experienced in some dream-states. As I was walking,

---

[1]In Ewers's *Der Student von Prag*, which serves as the starting-point of Rank's study on the 'double', the hero has promised his beloved not to kill his antagonist in a duel. But on his way to the duelling-ground he meets his 'double', who has already killed his rival.

[2]Heine, *Die Götter im Exil.*

one hot summer afternoon, through the deserted streets of a provincial town in Italy which was unknown to me, I found myself in a quarter of whose character I could not long remain in doubt. Nothing but painted women were to be seen at the windows of the small houses, and I hastened to leave the narrow street at the next turning. But after having wandered about for a time without enquiring my way, I suddenly found myself back in the same street, where my presence was now beginning to excite attention. I hurried away once more, only to arrive by another *détour* at the same place yet a third time. Now, however, a feeling overcame me which I can only describe as uncanny, and I was glad enough to find myself back at the piazza I had left a short while before, without any further voyages of discovery. Other situations which have in common with my adventure an unintended recurrence of the same situation, but which differ radically from it in other respects, also result in the same feeling of helplessness and of uncanniness. So, for instance, when, caught in a mist perhaps, one has lost one's way in a mountain forest, every attempt to find the marked or familiar path may bring one back again and again to one and the same spot, which one can identify by some particular landmark. Or one may wander about in a dark, strange room, looking for the door or the electric switch, and collide time after time with the same piece of furniture—though it is true that Mark Twain succeeded by wild exaggeration in turning this latter situation into something irresistibly comic.[1]

If we take another class of things, it is easy to see that there, too, it is only this factor of involuntary repetition which surrounds what would otherwise be innocent enough with an uncanny atmosphere, and forces upon us the idea of something fateful and inescapable when otherwise we should have spoken only of 'chance'. For instance, we naturally attach no importance to the event when we hand in an overcoat and get a cloak-room ticket with the number, let us say, 62; or when we find that our cabin on a ship bears that number. But the impression is altered if two such events,

[1][Mark Twain, *A Tramp Abroad*, London, 1880, **1**, 107.]

[238]   each in itself indifferent, happen close together—if we come across
the number 62 several times in a single day, or if we begin to notice
that everything which has a number—addresses, hotel rooms, compartments in railway trains—invariably has the same one, or at all
events one which contains the same figures. We do feel this to be
uncanny. And unless a man is utterly hardened and proof against
the lure of superstition, he will be tempted to ascribe a secret
meaning to this obstinate recurrence of a number; he will take it,
perhaps, as an indication of the span of life allotted to him.[1] Or
suppose one is engaged in reading the works of the famous phys-
iologist, Hering, and within the space of a few days receives two
letters from two different countries, each from a person called
Hering, though one has never before had any dealings with anyone
of that name. Not long ago an ingenious scientist (Kammerer, 1919)
attempted to reduce coincidences of this kind to certain laws, and
so deprive them of their uncanny effect. I will not venture to decide
whether he has succeeded or not.

How exactly we can trace back to infantile psychology the
uncanny effect of such similar recurrences is a question I can only
lightly touch on in these pages; and I must refer the reader instead
to another work,[2] already completed, in which this has been gone
into in detail, but in a different connection. For it is possible to
recognize the dominance in the unconscious mind of a 'compulsion to repeat' proceeding from the instinctual impulses and probably inherent in the very nature of the instincts—a compulsion
powerful enough to overrule the pleasure principle, lending to
certain aspects of the mind their daemonic character, and still very
clearly expressed in the impulses of small children; a compulsion,
too, which is responsible for a part of the course taken by the
analyses of neurotic patients. All these considerations prepare us for

[1] [Freud had himself reached the age of 62 a year earlier, in 1918.]
[2] [This was published a year later as *Beyond the Pleasure Principle* (1920g). The
various manifestations of the 'compulsion to repeat' enumerated here are en-
larged upon in Chapters II and III of that work. The 'compulsion to repeat' had
already been described by Freud as a clinical phenomenon, in a technical paper
published five years earlier (1914g).]

the discovery that whatever reminds us of this inner 'compulsion to repeat' is perceived as uncanny.

Now, however, it is time to turn from these aspects of the matter, which are in any case difficult to judge, and look for some undeniable instances of the uncanny, in the hope that an analysis of them [239] will decide whether our hypothesis is a valid one.

In the story of 'The Ring of Polycrates',[1] the King of Egypt turns away in horror from his host, Polycrates, because he sees that his friend's every wish is at once fulfilled, his every care promptly removed by kindly fate. His host has become 'uncanny' to him. His own explanation, that the too fortunate man has to fear the envy of the gods, seems obscure to us; its meaning is veiled in mythological language. We will therefore turn to another example in a less grandiose setting. In the case history of an obsessional neurotic,[2] I have described how the patient once stayed in a hydropathic establishment and benefited greatly by it. He had the good sense, however, to attribute his improvement not to the therapeutic properties of the water, but to the situation of his room, which immediately adjoined that of a very accommodating nurse. So on his second visit to the establishment he asked for the same room, but was told that it was already occupied by an old gentleman, whereupon he gave vent to his annoyance in the words: 'I wish he may be struck dead for it.' A fortnight later the old gentleman really did have a stroke. My patient thought this an 'uncanny' experience. The impression of uncanniness would have been stronger still if less time had elapsed between his words and the untoward event, or if he had been able to report innumerable similar coincidences. As a matter of fact, he had no difficulty in producing coincidences of this sort; but then not only he but every obsessional neurotic I have observed has been able to relate analogous experiences. They are never surprised at their invariably running up against someone they have just been thinking of, perhaps for the first time for a long

[1][Schiller's poem based on Herodotus.]
[2]'Notes upon a Case of Obsessional Neurosis' (1909*d*) [*Standard Ed.*, **10**, 234].

while. If they say one day 'I haven't had any news of so-and-so for a
long time', they will be sure to get a letter from him the next
morning, and an accident or a death will rarely take place without
having passed through their mind a little while before. They are in
[240]   the habit of referring to this state of affairs in the most modest
manner, saying that they have 'presentiments' which 'usually' come
true.

One of the most uncanny and wide-spread forms of superstition
is the dread of the evil eye, which has been exhaustively studied by
the Hamburg oculist Seligmann (1910–11). There never seems to
have been any doubt about the source of this dread. Whoever
possesses something that is at once valuable and fragile is afraid of
other people's envy, in so far as he projects on to them the envy he
would have felt in their place. A feeling like this betrays itself by a
look[1] even though it is not put into words; and when a man is
prominent owing to noticeable, and particularly owing to unat-
tractive, attributes, other people are ready to believe that his envy is
rising to a more than usual degree of intensity and that this
intensity will convert it into effective action. What is feared is thus
a secret intention of doing harm, and certain signs are taken to
mean that that intention has the necessary power at its command.

These last examples of the uncanny are to be referred to the
principle which I have called 'omnipotence of thoughts', taking
the name from an expression used by one of my patients.[2] And now
we find ourselves on familiar ground. Our analysis of instances of
the uncanny has led us back to the old, animistic conception of the
universe. This was characterized by the idea that the world was
peopled with the spirits of human beings; by the subject's narcissistic overvaluation of his own mental processes; by the belief in the
omnipotence of thoughts and the technique of magic based on that
belief; by the attribution to various outside persons and things of
carefully graded magical powers, or '*mana*'; as well as by all the

[1] ['The evil eye' in German is '*der böse Blick*', literally 'the evil look'.]
[2] [The obsessional patient referred to just above—the 'Rat Man' (1909*d*),
Standard Ed., **10**, 233f.]

other creations with the help of which man, in the unrestricted narcissism of that stage of development, strove to fend off the manifest prohibitions of reality. It seems as if each one of us has been through a phase of individual development corresponding to this animistic stage in primitive men, that none of us has passed through it without preserving certain residues and traces of it which are still capable of manifesting themselves, and that everything which now strikes us as 'uncanny' fulfils the condition of touching those residues of animistic mental activity within us and [241] bringing them to expression.[1]

At this point I will put forward two considerations which, I think, contain the gist of this short study. In the first place, if psycho-analytic theory is correct in maintaining that every affect belonging to an emotional impulse, whatever its kind, is transformed, if it is repressed, into anxiety, then among instances of frightening things there must be one class in which the frightening element can be shown to be something repressed which *recurs*. This class of frightening things would then constitute the uncanny; and it must be a matter of indifference whether what is uncanny was itself originally frightening or whether it carried some *other* affect. In the second place, if this is indeed the secret nature of the uncanny, we can understand why linguistic usage has extended *das Heimliche* ['homely'] into its opposite, *das Unheimliche* (p. 226); for this uncanny is in reality nothing new or alien, but something which is familiar and old-established in the mind and which has become alienated from it only through the process of repression. This reference to the factor of repression enables us, furthermore, to understand Schelling's definition [p. 224] of the uncanny as something which ought to have remained hidden but has come to light.

---

[1] Cf. my book *Totem and Taboo* (1912–13), Essay III, 'Animism, Magic and the Omnipotence of Thoughts', where the following footnote will be found: 'We appear to attribute an "uncanny" quality to impressions that seek to confirm the omnipotence of thoughts and the animistic mode of thinking in general, after we have reached a stage at which, in our *judgement*, we have abandoned such beliefs.' [*Standard Ed.*, **13**, 86.]

It only remains for us to test our new hypothesis on one or two more examples of the uncanny.

Many people experience the feeling in the highest degree in relation to death and dead bodies, to the return of the dead, and to spirits and ghosts. As we have seen [p. 221] some languages in use to-day can only render the German expression 'an *unheimlich* house' by 'a *haunted* house'. We might indeed have begun our investigation with this example, perhaps the most striking of all, of something uncanny, but we refrained from doing so because the uncanny in it is too much intermixed with what is purely gruesome and is in part overlaid by it. There is scarcely any other matter, however, upon [242] which our thoughts and feelings have changed so little since the very earliest times, and in which discarded forms have been so completely preserved under a thin disguise, as our relation to death. Two things account for our conservatism: the strength of our original emotional reaction to death and the insufficiency of our scientific knowledge about it. Biology has not yet been able to decide whether death is the inevitable fate of every living being or whether it is only a regular but yet perhaps avoidable event in life.[1] It is true that the statement 'All men are mortal' is paraded in textbooks of logic as an example of a general proposition; but no human being really grasps it, and our unconscious has as little use now as it ever had for the idea of its own mortality.[2] Religions continue to dispute the importance of the undeniable fact of individual death and to postulate a life after death; civil governments still believe that they cannot maintain moral order among the living if they do not uphold the prospect of a better life hereafter as a recompense for mundane existence. In our great cities, placards announce lectures that undertake to tell us how to get into touch with the souls of the departed; and it cannot be denied that not a few of the most able and penetrating minds among our men of science

[1] [This problem figures prominently in *Beyond the Pleasure Principle* (1920g), on which Freud was engaged while writing the present paper. See *Standard Ed.*, **18**, 44 ff.]

[2] [Freud had discussed the individual's attitude to death at greater length in the second part of his paper 'Thoughts for the Times on War and Death' (1915b).]

have come to the conclusion, especially towards the close of their own lives, that a contact of this kind is not impossible. Since almost all of us still think as savages do on this topic, it is no matter for surprise that the primitive fear of the dead is still so strong within us and always ready to come to the surface on any provocation. Most likely our fear still implies the old belief that the dead man becomes the enemy of his survivor and seeks to carry him off to share his new life with him. Considering our unchanged attitude towards death, we might rather enquire what has become of the repression, which is the necessary condition of a primitive feeling recurring in the shape of something uncanny. But repression is there, too. All supposedly educated people have ceased to believe officially that the dead can become visible as spirits, and have made any such appearances dependent on improbable and remote conditions; their emotional attitude towards their dead, moreover, once a highly ambiguous and ambivalent one, has been toned down in the higher strata of the mind into an unambiguous feeling of piety.[1]

[243]

We have now only a few remarks to add—for animism, magic and sorcery, the omnipotence of thoughts, man's attitude to death, involuntary repetition and the castration complex comprise practically all the factors which turn something frightening into something uncanny.

We can also speak of a living person as uncanny, and we do so when we ascribe evil intentions to him. But that is not all; in addition to this we must feel that his intentions to harm us are going to be carried out with the help of special powers. A good instance of this is the '*Gettatore*',[2] that uncanny figure of Romanic superstition which Schaeffer, with intuitive poetic feeling and profound psycho-analytic understanding, has transformed into a sympathetic character in his *Josef Montfort*. But the question of these secret powers bring us back again to the realm of animism. It was the pious Gretchen's intuition that Mephistopheles possessed secret powers of this kind that made him so uncanny to her.

[1]Cf. *Totem and Taboo* [*Standard Ed.*, **13**, 66].
[2][Literally 'thrower' (of bad luck), or 'one who casts' (the evil eye).—Schaeffer's novel was published in 1918.]

>Sie fühlt dass ich ganz sicher ein Genie,
>Vielleicht sogar der Teufel bin.[1]

The uncanny effect of epilepsy and of madness has the same origin. The layman sees in them the working of forces hitherto unsuspected in his fellow-men, but at the same time he is dimly aware of them in remote corners of his own being. The Middle Ages quite consistently ascribed all such maladies to the influence of demons, and in this their psychology was almost correct. Indeed, I should not be surprised to hear that psycho-analysis, which is concerned with laying bare these hidden forces, has itself become uncanny to many people for that very reason. In one case, after I had succeeded—though none too rapidly—in effecting a cure in a [244] girl who had been an invalid for many years, I myself heard this view expressed by the patient's mother long after her recovery.

Dismembered limbs, a severed head, a hand cut off at the wrist, as in a fairy tale of Hauff's,[2] feet which dance by themselves, as in the book by Schaeffer which I mentioned above—all these have something peculiarly uncanny about them, especially when, as in the last instance, they prove capable of independent activity in addition. As we already know, this kind of uncanniness springs from its proximity to the castration complex. To some people the idea of being buried alive by mistake is the most uncanny thing of all. And yet psycho-analysis has taught us that this terrifying phantasy is only a transformation of another phantasy which had originally nothing terrifying about it at all, but was qualified by a certain lasciviousness—the phantasy, I mean, of intra-uterine existence.[3]

There is one more point of general application which I should like to add, though, strictly speaking, it has been included in what

[1][She feels that surely I'm a genius now,—
Perhaps the very Devil indeed!
    Goethe, *Faust*, Part I (Scene 16),
        (Bayard Taylor's translation).]
[2][*Die Geschichte von der abgehauenen Hand* ('The Story of the Severed Hand').]
[3][See Section VIII of Freud's analysis of the 'Wolf Man' (1918*b*), above p. 101 ff.]

has already been said about animism and modes of working of the mental apparatus that have been surmounted; for I think it deserves special emphasis. This is that an uncanny effect is often and easily produced when the distinction between imagination and reality is effaced, as when something that we have hitherto regarded as imaginary appears before us in reality, or when a symbol takes over the full functions of the thing it symbolizes, and so on. It is this factor which contributes not a little to the uncanny effect attaching to magical practices. The infantile element in this, which also dominates the minds of neurotics, is the over-accentuation of psychical reality in comparison with material reality—a feature closely allied to the belief in the omnipotence of thoughts. In the middle of the isolation of war-time a number of the English *Strand Magazine* fell into my hands; and, among other somewhat redundant matter, I read a story about a young married couple who move into a furnished house in which there is a curiously shaped table with carvings of crocodiles on it. Towards evening an intolerable and very specific smell begins to pervade the house; they stumble over something in the dark; they seem to see a vague form gliding over the stairs—in short, we are given to understand that the presence of the table causes ghostly crocodiles to haunt the place, or that the wooden monsters come to life in the dark, or something of the sort. It was a naïve enough story, but the uncanny feeling it produced was quite remarkable. [245]

To conclude this collection of examples, which is certainly not complete, I will relate an instance taken from psycho-analytic experience; if it does not rest upon mere coincidence, it furnishes a beautiful confirmation of our theory of the uncanny. It often happens that neurotic men declare that they feel there is something uncanny about the female genital organs. This *unheimlich* place, however, is the entrance to the former *Heim* [home] of all human beings, to the place where each one of us lived once upon a time and in the beginning. There is a joking saying that 'Love is homesickness'; and whenever a man dreams of a place or a country and says to himself, while he is still dreaming: 'this place is familiar to me, I've been here before', we may interpret the place as being his

mother's genitals or her body.[1] In this case too, then, the *unheimlich*
is what was once *heimisch*, familiar; the prefix '*un*' ['un-'] is the
token of repression.[2]

III

In the course of this discussion the reader will have felt certain
doubts arising in his mind; and he must now have an opportunity
of collecting them and bringing them forward.

It may be true that the uncanny [*unheimlich*] is something
which is secretly familiar [*heimlich-heimisch*], which has undergone repression and then returned from it, and that everything that
is uncanny fulfils this condition. But the selection of material on
this basis does not enable us to solve the problem of the uncanny.
For our proposition is clearly not convertible. Not everything that
fulfils this condition—not everything that recalls repressed desires
and surmounted modes of thinking belonging to the prehistory of
the individual and of the race—is on that account uncanny.

[246]   Nor shall we conceal the fact that for almost every example
adduced in support of our hypothesis one may be found which
rebuts it. The story of the severed hand in Hauff's fairy tale [p. 244]
certainly has an uncanny effect, and we have traced that effect back
to the castration complex; but most readers will probably agree
with me in judging that no trace of uncanniness is provoked by
Herodotus's story of the treasure of Rhampsinitus, in which the
master-thief, whom the princess tries to hold fast by the hand,
leaves his brother's severed hand behind with her instead. Again,
the prompt fulfilment of the wishes of Polycrates [p. 239] undoubtedly affects us in the same uncanny way as it did the king of Egypt;
yet our own fairy stories are crammed with instantaneous wish-
fulfilments which produce no uncanny effect whatever. In the story
of 'The Three Wishes', the woman is tempted by the savoury smell
of a sausage to wish that she might have one too, and in an instant

[1][Cf. *The Interpretation of Dreams* (1900*a*), *Standard Ed.*, **5**, 399.]
[2][See Freud's paper on 'Negation' (1925*h*).]

it lies on a plate before her. In his annoyance at her hastiness her husband wishes it may hang on her nose. And there it is, dangling from her nose. All this is very striking but not in the least uncanny. Fairy tales quite frankly adopt the animistic standpoint of the omnipotence of thoughts and wishes, and yet I cannot think of any genuine fairy story which has anything uncanny about it. We have heard that it is in the highest degree uncanny when an inanimate object—a picture or a doll—comes to life; nevertheless in Hans Andersen's stories the household utensils, furniture and tin soldiers are alive, yet nothing could well be more remote from the uncanny. And we should hardly call it uncanny when Pygmalion's beautiful statue comes to life.

Apparent death and the re-animation of the dead have been represented as most uncanny themes. But things of this sort too are very common in fairy stories. Who would be so bold as to call it uncanny, for instance, when Snow-White opens her eyes once more? And the resuscitation of the dead in accounts of miracles, as in the New Testament, elicits feelings quite unrelated to the uncanny. Then, too, the theme that achieves such an indubitably uncanny effect, the unintended recurrence of the same thing, serves other and quite different purposes in another class of cases. We have already come across one example [p. 237] in which it is employed to call up a feeling of the comic; and we could multiply instances of this kind. Or again, it works as a means of emphasis, and so on. And once more: what is the origin of the uncanny effect of silence, darkness and solitude? Do not these factors point to the [247] part played by danger in the genesis of what is uncanny, notwithstanding that in children these same factors are the most frequent determinants of the expression of fear [rather than of the uncanny]? And are we after all justified in entirely ignoring intellectual uncertainty as a factor, seeing that we have admitted its importance in relation to death [p. 242]?

It is evident therefore, that we must be prepared to admit that there are other elements besides those which we have so far laid down as determining the production of uncanny feelings. We might say that these preliminary results have satisfied *psycho-*

analytic interest in the problem of the uncanny, and that what remains probably calls for an *aesthetic* enquiry. But that would be to open the door to doubts about what exactly is the value of our German contention that the uncanny proceeds from something familiar which has been repressed.

We have noticed one point which may help us to resolve these uncertainties: nearly all the instances that contradict our hypothesis are taken from the realm of fiction, of imaginative writing. This suggests that we should differentiate between the uncanny that we actually experience and the uncanny that we merely picture or read about.

What is *experienced* as uncanny is much more simply conditioned but comprises far fewer instances. We shall find, I think, that it fits in perfectly with our attempt at a solution, and can be traced back without exception to something familiar that has been repressed. But here, too, we must make a certain important and psychologically significant differentiation in our material, which is best illustrated by turning to suitable examples.

Let us take the uncanny associated with the omnipotence of thoughts, with the prompt fulfilment of wishes, with secret injurious powers and with the return of the dead. The condition under which the feeling of uncanniness arises here is unmistakable. We—or our primitive forefathers—once believed that these possibilities were realities, and were convinced that they actually happened. Nowadays we no longer believe in them, we have *surmounted* these modes of thought; but we do not feel quite sure of our new beliefs, and the old ones still exist within us ready to seize upon any confirmation. As soon as something *actually happens* in our lives which seems to confirm the old, discarded beliefs we get a feeling of the uncanny; it is as though we were making a judgement something like this: 'So, after all, it is *true* that one can kill a person by the mere wish!' or, 'So the dead *do* live on and appear on the scene of their former activities!' and so on. Conversely, anyone who has completely and finally rid himself of animistic beliefs will be insensible to this type of the uncanny. The most remarkable coincidences of wish and fulfilment, the most mysterious repetition of

[248]

similar experiences in a particular place or on a particular date, the most deceptive sights and suspicious noises—none of these things will disconcert him or raise the kind of fear which can be described as 'a fear of something uncanny'. The whole thing is purely an affair of 'reality-testing', a question of the material reality of the phenomena.[1]

The state of affairs is different when the uncanny proceeds from repressed infantile complexes, from the castration complex, womb-phantasies, etc.; but experiences which arouse this kind of uncanny feeling are not of very frequent occurrence in real life. The uncanny which proceeds from actual experience belongs for the most part to the first group [the group dealt with in the previous paragraph]. Nevertheless the distinction between the two is theoretically very important. Where the uncanny comes from infantile complexes [249] the question of material reality does not arise; its place is taken by psychical reality. What is involved is an actual repression of some content of thought and a return of this repressed content, not a cessation of *belief in the reality* of such a content. We might say that in the one case what had been repressed is a particular ideational content, and in the other the belief in its (material) reality. But this

---

[1]Since the uncanny effect of a 'double' also belongs to this same group it is interesting to observe what the effect is of meeting one's own image unbidden and unexpected. Ernst Mach has related two such observations in his *Analyse der Empfindungen* (1900, 3). On the first occasion he was not a little startled when he realized that the face before him was his own. The second time he formed a very unfavourable opinion about the supposed stranger who entered the omnibus, and thought 'What a shabby-looking school-master that man is who is getting in!'—I can report a similar adventure. I was sitting alone in my *wagon-lit* compartment when a more than usually violent jolt of the train swung back the door of the adjoining washing-cabinet, and an elderly gentleman in a dressing-gown and a travelling cap came in. I assumed that in leaving the washing-cabinet, which lay between the two compartments, he had taken the wrong direction and come into my compartment by mistake. Jumping up with the intention of putting him right, I at once realized to my dismay that the intruder was nothing but my own reflection in the looking-glass on the open door. I can still recollect that I thoroughly disliked his appearance. Instead, therefore, of being *frightened* by our 'doubles', both Mach and I simply failed to recognize them as such. Is it not possible, though, that our dislike of them was a vestigial trace of the archaic reaction which feels the 'double' to be something uncanny?

last phrase no doubt extends the term 'repression' beyond its
legitimate meaning. It would be more correct to take into account a
psychological distinction which can be detected here, and to say
that the animistic beliefs of civilized people are in a state of having
been (to a greater or lesser extent) *surmounted* [rather than re-
pressed]. Our conclusion could then be stated thus: an uncanny
experience occurs either when infantile complexes which have
been repressed are once more revived by some impression, or when
primitive beliefs which have been surmounted seem once more to
be confirmed. Finally, we must not let our predilection for smooth
solutions and lucid exposition blind us to the fact that these two
classes of uncanny experience are not always sharply distinguish-
able. When we consider that primitive beliefs are most intimately
connected with infantile complexes, and are, in fact, based on
them, we shall not be greatly astonished to find that the distinction
is often a hazy one.

The uncanny as it is depicted in *literature*, in stories and imaginative productions, merits in truth a separate discussion. Above
all, it is a much more fertile province than the uncanny in real life,
for it contains the whole of the latter and something more besides,
something that cannot be found in real life. The contrast between
what has been repressed and what has been surmounted cannot be
transposed on to the uncanny in fiction without profound modification; for the realm of phantasy depends for its effect on the fact
that its content is not submitted to reality-testing. The somewhat
paradoxical result is that *in the first place a great deal that is not
uncanny in fiction would be so if it happened in real life; and in the
second place that there are many more means of creating uncanny
effects in fiction than there are in real life.*

The imaginative writer has this licence among many others, that
he can select his world of representation so that it either coincides
with the realities we are familiar with or departs from them in what
particulars he pleases. We accept his ruling in every case. In fairy
tales, for instance, the world of reality is left behind from the very
start, and the animistic system of beliefs is frankly adopted. Wish-
fulfilments, secret powers, omnipotence of thoughts, animation of
inanimate objects, all the elements so common in fairy stories, can

[250]

exert no uncanny influence here; for, as we have learnt, that feeling cannot arise unless there is a conflict of judgement as to whether things which have been 'surmounted' and are regarded as incredible may not, after all, be possible; and this problem is eliminated from the outset by the postulates of the world of fairy tales. Thus we see that fairy stories, which have furnished us with most of the contradictions to our hypothesis of the uncanny, confirm the first part of our proposition—that in the realm of fiction many things are not uncanny which would be so if they happened in real life. In the case of these stories there are other contributory factors, which we shall briefly touch upon later.

The creative writer can also choose a setting which though less imaginary than the world of fairy tales, does yet differ from the real world by admitting superior spiritual beings such as daemonic spirits or ghosts of the dead. So long as they remain within their setting of poetic reality, such figures lose any uncanniness which they might possess. The souls in Dante's *Inferno*, or the supernatural apparitions in Shakespeare's *Hamlet, Macbeth* or *Julius Caesar*, may be gloomy and terrible enough, but they are no more really uncanny than Homer's jovial world of gods. We adapt our judgement to the imaginary reality imposed on us by the writer, and regard souls, spirits and ghosts as though their existence had the same validity as our own has in material reality. In this case too we avoid all trace of the uncanny.

The situation is altered as soon as the writer pretends to move in the world of common reality. In this case he accepts as well all the conditions operating to produce uncanny feelings in real life; and everything that would have an uncanny effect in reality has it in his story. But in this case he can even increase his effect and multiply it far beyond what could happen in reality, by bringing about events which never or very rarely happen in fact. In doing this he is in a sense betraying us to the superstitiousness which we have ostensibly surmounted; he deceives us by promising to give us the sober truth, and then after all overstepping it. We react to his inventions as we would have reacted to real experiences; by the time we have [251] seen through his trick it is already too late and the author has achieved his object. But it must be added that his success is not unalloyed. We retain a feeling of dissatisfaction, a kind of grudge against the attempted deceit. I have noticed this particularly after reading Schnitzler's *Die Weissagung* [*The Prophecy*] and similar stories which flirt with the supernatural. However, the writer has one more means which he can use in order to avoid our recalcitrance and at the same time to improve his chances of success. He can keep us in the dark for a long time about the precise nature of the presuppositions on which the world he writes about is based, or he can cunningly and ingeniously avoid any definite information on the point to the last. Speaking generally, however, we find a confirmation of the second part of our proposition—that fiction presents more opportunities for creating uncanny feelings than are possible in real life.

Strictly speaking, all these complications relate only to that class of the uncanny which proceeds from forms of thought that have been surmounted. The class which proceeds from repressed complexes is more resistant and remains as powerful in fiction as in real experience, subject to one exception [see p. 252]. The uncanny belonging to the first class—that proceeding from forms of thought that have been surmounted—retains its character not only in experience but in fiction as well, so long as the setting is one of material reality; but where it is given an arbitrary and artificial setting in fiction, it is apt to lose that character.

We have clearly not exhausted the possibilities of poetic licence and the privileges enjoyed by story-writers in evoking or in excluding an uncanny feeling. In the main we adopt an unvarying passive attitude towards real experience and are subject to the influence of our physical environment. But the story-teller has a *peculiarly* directive power over us; by means of the moods he can put us into, he is able to guide the current of our emotions, to dam it up in one direction and make it flow in another, and he often obtains a great variety of effects from the same material. All this is nothing new, and has doubtless long since been fully taken into account by students of aesthetics. We have drifted into this field of research half involuntarily, through the temptation to explain certain instances which [252] contradicted our theory of the causes of the uncanny. Accordingly we will now return to the examination of a few of those instances.

We have already asked [p. 246] why it is that the severed hand in the story of the treasure of Rhampsinitus has no uncanny effect in the way that the severed hand has in Hauff's story. The question seems to have gained in importance now that we have recognized that the class of the uncanny which proceeds from repressed complexes is the more resistant of the two. The answer is easy. In the Herodotus story our thoughts are concentrated much more on the superior cunning of the master-thief than on the feelings of the princess. The princess may very well have had an uncanny feeling, indeed she very probably fell into a swoon; but *we* have no such sensations, for we put ourselves in the thief's place, not in hers. In Nestroy's farce, *Der Zerrissene* [*The Torn Man*], another means is used to avoid any impression of the uncanny in the scene in which the fleeing man, convinced that he is a murderer, lifts up one trap-door after another and each time sees what he takes to be the ghost of his victim rising up out of it. He calls out in despair, 'But I've only killed *one* man. Why this ghastly multiplication?' We know what went before this scene and do not share his error, so what must be uncanny to him has an irresistibly comic effect on us. Even a 'real' ghost, as in Oscar Wilde's *Canterville Ghost*, loses all power of at least arousing *gruesome* feelings in us as soon as the author begins to amuse himself by being ironical about it and allows liberties to be taken with it. Thus we see how independent emotional effects can be of the actual subject-matter in the world of fiction. In fairy stories feelings of fear—including therefore uncanny feelings—are ruled out altogether. We understand this, and that is why we ignore any opportunities we find in them for developing such feelings.

Concerning the factors of silence, solitude and darkness [pp. 246–7], we can only say that they are actually elements in the production of the infantile anxiety from which the majority of human beings have never become quite free. This problem has been discussed from a psycho-analytic point of view elsewhere.[1]

[1] [See the discussion of children's fear of the dark in Section V of the third of Freud's *Three Essays* (1905*d*), *Standard Ed.*, 7, 224 *n.*]

Appendix
Extract from Daniel Sanders's *Wörterbuch der Deutschen Sprache*[1]

[253] Heimlich, a. (-keit, f. -en): **1.** auch Heimelich, heimelig, zum Hause gehörig, nicht fremd, vertraut, zahm, traut und traulich, anheimelnd etc. (*a*) (veralt.) zum Haus, zur Familie gehörig oder: wie dazu gehörig betrachtet, vgl. lat. familiaris, vertraut: Die Heimlichen, die Hausgenossen; Der heimliche Rath. 1. Mos. 41, 45; 2. Sam. 23, 23. 1 Chr. 12, 25. Weish. 8, 4., wofür jetzt: Geheimer (s. *d***1.**) Rath üblich ist, s. Heimlicher—(*b*) von Thieren zahm, sich den Menschen traulich anschließend. Ggstz. wild, z. B.: Thier, die weder wild noch heimlich sind, etc. Eppendorf. 88; Wilde Thier . . . so man sie h. und gewohnsam um die Leute aufzeucht. 92. So diese Thierle von Jugend bei den Menschen erzogen, werden sie ganz h., freundlich etc., Stumpf 608a etc.—So noch: So h. ist's (das Lamm) und frißt aus meiner Hand. Hölty; Ein schöner, heimelicher (s. *c*) Vogel bleibt der Storch immerhin. Linck, Schl. 146. s. Häuslich **1** etc.—(*c*) traut, traulich anheimelnd; das Wohlgefühl stiller Befriedigung etc., behaglicher Ruhe u. sichern Schutzes, wie das umschlossne, wohnliche Haus erregend (vgl. Geheuer): Ist dir's h. noch im Lande, wo die Fremden deine Wälder roden? Alexis H. 1, 1, 289; Es war ihr nicht allzu h. bei ihm. Brentano Wehm. 92; Auf einem hohen h—en Schattenpfade . . ., längs dem rieselnden rauschenden und plätschernden Waldbach. Forster B. 1, 417. Die H—keit der Heimath zerstören. Gervinus Lit. 5, 375. So vertraulich und h. habe ich nicht leicht ein Plätzchen gefunden. G[oethe], 14, 14; Wir dachten es uns so bequem, so artig, so gemüthlich und h. 15, 9; In stiller H—keit, umzielt von engen Schranken. Haller; Einer sorglichen Hausfrau, die mit dem Wenigsten eine vergnügliche H—keit (Häuslichkeit) zu schaffen versteht. Hartmann Unst. 1, 188; Desto h—er kam ihm jetzt der ihm erst kurz noch so fremde Mann vor. Kerner 540; Die protestantischen Besitzer fühlen sich . . . nicht h. unter ihren katholischen Unterthanen. Kohl. Irl. 1,

[1][Cf. p. 196.]

230

172; Wenns h. wird und leise/die Abendstille nur an deiner Zelle
lauscht. Tiedge 2, 39; Still und lieb und h., als sie sich/zum Ruhen
einen Platz nur wünschen möchten. W[ieland], 11, 144; Es war ihm
garnicht h. dabei 27. 170, etc.—Auch: Der Platz war so still, so
einsam, so schatten-h. Scherr Pilg. 1, 170; Die ab- und zuströ-
menden Fluthwellen, träumend und wiegenlied-h. Körner, Sch. 3,
320, etc.—Vgl. namentl. Un-h.—Namentl. bei schwäb., schwzr.
Schriftst. oft dreisilbig: Wie 'heimelich' war es dann Ivo Abends
wieder, als er zu Hause lag. Auerbach, D. 1, 249; In dem Haus ist
mir's so heimelig gewesen. 4. 307; Die warme Stube, der heimelige
Nachmittag. Gotthelf, Sch. 127, 148; Das ist das wahre Heimelig,
wenn der Mensch so von Herzen fühlt, wie wenig er ist, wie groß
der Herr ist. 147; Wurde man nach und nach recht gemüthlich und
heimelig mit einander. U. 1, 297; Die trauliche Heimeligkeit. 380,
2, 86; Heimelicher wird es mir wohl nirgends werden als hier. 327;
Pestalozzi 4, 240; Was von ferne herkommt . . . lebt gw. nicht ganz
heimelig (heimatlich, freundnachbarlich) mit den Leuten. 325; Die
Hütte, wo/er sonst so heimelig, so froh/ . . . im Kreis der Seinen oft
gesessen. Reithard 20; Da klingt das Horn des Wächters so
heimelig vom Thurm/da ladet seine Stimme so gastlich. 49; Es
schläft sich da so lind und warm/so wunderheim'lig ein. 23, etc.—
Diese Weise verdiente allgemein zu werden, um das
gute Wort vor dem Veralten wegen nahe liegender Ver-
wechslung mit 2 zu bewahren. vgl.: 'Die Zecks sind alle
h. (2)' H.? . . Was verstehen sie unter h.? . .—'Nun . . . es
kommt mir mit ihnen vor, wie mit einem zugegrabenen
Brunnen oder einem ausgetrockneten Teich. Man kann
nicht darüber gehen, ohne daß es Einem immer ist, als
könnte da wieder einmal Wasser zum Vorschein kom-
men.' Wir nennen das un-h.; Sie nennen's h. Worin
finden Sie denn, daß diese Familie etwas Verstecktes
und Unzuverlässiges hat? etc. Gutzkow R. 2, 61.[1]—(d)
(s. c) namentl. schles.: fröhlich, heiter, auch vom Wetter, s. Ade-
lung und Weinhold.

[1][Spaced type, here and below, is introduced by Freud.]

2. versteckt, verborgen gehalten, so daß man Andre nicht davon oder darum wissen lassen, es ihnen verbergen will, vgl. Geheim (**2**), von welchem erst nhd. Ew. es doch zumal in der älteren [255] Sprache, z. B. in der Bibel, wie Hiob 11, 6; 15, 8; Weish. 2, 22; 1. Kor. 2, 7 etc., und so auch H—keit statt Geheimnis. Math. 13, 35 etc., nicht immer genau geschieden wird: H. (hinter Jemandes Rücken) Etwas thun, treiben; Sich h. davon schleichen; H—e Zusammenkünfte, Verabredungen; Mit h—er Schadenfreude zusehen; H. seufzen, weinen; H. thun, als ob man etwas zu verbergen hätte; H—e Liebschaft, Liebe, Sünde; H—e Orte (die der Wohlstand zu verhüllen gebietet). 1. Sam. 5, 6; Das h—e Gemach (Abtritt). 2. Kön. 10, 27; W[ieland], 5, 256 etc., auch: Der h—e Stuhl. Zinkgräf 1, 249; In Graben, in H—keiten werfen. 3, 75; Rollenhagen Fr. 83 etc.—Führte h. vor Laomedon/die Stuten vor. B[ürger], 161 b etc.—Ebenso versteckt, h., hinterlistig und boshaft gegen grausame Herren . . . wie offen, frei, theilnehmend und dienstwillig gegen den leidenden Freund. Burmeister gB 2, 157; Du sollst mein h. Heiligstes noch wissen. Chamisso 4, 56; Die h—e Kunst (der Zauberei). 3, 224; Wo die öffentliche Ventilation aufhören muß, fängt die h—e Machination an. Forster, Br. 2, 135; Freiheit ist die leise Parole h. Verschworener, das laute Feldgeschrei der öffentlich Umwälzenden. G[oethe], 4, 222; Ein heilig, h. Wirken. 15; Ich habe Wurzeln/die sind gar h.,/im tiefen Boden/bin ich gegründet. 2, 109; Meine h—e Tücke (vgl. Heimtücke). 30, 344; Empfängt er es nicht offenbar und gewissenhaft, so mag er es h. und gewissenlos ergreifen. 39, 33; Ließ h. und geheimnisvoll achromatische Fernröhre zusammensetzen. 375; Von nun an, will ich, sei nichts H—es/mehr unter uns. Sch[iller], 369 b.—Jemandes H—keiten entdecken, offenbaren, verrathen; H—keiten hinter meinem Rücken zu brauen. Alexis. H. 2, 3, 168; Zu meiner Zeit/befliß man sich der H—keit. Hagedorn 3, 92; Die H—keit und das Gepuschele unter der Hand. Immermann, M. 3, 289; Der H—keit (des verborgnen Golds) unmächtigen Bann/kann nur die Hand der Einsicht lösen. Novalis. 1, 69; /Sag'an, wo du sie . . . verbirgst, in welches Ortes verschwiegener H. Sch[iller], 495 b; Ihr Bienen, die ihr knetet/der H—keiten Schloß (Wachs zum Siegeln). Tieck,

Cymb. 3, 2; Erfahren in seltnen H—keiten (Zauberkünsten).
Schlegel Sh. 6, 102 etc., vgl. Geheimnis L[essing], 10: 291 ff.
   Zsstzg. s. 1 *c*, so auch nam. der Ggstz.: Un-: unbehagliches,
banges Grauen erregend: Der schier ihm un-h., gespenstisch
erschien. Chamisso 3, 238; Der Nacht un-h., bange Stunden. 4, 148;
Mir war schon lang' un-h., ja graulich zu Muthe. 242; Nun fängts   [256]
mir an, un-h. zu werden. G[oethe], 6, 330; . . . Empfindet ein u—es
Grauen. Heine, Verm. 1, 51; Un-h. und starr wie ein Steinbild. Reis,
1, 10; Den u—en Nebel, Haarrauch geheißen. Immermann M., 3,
299; Diese blassen Jungen sind un-h. und brauen Gott weiß was
Schlimmes. Laube, Band. 1, 119; Un-h. nennt man Alles, was
im Geheimnis, im Verborgnen . . . bleiben sollte und
hervorgetreten ist. Schelling, 2, 2, 649 etc.—Das Göttliche
zu verhüllen, mit einer gewissen U—keit zu umgeben 658, etc.—
Unüblich als Ggstz. von (**2**), wie es Campe ohne Beleg anführt.

§ Dostoevsky and Parricide

[177] FOUR facets may be distinguished in the rich personality of Dostoevsky: the creative artist, the neurotic, the moralist and the sinner. How is one to find one's way in this bewildering complexity?

The creative artist is the least doubtful: Dostoevsky's place is not far behind Shakespeare. *The Brothers Karamazov* is the most magnificent novel ever written; the episode of the Grand Inquisitor, one of the peaks in the literature of the world, can hardly be valued too highly. Before the problem of the creative artist analysis must, alas, lay down its arms.

The moralist in Dostoevsky is the most readily assailable. If we seek to rank him high as a moralist on the plea that only a man who has gone through the depths of sin can reach the highest summit of morality, we are neglecting a doubt that arises. A moral man is one who reacts to temptation as soon as he feels it in his heart, without yielding to it. A man who alternately sins and then in his remorse erects high moral standards lays himself open to the reproach that he has made things too easy for himself. He has not achieved the essence of morality, renunciation, for the moral conduct of life is a practical human interest. He reminds one of the barbarians of the great migrations, who murdered and did penance for it, till penance became an actual technique for enabling murder to be done. Ivan the Terrible behaved in exactly this way; indeed this compro-

SOURCE: *Standard Ed.*, **21**, 177–96.

234

mise with morality is a characteristic Russian trait. Nor was the
final outcome of Dostoevsky's moral strivings anything very glori-
ous. After the most violent struggles to reconcile the instinctual
demands of the individual with the claims of the community, he
landed in the retrograde position of submission both to temporal
and spiritual authority, of veneration both for the Tsar and for the
God of the Christians, and of a narrow Russian nationalism—a
position which lesser minds have reached with smaller effort. This
is the weak point in that great personality. Dostoevsky threw away
the chance of becoming a teacher and liberator of humanity and
made himself one with their gaolers. The future of human civilization will have little to thank him for. It seems probable that he was
condemned to this failure by his neurosis. The greatness of his   [178]
intelligence and the strength of his love for humanity might have
opened to him another, an apostolic, way of life.

To consider Dostoevsky as a sinner or a criminal rouses violent
opposition, which need not be based upon a philistine assessment
of criminals. The real motive for this opposition soon becomes
apparent. Two traits are essential in a criminal: boundless egoism
and a strong destructive urge. Common to both of these, and a
necessary condition for their expression, is absence of love, lack of
an emotional appreciation of (human) objects. One at once recalls
the contrast to this presented by Dostoevsky—his great need of love
and his enormous capacity for love, which is to be seen in manifestations of exaggerated kindness and caused him to love and to
help where he had a right to hate and to be revengeful, as, for
example, in his relations with his first wife and her lover. That
being so, it must be asked why there is any temptation to reckon
Dostoevsky among the criminals. The answer is that it comes from
his choice of material, which singles out from all others violent,
murderous and egoistic characters, thus pointing to the existence of
similar tendencies within himself, and also from certain facts in his
life, like his passion for gambling and his possible confession to a
sexual assault upon a young girl.[1] The contradiction is resolved by

---

[1] See the discussion of this in Fülöp-Miller and Eckstein (1926). Stefan Zweig
(1920) writes: 'He was not halted by the barriers of bourgeois morality; and no

the realization that Dostoevsky's very strong destructive instinct, which might easily have made him a criminal, was in his actual life directed mainly against his own person (inward instead of outward) and thus found expression as masochism and a sense of guilt. Nevertheless, his personality retained sadistic traits in plenty, which show themselves in his irritability, his love of tormenting and his intolerance even towards people he loved, and which [179] appear also in the way in which, as an author, he treats his readers. Thus in little things he was a sadist towards others, and in bigger things a sadist towards himself, in fact a masochist—that is to say the mildest, kindliest, most helpful person possible.

We have selected three factors from Dostoevsky's complex personality, one quantitative and two qualitative: the extraordinary intensity of his emotional life, his perverse innate instinctual disposition, which inevitably marked him out to be a sado-masochist or a criminal, and his unanalysable artistic gift. This combination might very well exist without neurosis; there are people who are complete masochists without being neurotic. Nevertheless, the balance of forces between his instinctual demands and the inhibitions opposing them (plus the available methods of sublimation) would even so make it necessary to classify Dostoevsky as what is known as an 'instinctual character'. But the position is obscured by the simultaneous presence of neurosis, which, as we have said, was not in the circumstances inevitable, but which comes into being the more readily, the richer the complication which has to be mastered by the ego. For neurosis is after all only a sign that the ego has not succeeded in making a synthesis, that in attempting to do so it has forfeited its unity.

---

one can say exactly how far he transgressed the bounds of law in his own life or how much of the criminal instincts of his heroes was realized in himself.' For the intimate connection between Dostoevsky's characters and his own experiences, see René Fülöp-Miller's remarks in the introductory section of Fülöp-Miller and Eckstein (1925), which are based upon N. Strakhov [1921].—[The topic of a sexual assault on an immature girl appears several times in Dostoevsky's writings—especially in the posthumous *Stavrogin's Confession* and *The Life of a Great Sinner.*]

How then, strictly speaking, does his neurosis show itself? Dostoevsky called himself an epileptic, and was regarded as such by other people, on account of his severe attacks, which were accompanied by loss of consciousness, muscular convulsions and subsequent depression. Now it is highly probable that this so-called epilepsy was only a symptom of his neurosis and must accordingly be classified as hystero-epilepsy—that is, as severe hysteria. We cannot be completely certain on this point for two reasons—firstly, because the anamnestic data on Dostoevsky's alleged epilepsy are defective and untrustworthy, and secondly, because our understanding of pathological states combined with epileptiform attacks is imperfect.

To take the second point first. It is unnecessary here to reproduce the whole pathology of epilepsy, for it would throw no decisive light on the problem. But this may be said. The old *morbus sacer* is still in evidence as an ostensible clinical entity, the uncanny disease with its incalculable, apparently unprovoked convulsive attacks, its changing of the character into irritability and aggressiveness, and its progressive lowering of all the mental faculties. But the outlines [180] of this picture are quite lacking in precision. The attacks, so savage in their onset, accompanied by biting of the tongue and incontinence of urine and working up to the dangerous *status epilepticus* with its risk of severe self-injuries, may, nevertheless, be reduced to brief periods of *absence*, or rapidly passing fits of vertigo or may be replaced by short spaces of time during which the patient does something out of character, as though he were under the control of his unconscious. These attacks, though as a rule determined, in a way we do not understand, by purely physical causes, may nevertheless owe their first appearance to some purely mental cause (a fright, for instance) or may react in other respects to mental excitations. However characteristic intellectual impairment may be in the overwhelming majority of cases, at least *one* case is known to us (that of Helmholtz) in which the affliction did not interfere with the highest intellectual achievement. (Other cases of which the same assertion has been made are either disputable or open to the same doubts as the case of Dostoevsky himself.) People who are victims of epilepsy may give an impression of dullness and arrested

development just as the disease often accompanies the most palpa-
ble idiocy and the grossest cerebral defects, even though not as a
necessary component of the clinical picture. But these attacks, with
all their variations, also occur in other people who display complete
mental development and, if anything, an excessive and as a rule
insufficiently controlled emotional life. It is no wonder in these
circumstances that it has been found impossible to maintain that
'epilepsy' is a single clinical entity. The similarity that we find in the
manifest symptoms seems to call for a functional view of them. It is
as though a mechanism for abnormal instinctual discharge had
been laid down organically, which could be made use of in quite
different circumstances—both in the case of disturbances of cerebral activity due to severe histolytic or toxic affections, and also in
the case of inadequate control over the mental economy and at
times when the activity of the energy operating in the mind reaches
crisis-pitch. Behind this dichotomy we have a glimpse of the
identity of the underlying mechanism of instinctual discharge. Nor
can that mechanism stand remote from the sexual processes, which
are fundamentally of toxic origin: the earliest physicians described
[181]   coition as a minor epilepsy, and thus recognized in the sexual act a
mitigation and adaptation of the epileptic method of discharging
stimuli.[1]

The 'epileptic reaction', as this common element may be called,
is also undoubtedly at the disposal of the neurosis whose essence it
is to get rid by somatic means of amounts of excitation which it
cannot deal with psychically. Thus the epileptic attack becomes a
symptom of hysteria and is adapted and modified by it just as it is
by the normal sexual process of discharge. It is therefore quite right
to distinguish between an organic and an 'affective' epilepsy. The
practical significance of this is that a person who suffers from the
first kind has a disease of the brain, while a person who suffers from
the second kind is a neurotic. In the first case his mental life is
subjected to an alien disturbance from without, in the second case
the disturbance is an expression of his mental life itself.

[1][Cf. Freud's earlier paper on hysterical attacks (1909a), *Standard Ed.*, **9**, 234.]

It is extremely probable that Dostoevsky's epilepsy was of the second kind. This cannot, strictly speaking, be proved. To do so we should have to be in a position to insert the first appearance of the attacks and their subsequent fluctuations into the thread of his mental life; and for that we know too little. The descriptions of the attacks themselves teach us nothing and our information about the relations between them and Dostoevsky's experiences is defective and often contradictory. The most probable assumption is that the attacks went back far into his childhood, that their place was taken to begin with by milder symptoms and that they did not assume an epileptic form until after the shattering experience of his eighteenth year—the murder of his father.[1] It would be very much to the point if it could be established that they ceased completely   [182] during his exile in Siberia, but other accounts contradict this.[2]

The unmistakable connection between the murder of the father in *The Brothers Karamazov* and the fate of Dostoevsky's own father has struck more than one of his biographers, and has led them to refer to 'a certain modern school of psychology'. From the standpoint of psycho-analysis (for that is what is meant), we are tempted

---

[1]See René Fülöp-Miller (1924). [Cf. also the account given by Aimée Dostoevsky (1921) in her life of her father.] Of especial interest is the information that in the novelist's childhood 'something terrible, unforgettable and agonizing' happened, to which the first signs of his illness were to be traced (from an article by Suvorin in the newspaper *Novoe Vremya*, 1881, quoted in the introduction to Fülöp-Miller and Eckstein, 1925, xlv). See also Orest Miller (1921, 140): 'There is, however, another special piece of evidence about Fyodor Mikhailovich's illness, which relates to his earliest youth and brings the illness into connection with a tragic event in the family life of his parents. But, although this piece of evidence was given to me orally by one who was a close friend of Fyodor Mikhailovich, I cannot bring myself to reproduce it fully and precisely since I have had no confirmation of this rumour from any other quarter.' Biographers and scientific research workers cannot feel grateful for this discretion.

[2]Most of the accounts, including Dostoevsky's own, assert on the contrary that the illness only assumed its final, epileptic character during the Siberian exile. Unfortunately there is reason to distrust the autobiographical statements of neurotics. Experience shows that their memories introduce falsifications which are designed to interrupt disagreeable causal connections. Nevertheless, it appears certain that Dostoevsky's detention in the Siberian prison markedly altered his pathological condition. Cf. Fülöp-Miller (1924, 1186).

to see in that event the severest trauma and to regard Dostoevsky's reaction to it as the turning-point of his neurosis. But if I undertake to substantiate this view psycho-analytically, I shall have to risk the danger of being unintelligible to all those readers who are unfamiliar with the language and theories of psycho-analysis.

We have one certain starting-point. We know the meaning of the first attacks from which Dostoevsky suffered in his early years, long before the incidence of the 'epilepsy'. These attacks had the significance of death: they were heralded by a fear of death and consisted of lethargic, somnolent states. The illness first came over him while he was still a boy, in the form of a sudden, groundless melancholy, a feeling, as he later told his friend Soloviev, as though he were going to die on the spot. And there in fact followed a state exactly similar to real death. His brother Andrey tells us that even when he was quite young Fyodor used to leave little notes about before he went to sleep, saying that he was afraid he might fall into this death-like sleep during the night and therefore begged that his burial should be postponed for five days. (Fülöp-Miller and Eckstein, 1925, lx.)

[183]   We know the meaning and intention of such deathlike attacks.[1] They signify an identification with a dead person, either with someone who is really dead or with someone who is still alive and whom the subject wishes dead. The latter case is the more significant. The attack then has the value of a punishment. One has wished another person dead, and now one *is* this other person and is dead oneself. At this point psycho-analytical theory brings in the assertion that for a boy this other person is usually his father and that the attack (which is termed hysterical) is thus a self-punishment for a death-wish against a hated father.

Parricide, according to a well-known view, is the principal and primal crime of humanity as well as of the individual. (See my *Totem and Taboo*, 1912–13.) It is in any case the main source of the sense of guilt, though we do not know if it is the only one: researches have not yet been able to establish with certainty the

[1][The explanation was already given by Freud in a letter to Fliess of February 8, 1897 (Freud, 1950*a*, Letter 58).]

mental origin of guilt and the need for expiation. But it is not necessary for it to be the only one. The psychological situation is complicated and requires elucidation. The relation of a boy to his father is, as we say, an 'ambivalent' one. In addition to the hate which seeks to get rid of the father as a rival, a measure of tenderness for him is also habitually present. The two attitudes of mind combine to produce identification with the father; the boy wants to be in his father's place because he admires him and wants to be like him, and also because he wants to put him out of the way. This whole development now comes up against a powerful obstacle. At a certain moment the child comes to understand that an attempt to remove his father as a rival would be punished by him with castration. So from fear of castration—that is, in the interests of preserving his masculinity—he gives up his wish to possess his mother and get rid of his father. In so far as this wish remains in the unconscious it forms the basis of the sense of guilt. We believe that what we have here been describing are normal processes, the normal fate of the so-called 'Oedipus complex'; nevertheless it requires an important amplification.

A further complication arises when the constitutional factor we call bisexuality is comparatively strongly developed in a child. For then, under the threat to the boy's masculinity by castration, his inclination becomes strengthened to diverge in the direction of femininity, to put himself instead in his mother's place and take over her role as object of his father's love. But the fear of castration makes *this* solution impossible as well. The boy understands that he must also submit to castration if he wants to be loved by his father as a woman. Thus both impulses, hatred of the father and being in love with the father, undergo repression. There is a certain psychological distinction in the fact that the hatred of the father is given up on account of fear of an *external* danger (castration), while the being in love with the father is treated as an *internal* instinctual danger, though fundamentally it goes back to the same external danger. [184]

What makes hatred of the father unacceptable is *fear* of the father; castration is terrible, whether as a punishment or as the price of love. Of the two factors which repress hatred of the father, the first, the direct fear of punishment and castration, may be called the normal one; its pathogenic intensification seems to come only with the addition of the second factor, the fear of the feminine attitude. Thus a strong innate bisexual disposition becomes one of the preconditions or reinforcements of neurosis. Such a disposition must certainly be assumed in Dostoevsky, and it shows itself in a viable form (as latent homosexuality) in the important part played by male friendships in his life, in his strangely tender attitude towards rivals in love and in his remarkable understanding of situations which are explicable only by repressed homosexuality, as many examples from his novels show.

I am sorry, though I cannot alter the facts, if this exposition of the attitudes of hatred and love towards the father and their transformations under the influence of the threat of castration seems to readers unfamiliar with psycho-analysis unsavoury and incredible. I should myself expect that it is precisely the castration complex that would be bound to arouse the most general repudiation. But I can only insist that psycho-analytic experience has put these matters in particular beyond the reach of doubt and has taught us to recognize in them the key to every neurosis. This key, then, we must apply to our author's so-called epilepsy. So alien to our consciousness are the things by which our unconscious mental life is governed!

But what has been said so far does not exhaust the consequences of the repression of the hatred of the father in the Oedipus complex. There is something fresh to be added: namely that in spite of everything the identification with the father finally makes a permanent place for itself in the ego. It is received into the ego, but [185] establishes itself there as a separate agency in contrast to the rest of the content of the ego. We then give it the name of super-ego and ascribe to it, the inheritor of the parental influence, the most important functions. If the father was hard, violent and cruel, the super-ego takes over those attributes from him and, in the relations between the ego and it, the passivity which was supposed to have been repressed is reestablished. The super-ego has become sadistic, and the ego becomes masochistic—that is to say, at bottom passive in a feminine way. A great need for punishment develops in the ego, which in part offers itself as a victim to Fate, and in part finds satisfaction in ill-treatment by the super-ego (that is, in the sense of guilt). For every punishment is ultimately castration and, as such, a fulfilment of the old passive attitude towards the father. Even Fate is, in the last resort, only a later projection of the father.

The normal processes in the formation of conscience must be similar to the abnormal ones described here. We have not yet succeeded in fixing the boundary line between them. It will be observed that here the largest share in the outcome is ascribed to the passive component of repressed femininity. In addition, it must be of importance as an accidental factor whether the father, who is feared in any case, is also especially violent in reality. This was true in Dostoevsky's case, and we can trace back the fact of his extraordinary sense of guilt and of his masochistic conduct of life to a specially strong feminine component. Thus the formula for Dostoevsky is as follows: a person with a specially strong innate bisexual disposition, who can defend himself with special intensity against dependence on a specially severe father. This characteristic of bisexuality comes as an addition to the components of his nature that we have already recognized. His early symptoms of death-like attacks can thus be understood as a father-identification on the part of his ego, which is permitted by his super-ego as a punishment. 'You wanted to kill your father in order to be your father yourself. Now you *are* your father, but a dead father'—the regular mechanism of hysterical symptoms. And further: 'Now your father is killing *you*.' For the ego the death symptom is a satisfaction in phantasy of the masculine wish and at the same time a masochistic satisfaction; for the super-ego it is a punitive satisfaction—that is, a sadistic satisfaction. Both of them, the ego and the super-ego, carry on the role of the father.

To sum up, the relation between the subject and his father-object, while retaining its content, has been transformed into a [186] relation between the ego and the super-ego—a new setting on a fresh stage. Infantile reactions from the Oedipus complex such as these may disappear if reality gives them no further nourishment. But the father's character remained the same, or rather, it deteriorated with the years, and thus Dostoevsky's hatred for his father and his death-wish against that wicked father were maintained. Now it is a dangerous thing if reality fulfils such repressed wishes. The phantasy has become reality and all defensive measures are thereupon reinforced. Dostoevsky's attacks now assumed an epileptic character; they still undoubtedly signified an identification with his father as a punishment, but they had become terrible, like his father's frightful death itself. What further content they had absorbed, particularly what sexual content, escapes conjecture.

One thing is remarkable: in the aura of the epileptic attack, one moment of supreme bliss is experienced. This may very well be a record of the triumph and sense of liberation felt on hearing the news of the death, to be followed immediately by an all the more cruel punishment. We have divined just such a sequence of triumph and mourning, of festive joy and mourning, in the brothers of the primal horde who murdered their father, and we find it repeated in the ceremony of the totem meal.[1] If it proved to be the case that Dostoevsky was free from his attacks in Siberia, that would merely substantiate the view that they were his punishment. He did not need them any longer when he was being punished in another way. But that cannot be proved. Rather does this necessity for punishment on the part of Dostoevsky's mental economy explain the fact that he passed unbroken through these years of misery and humiliation. Dostoevsky's condemnation as a political prisoner was unjust and he must have known it, but he accepted the undeserved punishment at the hands of the Little Father, the Tsar, as a substitute for the punishment he deserved for his sin against his real father. Instead of punishing himself, he got himself punished by his father's deputy. Here we have a glimpse of the psychological justification of the punishments inflicted by society.

[1]See *Totem and Taboo* [(1912–13), Section 5 of Essay IV, *Standard Ed.*, **13**, 140].

It is a fact that large groups of criminals want to be punished. Their super-ego demands it and so saves itself the necessity for inflicting the punishment itself.[1] [187]

Everyone who is familiar with the complicated transformation of meaning undergone by hysterical symptoms will understand that no attempt can be made here to follow out the meaning of Dostoevsky's attacks beyond this beginning.[2] It is enough that we may assume that their original meaning remained unchanged behind all later accretions. We can safely say that Dostoevsky never got free from the feelings of guilt arising from his intention of murdering his father. They also determined his attitude in the two other spheres in which the father-relation is the decisive factor, his attitude towards the authority of the State and towards belief in God. In the first of these he ended up with complete submission to his Little Father, the Tsar, who had once performed with him in *reality* the comedy of killing which his attacks had so often represented in *play*. Here penitence gained the upper hand. In the religious sphere he retained more freedom: according to apparently trustworthy reports he wavered, up to the last moment of his life, between faith and atheism. His great intellect made it impossible for him to overlook any of the intellectual difficulties to which faith leads. By an individual recapitulation of a development in world-history he hoped to find a way out and a liberation from guilt in the Christ ideal, and even to make use of his sufferings as a claim to be playing a Christ-like role. If on the whole he did not achieve freedom and became a reactionary, that was because the filial guilt,

[1][Cf. 'Criminals from a Sense of Guilt', the third essay in Freud's 'Some Character-Types Met with in Psycho-Analytic Work' (1916*d*), *Standard Ed.*, **14**, 332.]

[2]The best account of the meaning and content of his attacks was given by Dostoevsky himself, when he told his friend Strakhov that his irritability and depression after an epileptic attack were due to the fact that he seemed to himself a criminal and could not get rid of the feeling that he had a burden of unknown guilt upon him, that he had committed some great misdeed, which oppressed him. (Fülöp-Miller, 1924, 1188.) In self-accusations like these psycho-analysis sees signs of a recognition of 'psychical reality', and it endeavours to make the unknown guilt known to consciousness.

which is present in human beings generally and on which religious
feeling is built, had in him attained a super-individual intensity
and remained insurmountable even to his great intelligence. In
writing this we are laying ourselves open to the charge of having
abandoned the impartiality of analysis and of subjecting Dostoevsky to judgements that can only be justified from the partisan
standpoint of a particular *Weltanschauung.* A conservative would
take the side of the Grand Inquisitor and would judge Dostoevsky
differently. The objection is just; and one can only say in extenua-
tion that Dostoevsky's decision has every appearance of having
been determined by an intellectual inhibition due to his neurosis.

It can scarcely be owing to chance that three of the masterpieces
of the literature of all time—the *Oedipus Rex* of Sophocles, Shakespeare's *Hamlet* and Dostoevsky's *The Brothers Karamazov*—should
all deal with the same subject, parricide. In all three, moreover, the
motive for the deed, sexual rivalry for a woman, is laid bare.

The most straightforward is certainly the representation in the
drama derived from the Greek legend. In this it is still the hero
himself who commits the crime. But poetic treatment is impossible
without softening and disguise. The naked admission of an intention to commit parricide, as we arrive at it in analysis, seems
intolerable without analytic preparation. The Greek drama, while
retaining the crime, introduces the indispensable toning-down in a
masterly fashion by projecting the hero's unconscious motive into
reality in the form of a compulsion by a destiny which is alien to
him. The hero commits the deed unintentionally and apparently
uninfluenced by the woman; this latter element is however taken
into account in the circumstances that the hero can only obtain
possession of the queen mother after he has repeated his deed upon
the monster who symbolizes the father. After his guilt has been
revealed and made conscious, the hero makes no attempt to excul-
pate himself by appealing to the artificial expedient of the compulsion of destiny. His crime is acknowledged and punished as though
it were a full and conscious one—which is bound to appear unjust
to our reason, but which psychologically is perfectly correct.

In the English play the presentation is more indirect; the hero does not commit the crime himself; it is carried out by someone else, for whom it is not parricide. The forbidden motive of sexual rivalry for the woman does not need, therefore, to be disguised. Moreover, we see the hero's Oedipus complex, as it were, in a reflected light, by learning the effect upon him of the other's crime. He ought to avenge the crime, but finds himself, strangely enough, incapable of doing so. We know that it is his sense of guilt that is paralysing him; but, in a manner entirely in keeping with neurotic processes, the sense of guilt is displaced on to the perception of his inadequacy for fulfilling his task. There are signs that the hero feels this guilt as a super-individual one. He despises others no less than himself: 'Use every man after his desert, and who should 'scape whipping?'

The Russian novel goes a step further in the same direction. There also the murder is committed by someone else. This other person, however, stands to the murdered man in the same filial relation as the hero, Dmitri; in this other person's case the motive of sexual rivalry is openly admitted; he is a brother of the hero's, and it is a remarkable fact that Dostoevsky has attributed to him his own illness, the alleged epilepsy, as though he were seeking to confess that the epileptic, the neurotic, in himself was a parricide. Then, again, in the speech for the defence at the trial, there is the famous mockery of psychology—it is a 'knife that cuts both ways':[1] a splendid piece of disguise, for we have only to reverse it in order to discover the deepest meaning of Dostoevsky's view of things. It is not psychology that deserves the mockery, but the procedure of judicial enquiry. It is a matter of indifference who actually committed the crime; psychology is only concerned to know who desired it emotionally and who welcomed it when it was done.[2] And for that reason all of the brothers, except the contrasted figure

[1] [In the German (and in the original Russian) the simile is 'a stick with two ends'. The 'knife that cuts both ways' is derived from Constance Garnett's English translation. The phrase occurs in Book XII, Chapter X, of the novel.]

[2] [A practical application of this to an actual criminal case is to be found in Freud's comments on the Halsmann Case (1931*d*), p. 251 below, where *The Brothers Karamazov* is again discussed.]

of Alyosha, are equally guilty—the impulsive sensualist, the sceptical cynic and the epileptic criminal. In *The Brothers Karamazov* there is one particularly revealing scene. In the course of his talk with Dmitri, Father Zossima recognizes that Dmitri is prepared to commit parricide, and he bows down at his feet. It is impossible that this can be meant as an expression of admiration; it must mean that the holy man is rejecting the temptation to despise or detest [190]   the murderer and for that reason humbles himself before him. Dostoevsky's sympathy for the criminal is, in fact, boundless; it goes far beyond the pity which the unhappy wretch has a right to, and reminds us of the 'holy awe' with which epileptics and lunatics were regarded in the past. A criminal is to him almost a Redeemer, who has taken on himself the guilt which must else have been borne by others. There is no longer any need for one to murder, since *he* has already murdered; and one must be grateful to him, for, except for him, one would have been obliged oneself to murder. That is not kindly pity alone, it is identification on the basis of similar murderous impulses—in fact, a slightly displaced narcissism. (In saying this, we are not disputing the ethical value of this kindliness.) This may perhaps be quite generally the mechanism of kindly sympathy with other people, a mechanism which one can discern with especial ease in this extreme case of a guilt-ridden novelist. There is no doubt that this sympathy by identification was a decisive factor in determining Dostoevsky's choice of material. He dealt first with the common criminal (whose motives are egotistical) and the political and religious criminal; and not until the end of his life did he come back to the primal criminal, the parricide, and use him, in a work of art, for making his confession.

The publication of Dostoevsky's posthumous papers and of his wife's diaries has thrown a glaring light on one episode in his life, namely the period in Germany when he was obsessed with a mania for gambling (cf. Fülöp-Miller and Eckstein, 1925), which no one could regard as anything but an unmistakable fit of pathological passion. There was no lack of rationalizations for this remarkable and unworthy behaviour. As often happens with neurotics, Dostoevsky's sense of guilt had taken a tangible shape as a burden of debt, and he was able to take refuge behind the pretext that he was trying by his winnings at the tables to make it possible for him to return to Russia without being arrested by his creditors. But this was no more than a pretext and Dostoevsky was acute enough to recognize the fact and honest enough to admit it. He knew that the chief thing was gambling for its own sake—*le jeu pour le jeu*.[1] All the details of his impulsively irrational conduct show this and something more besides. He never rested until he had lost everything. For him gambling was a method of self-punishment as well. Time after time he gave his young wife his promise or his word of honour not to play any more or not to play any more on that particular day; and, as she says, he almost always broke it. When his losses had reduced himself and her to the direst need, he derived a second pathological satisfaction from that. He could then scold and humiliate himself before her, invite her to despise him and to feel sorry that she had married such an old sinner; and when he had thus unburdened his conscience, the whole business would begin again next day. His young wife accustomed herself to this cycle, for she had noticed that the one thing which offered any real hope of salvation—his literary production—never went better than when they had lost everything and pawned their last possessions. Naturally she did not understand the connection. When his sense of guilt was satisfied by the punishments he had inflicted on himself, the inhibition upon his work became less severe and he allowed himself to take a few steps along the road to success.[2]

What part of a gambler's long-buried childhood is it that forces its way to repetition in his obsession for play? The answer may be divined without difficulty from a story by one of our younger

[191]

[1]'The main thing is the play itself,' he writes in one of his letters. 'I swear that greed for money has nothing to do with it, although Heaven knows I am sorely in need of money.'

[2]'He always remained at the gaming tables till he had lost everything and was totally ruined. It was only when the damage was quite complete that the demon at last retired from his soul and made way for the creative genius.' (Fülöp-Miller and Eckstein, 1925, lxxxvi.)

writers. Stefan Zweig, who has incidentally devoted a study to Dostoevsky himself (1920), has included in his collection of three stories *Die Verwirrung der Gefühle* [*Confusion of Feelings*] (1927) one which he calls 'Vierundzwanzig Stunden aus dem Leben einer Frau' ['Four-and-Twenty Hours in a Woman's Life']. This little masterpiece ostensibly sets out only to show what an irresponsible creature woman is, and to what excesses, surprising even to herself, an unexpected experience may drive her. But the story tells far more than this. If it is subjected to an analytical interpretation, it will be found to represent (without any apologetic intent) some-thing quite different, something universally human, or rather something masculine. And such an interpretation is so extremely [192] obvious that it cannot be resisted. It is characteristic of the nature of artistic creation that the author, who is a personal friend of mine, was able to assure me, when I asked him, that the interpretation which I put to him had been completely strange to his knowledge and intention, although some of the details woven into the narra-tive seemed expressly designed to give a clue to the hidden secret.

In this story, an elderly lady of distinction tells the author about an experience she has had more than twenty years earlier. She has been left a widow when still young and is the mother of two sons, who no longer need her. In her forty-second year, expecting noth-ing further of life, she happens, on one of her aimless journeyings, to visit the Rooms at Monte Carlo. There, among all the remark-able impressions which the place produces, she is soon fascinated by the sight of a pair of hands which seem to betray all the feelings of the unlucky gambler with terrifying sincerity and intensity. These hands belong to a handsome young man—the author, as though unintentionally, makes him of the same age as the narrator's elder son—who, after losing everything, leaves the Rooms in the depth of despair, with the evident intention of ending his hopeless life in the Casino gardens. An inexplicable feeling of sympathy compels her to follow him and make every effort to save him. He takes her for one of the importunate women so common there and tries to shake her off; but she stays with him and finds herself obliged, in the most natural way possible, to join him in his apartment at the hotel, and finally to share his bed. After this improvised night of love, she exacts a most solemn vow from the young man, who has now apparently calmed down, that he will never play again, provides him with money for his journey home and promises to meet him at the station before the departure of his train. Now, however, she begins to feel a great tenderness for him, is ready to sacrifice all she has in order to keep him and makes up her mind to go with him instead of saying goodbye. Various mischances delay her, so that she misses the train. In her longing for the lost one she returns once more to the Rooms and there, to her horror, sees once more the hands which had first excited her sympathy: the faithless youth had gone back to his play. She reminds him of his promise, but, obsessed by his passion, he calls her a spoil-sport, tells her to go, and flings back the money with which she has tried to rescue him. She hurries away in deep [193] mortification and learns later that she has not succeeded in saving him from suicide.

The brilliantly told, faultlessly motivated story is of course complete in itself and is certain to make a deep effect upon the reader. But analysis shows us that its invention is based fundamentally upon a wishful phantasy belonging to the period of puberty, which a number of people actually remember consciously. The phantasy embodies a boy's wish that his mother should herself initiate him into sexual life in order to save him from the dreaded injuries caused by masturbation. (The numerous creative works that deal with the theme of redemption have the same origin.) The 'vice' of masturbation is replaced by the addiction to gambling;[1] and the emphasis laid upon the passionate activity of the hands betrays this derivation. Indeed, the passion for play is an equivalent of the old compulsion to masturbate; 'playing' is the actual word used in the nursery to describe the activity of the hands upon the genitals. The irresistible nature of the temptation, the solemn resolutions, which are nevertheless invariably broken, never to do it again, the stupefy-

[1] [In a letter to Fliess of December 22, 1897, Freud suggested that masturbation is the 'primal addiction', for which all later addictions are substitutes (Freud, 1950a, Letter 79).]

ing pleasure and the bad conscience which tells the subject that he is ruining himself (committing suicide)—all these elements remain unaltered in the process of substitution. It is true that Zweig's story is told by the mother, not by the son. It must flatter the son to think: 'if my mother only knew what dangers masturbation involves me in, she would certainly save me from them by allowing me to lavish all my tenderness on her own body'. The equation of the mother with a prostitute, which is made by the young man in the story, is linked up with the same phantasy. It brings the unattainable woman within easy reach. The bad conscience which accompanies the phantasy brings about the unhappy ending of the story. It is also interesting to notice how the *façade* given to the story by its author seeks to disguise its analytic meaning. For it is extremely questionable whether the erotic life of women is dominated by sudden and mysterious impulses. On the contrary, analysis reveals an adequate motivation for the surprising behaviour of this woman who had hitherto turned away from love. Faithful to [194] the memory of her dead husband, she had armed herself against all similar attractions; but—and here the son's phantasy is right—she did not, as a mother, escape her quite unconscious transference of love on to her son, and Fate was able to catch her at this undefended spot.

If the addiction to gambling, with the unsuccessful struggles to break the habit and the opportunities it affords for self-punishment, is a repetition of the compulsion to masturbate, we shall not be surprised to find that it occupied such a large space in Dostoevsky's life. After all, we find no cases of severe neurosis in which the auto-erotic satisfaction of early childhood and of puberty has not played a part; and the relation between efforts to suppress it and fear of the father are too well known to need more than a mention.[1]

[1]Most of the views which are here expressed are also contained in an excellent book by Jolan Neufeld (1923).

Appendix
A Letter from Freud to Theodor Reik

[A few months after the publication of Freud's essay on Dostoevsky, a discussion of it by Theodor Reik appeared in *Imago* (in the second issue for 1929, **15**, 232–42). Though Reik's comments were on the whole appreciative, he argued at considerable length that Freud's judgement on Dostoevsky's morals was unjustifiably severe and disagreed too with what Freud wrote about morality in the third paragraph of the essay. He also, incidentally, criticized the *form* of the essay, with its apparently disconnected tail-end. After reading these criticisms[1] Freud sent Reik a letter in reply; and when, not long afterwards, Reik reprinted his article in a book of collected papers (1930), Freud agreed that his letter should also be included. An English translation of the criticism and of the reply to it were published later in Reik's *From Thirty Years with Freud* (New York, 1940 and London, 1942). It is with Dr. Theodor Reik's kind permission that we publish Freud's letter to him in a revised translation.]

[1951]

April 14, 1929

. . . I have read your critical review of my Dostoevsky study with great pleasure. All your objections deserve consideration and must be recognized as in a sense apt. I can bring forward a little in my defence. But of course it will not be a question of who is right or who is wrong.

I think you are applying too high a standard to this triviality. It was written as a favour to someone[2] and written reluctantly. I always write reluctantly nowadays. No doubt you noticed this about it. This is not meant, of course, to excuse hasty or false judgements, but merely the careless architecture of the essay as a whole. I cannot dispute the unharmonious effect produced by the addition of the Zweig analysis; but deeper examination will per-

---

[1][See footnote 1 on p. 255 below.]
[2][No doubt Eitingon, who had persistently pressed Freud to finish the essay (Jones, 1957, 152).]

haps show some justification for it. If I had not been hampered by considerations of the place where my essay was to appear, I should certainly have written: 'We may expect that in the history of a neurosis accompanied by such a severe sense of guilt a special part will be played by the struggle against masturbation. This expectation is completely fulfilled by Dostoevsky's pathological addiction to gambling. For, as we can see from a short story of Zweig's . . . etc.' That is to say, the amount of space given to the short story corresponds not to the relation: Zweig—Dostoevsky, but to the other one: masturbation—neurosis. All the same, the outcome was clumsy.

I hold firmly to a scientifically objective social assessment of ethics, and for that reason I should not wish to deny the excellent Philistine a certificate of good ethical conduct, even though it has cost him little self-discipline.[1] But alongside of this I grant the validity of the subjective psychological view of ethics which you support. Though I agree with your judgement of the world and mankind as they are to-day, I cannot, as you know, regard your pessimistic dismissal of a better future as justified.

As you suggest, I included Dostoevsky the psychologist under the creative artist. Another objection I might have raised against him was that his insight was so much restricted to abnormal mental life. Consider his astonishing helplessness in face of the phenomena of love. All he really knew were crude, instinctual desire, masochistic subjection and loving out of pity. You are right, too, in suspecting that, in spite of all my admiration for Dostoevsky's intensity and pre-eminence, I do not really like him. That is because my patience with pathological natures is exhausted in analysis. In art and life I am intolerant of them. Those are character traits personal to me and not binding on others.

---

[1][Reik had written: 'Renunciation was once the criterion of morality; to-day it is only one of many. If it were the only one, then the excellent citizen and Philistine, who, with his dull sensibility, submits to the authorities and for whom renunciation is made much easier by his lack of imagination, would be far superior to Dostoevsky in morality.']

Where are you going to publish your essay?[1] I rate it very highly. It is only scientific research that must be without presumptions. In every other kind of thinking the choice of a point of view cannot be avoided; and there are, of course, several of these . . .

[1][This seems to show that Reik had shown Freud his criticism before its publication in *Imago*, though it is possible that what Freud had in mind was the question of the reprint.]

§ The Goethe Prize

Letter to Dr. Alfons Paquet

Grundlsee, 3.8.1930

My dear Dr. Paquet,

I have not been spoilt by public marks of honour and I have so adapted myself to this state of things that I have been able to do without them. I should not like to deny, however, that the award of the Goethe Prize of the City of Frankfurt has given me great pleasure. There is something about it that especially fires the imagination and one of its stipulations dispels the feeling of humiliation which in other cases is a concomitant of such distinctions.

I must particularly thank you for your letter; it moved and astonished me. Apart from your sympathetic penetration into the nature of my work, I have never before found the secret, personal intentions behind it recognized with such clarity as by you, and I should very much like to ask you how you come by such knowledge.

I am sorry to learn from your letter to my daughter that I am not to see you in the near future, and postponement is always a chancy affair at my time of life. Of course I shall be most ready to receive the gentleman (Dr. Michel) whose visit you announce.

Unfortunately I shall not be able to attend the ceremony in

SOURCE: *Standard Ed.*, **21**, 207–14.

Frankfurt; I am too frail for such an undertaking. The company there will lose nothing by that: my daughter Anna is certainly pleasanter to look at and to listen to than I am. We propose that she shall read out a few sentences of mine which deal with Goethe's connections with psycho-analysis and defend the analysts themselves against the reproach of having offended against the respect due to the great man by the analytic attempts they have made on him. I hope it will be acceptable if I thus adapt the theme that has been proposed to me—my 'inner relations as a man and a scientist to Goethe'—or else that you will be kind enough to let me know.

Yours very sincerely,

Freud

Address Delivered in the Goethe House at Frankfurt

MY life's work has been directed to a single aim. I have observed [208] the more subtle disturbances of mental function in healthy and sick people and have sought to infer—or, if you prefer it, to guess—from signs of this kind how the apparatus which serves these functions is constructed and what concurrent and mutually opposing forces are at work in it. What we—I, my friends and collaborators—have managed to learn in following this path has seemed to us of importance for the construction of a mental science which makes it possible to understand both normal and pathological processes as parts of the same natural course of events.

I was recalled from such narrow considerations by the astonishing honour which you do me. By evoking the figure of the great universal personality who was born in this house and who spent his childhood in these rooms, your distinction prompts one as it were to justify oneself before him and raises the question of how *he* would have reacted if his glance, attentive to every innovation in science, had fallen on psycho-analysis.

Goethe can be compared in versatility to Leonardo da Vinci, the Renaissance master, who like him was both artist and scientific investigator. But human images can never be repeated, and profound differences between the two great men are not lacking. In

Leonardo's nature the scientist did not harmonize with the artist, he interfered with him and perhaps in the end stifled him. In Goethe's life both personalities found room side by side: at different times each allowed the other to predominate. In Leonardo it is plausible to associate his disturbance with that inhibition in his development which withdrew everything erotic, and hence psychology too, from his sphere of interest. In this respect Goethe's character was able to develop more freely.

I think that Goethe would not have rejected psycho-analysis in an unfriendly spirit, as so many of our contemporaries have done. He himself approached it at a number of points, recognized much through his own insight that we have since been able to confirm, [209] and some views, which have brought criticism and mockery down upon us, were expounded by him as self-evident. Thus he was familiar with the incomparable strength of the first affective ties of human creatures. He celebrated them in the Dedication to his *Faust* poem, in words which we could repeat for each of our analyses:

> Ihr naht euch wieder, schwankende Gestalten,
> Die früh sich einst dem trüben Blick gezeigt,
> Versuch' ich wohl, euch diesmal festzuhalten?
>
> . . . .
>
> Gleich einer alten, halbverklungenen Sage
> Kommt erste Lieb' und Freundschaft mit herauf.[1]

He explained to himself the strongest impulse of love that he experienced as a mature man by apostrophizing his beloved: 'Ach, du warst in abgelebten Zeiten meine Schwester oder meine Frau.'[2]

[1] [Again ye come, ye hovering forms! I find ye,
As early to my clouded sight ye shone!
Shall I attempt, this once, to seize and bind ye?

. . . .

And, like an old and half-extinct tradition,
First love returns, with friendship in his train.
From the opening lines of the Dedication to *Faust*, in Bayard Taylor's translation.]

[2] ['Ah, you were, in a past life, my sister or my wife.' From a poem to Charlotte von Stein, 'Warum gabst du uns die tiefen Blicke'.]

Thus he does not deny that these perennial first inclinations take figures from one's own family circle as their object.

Goethe paraphrases the content of dream-life in the evocative words:

> Was von Menschen nicht gewusst
> Oder nicht bedacht,
> Durch das Labyrinth der Brust
> Wandelt in der Nacht.[1]

Behind this magic we recognize the ancient, venerable and incontestably correct pronouncement of Aristotle—that dreaming is the continuation of our mental activity into the state of sleep—combined with the recognition of the unconscious which psychoanalysis first added to it. Only the riddle of dream-distortion finds no solution here.

In what is perhaps his most sublime poetical creation, *Iphigenie,* [210] Goethe shows us a striking instance of expiation, of the freeing of a suffering mind from the burden of guilt, and he makes this catharsis come about through a passionate outburst of feeling under the beneficent influence of loving sympathy. Indeed, he himself repeatedly made attempts at giving psychological help—as for example to the unfortunate man who is named as Kraft in the Letters, and to Professor Plessing, of whom he tells in the *Campagne in Frankreich* [*Campaign in France*]; and the procedure which he applied goes beyond the method of the Catholic Confessional and approximates in some remarkable details to the technique of our psycho-analysis. There is an example of psychotherapeutic influence which is described by Goethe as a jest, but which I should like to quote in full since it may not be well known and yet is very characteristic. It is from a letter to Frau von Stein (No. 1444, of September 5, 1785):

> Yesterday evening I performed a psychological feat. Frau Herder was still in a state of tension of the most hypochondriacal kind over all

[1]['That which, not known or not heeded by men, wanders in the night through the labyrinth of the heart.' From the final version of the poem 'An den Mond', which begins: 'Füllest wieder Busch und Tal'.]

the unpleasant things that had happened to her at Carlsbad. Particularly through the woman who was her companion in the house. I made her tell and confess everything to me, other people's misdeeds and her own faults with their most minute circumstances and consequences, and at the end I absolved her and made it clear to her, jestingly, in this formula, that these things were now done with and cast into the depths of the sea. She herself made fun of it all and is really cured.

Goethe always rated Eros high, never tried to belittle its power, followed its primitive and even wanton expressions with no less attentiveness than its highly sublimated ones and has, as it seems to me, expounded its essential unity throughout all its manifestations no less decisively than Plato did in the remote past. Indeed, it is perhaps more than a chance coincidence when in *Die Wahlverwandtschaften* [*The Elective Affinities*] he applies to love an idea taken from the sphere of chemistry—a connection to which the name of psycho-analysis itself bears witness.

I am prepared for the reproach that we analysts have forfeited the right to place ourselves under the patronage of Goethe because we [211] have offended against the respect due to him by trying to apply analysis to him himself: we have degraded the great man to the position of an object of analytic investigation. But I would dispute at once that any degradation is intended or implied by this.

We all, who revere Goethe, put up, without too much protest, with the efforts of his biographers, who try to recreate his life from existing accounts and indications. But what can these biographies achieve for us? Even the best and fullest of them could not answer the two questions which alone seem worth knowing about. It would not throw any light on the riddle of the miraculous gift that makes an artist, and it could not help us to comprehend any better the value and the effect of his works. And yet there is no doubt that such a biography does satisfy a powerful need in us. We feel this very distinctly if the legacy of history unkindly refuses the satisfaction of this need—for example in the case of Shakespeare. It is undeniably painful to all of us that even now we do not know who was the author of the Comedies, Tragedies and Sonnets of Shakespeare; whether it was in fact the untutored son of the provincial citizen of Stratford, who attained a modest position as an actor in London, or whether it was, rather, the nobly-born and highly cultivated, passionately wayward, to some extent *déclassé* aristocrat, Edward de Vere, Seventeenth Earl of Oxford, hereditary Lord Great Chamberlain of England.[1] But how can we justify a need of this kind to obtain knowledge of the circumstances of a man's life when his works have become so full of importance to us? People generally say that it is our desire to bring ourselves nearer to such a man in a human way as well. Let us grant this; it is, then, the need to acquire affective relations with such men, to add them to the fathers, teachers, exemplars whom we have known or whose influence we have already experienced, in the expectation that their personalities will be just as fine and admirable as those works of art of theirs which we possess.

All the same, we may admit that there is still another motive-force at work. The biographer's justification also contains a confession. It is true that the biographer does not want to depose his [212] hero, but he does want to bring him nearer to us. That means, however, reducing the distance that separates him from us: it still tends in effect towards degradation. And it is unavoidable that if we learn more about a great man's life we shall also hear of occasions on which he has in fact done no better than we, has in fact come near to us as a human being. Nevertheless, I think we may declare the efforts of biography to be legitimate. Our attitude to fathers and teachers is, after all, an ambivalent one since our reverence for them regularly conceals a component of hostile rebellion. That is a psychological fatality; it cannot be altered without forcible suppression of the truth and is bound to extend to our relations with the great men whose life histories we wish to investigate.[2]

[1][This was Freud's first published expression of his views on the authorship of Shakespeare's works. He returned to the question in a footnote added in 1935 to Chapter VI of his *Autobiographical Study* (1925*d*), *Standard Ed.*, **20**, 63–4, and again at the end of Part II of his posthumous *Outline* (1940*a* [1938]).]

[2][Freud had made some remarks on the relation of psycho-analysis to biography in his essay on Leonardo (1910*c*), *Standard Ed.*, **11**, 134–5. He had also discussed the question at a meeting of the Vienna Psycho-Analytical Society on December 11, 1907. (Cf. Jones, 1955, 383.)]

When psycho-analysis puts itself at the service of biography, it naturally has the right to be treated no more harshly than the latter itself. Psycho-analysis can supply some information which cannot be arrived at by other means, and can thus demonstrate new connecting threads in the 'weaver's masterpiece'[1] spread between the instinctual endowments, the experiences and the works of an artist. Since it is one of the principal functions of our thinking to master the material of the external world psychically, it seems to me that thanks are due to psycho-analysis if, when it is applied to a great man, it contributes to the understanding of his great achievement. But, I admit, in the case of Goethe we have not yet succeeded very far. This is because Goethe was not only, as a poet, a great self-revealer, but also, in spite of the abundance of autobiographical records, a careful concealer. We cannot help thinking here of the words of Mephistopheles:

> Das Beste, was du wissen kannst,
> Darfst du den Buben doch nicht sagen.[2]

[1] [A quotation from Mephistopheles's description of the fabric of thought, in *Faust*, Part I, Scene 4. Freud had quoted the whole passage, in connection with the complexity of dream-associations, in Chapter VI (A) of *The Interpretation of Dreams* (1900a), *Standard Ed.*, 4, 283.]

[2] [The best of what you know may not, after all, be told to boys.
(*Faust*, Part I, Scene 4.)

Freud had often quoted these lines. For other instances see *The Interpretation of Dreams* (1900a), *Standard Ed.*, 4, 142 *n*. 1.]

Appendix
List of Writings by Freud Dealing Mainly or Largely with Art, Literature or the Theory of Aesthetics

[*The date at the beginning of each entry is that of the year during* [213] *which the work in question was probably written. The date at the end is that of publication, and under that date fuller particulars of the work will be found in the* Bibliography and Author Index. *The items in square brackets were published posthumously.*]

[1897   On *Oedipus Rex* and *Hamlet* in Letter 71 to Fliess of October 15, 1897. (1950*a*)]

[1898   'Die Richterin' ('The Woman Judge'), in Letter 91 to Fliess of June 20, 1898. (1950*a*)]

1899   *The Interpretation of Dreams*, Chapter V, Section D (ß), on *Oedipus Rex* and *Hamlet*. (1900*a*)

1905   *Jokes and their Relation to the Unconscious*. (1905*c*)

[1905–6   'Psychopathic Characters on the Stage.' (1942*a*)]

1906   *Delusions and Dreams in Jensen's 'Gradiva'*. (1907*a*)

1907   'Contribution to a Questionnaire on Reading.' (1907*d*)

1907   'Creative Writers and Day-Dreaming.' (1908*e*)

1910   *Leonardo da Vinci and a Memory of his Childhood*. (1910*c*)

1913   'The Theme of the Three Caskets.' (1913*f*)

1913   'The Claims of Psycho-Analysis to Scientific Interest', Part II, Section F. (1913*j*)

1914   'The Moses of Michelangelo.' (1914*b*)

1915   'On Transience.' (1916*a*)

1916   'Some Character-Types Met with in Psycho-Analytic Work.' (1916*d*)

1917   'A Childhood Recollection from *Dichtung und Wahrheit*.' (1917*b*)

1919   'The "Uncanny".' (1919*h*)

1927   Postscript to 'The Moses of Michelangelo'. (1927*b*)

1927   'Humour.' (1927*d*)

1927   'Dostoevsky and Parricide.' (1928*b*)

1929   Letter to Reik on Dostoevsky. (1930*f*)   [214]

1930   'The Goethe Prize.' (1930*d* and *e*)

1933   Preface to Marie Bonaparte's *Edgar Allan Poe*. (1933*d*)

§ Medusa's Head

WE have not often attempted to interpret individual mythological themes, but an interpretation suggests itself easily in the case of the horrifying decapitated head of Medusa.

To decapitate = to castrate. The terror of Medusa is thus a terror of castration that is linked to the sight of something. Numerous analyses have made us familiar with the occasion for this: it occurs when a boy, who has hitherto been unwilling to believe the threat of castration, catches sight of the female genitals, probably those of an adult, surrounded by hair, and essentially those of his mother.

The hair upon Medusa's head is frequently represented in works of art in the form of snakes, and these once again are derived from the castration complex. It is a remarkable fact that, however frightening they may be in themselves, they nevertheless serve actually as a mitigation of the horror, for they replace the penis, the absence of which is the cause of the horror. This is a confirmation of the technical rule according to which a multiplication of penis symbols signifies castration.[1]

The sight of Medusa's head makes the spectator stiff with terror, turns him to stone. Observe that we have here once again the same origin from the castration complex and the same transformation of

SOURCE: *Standard Ed.*, **18**, 273–74.
[1][This is referred to in Freud's paper on 'The "Uncanny"' (1919*h*), middle of Section II.]

264

affect! For becoming stiff means an erection. Thus in the original situation it offers consolation to the spectator: he is still in possession of a penis, and the stiffening reassures him of the fact.

This symbol of horror is worn upon her dress by the virgin goddess Athene. And rightly so, for thus she becomes a woman who is unapproachable and repels all sexual desires—since she displays the terrifying genitals of the Mother. Since the Greeks were [274] in the main strongly homosexual, it was inevitable that we should find among them a representation of woman as a being who frightens and repels because she is castrated.

If Medusa's head takes the place of a representation of the female genitals, or rather if it isolates their horrifying effects from their pleasure-giving ones, it may be recalled that displaying the genitals is familiar in other connections as an apotropaic act. What arouses horror in oneself will produce the same effect upon the enemy against whom one is seeking to defend oneself. We read in Rabelais of how the Devil took to flight when the woman showed him her vulva.

The erect male organ also has an apotropaic effect, but thanks to another mechanism. To display the penis (or any of its surrogates) is to say: 'I am not afraid of you. I defy you. I have a penis.' Here, then, is another way of intimidating the Evil Spirit.[1]

In order seriously to substantiate this interpretation it would be necessary to investigate the origin of this isolated symbol of horror in Greek mythology as well as parallels to it in other mythologies.[2]

---

[1][It may be worth quoting a footnote added by Freud to a paper of Stekel's, 'Zur Psychologie des Exhibitionismus', in *Zentralbl. Psychoanal.*, **1** (1911*b*), 495: 'Dr. Stekel here proposes to derive exhibitionism from unconscious narcissistic motive forces. It seems to me probable that the same explanation can be applied to the apotropaic exhibiting found among the peoples of antiquity.']

[2][The same topic was dealt with by Ferenczi (1923) in a very short paper which was itself briefly commented upon by Freud in his 'Infantile Genital Organization of the Libido' (1923*e*).]

Reference Matter

Editor's Notes

The following notes were prepared by James Strachey for *The Standard Edition of the Complete Psychological Works of Sigmund Freud*.

Delusion and Dreams in Jensen's *Gradiva* (Der Wahn und die Träume in W. Jensens *Gradiva*)

(*a*) German Editions:

1907   Leipzig and Vienna: Heller. Pp. 81. (*Schriften zur angewandten Seelenkunde*, Heft 1) (Re-issued unchanged with the same title page but a new paper outer cover: Leipzig and Vienna: Deuticke, 1908.)

1912   2nd ed. Leipzig and Vienna: Deuticke. With 'Postscript'. Pp. 87.

1924   3rd ed. Same publishers. Unchanged.

1925   *G.S.*, **9**, 273–367.

1941   *G.W.*, **7**, 31–125.

(*b*) English Translation:

    Delusion and Dream

1917   New York: Moffat, Yard. Pp. 243. (Tr. H. M. Downey.) (With an introduction by G. Stanley Hall. Omits Freud's 'Postscript'. Includes translation of Jensen's story.)

1921   London: George Allen & Unwin. Pp. 213. (A reprint of the above.)

The present translation is an entirely new one, with a modified title, by James Strachey. The 'Postscript' appears in English for the first time.

This was Freud's first published analysis of a work of literature, apart, of course, from his comments on *Oedipus Rex* and *Hamlet* in *The Interpretation of Dreams* (1900*a*), *Standard Ed.*, **4**, 261–6. At an earlier date, however, he had written a short analysis of Conrad Ferdinand Meyer's story, 'Die Richterin' ['The Woman Judge'], and had sent it to Fliess, enclosed in a letter dated June 20, 1898 (Freud, 1950*a*, Letter 91).

It was Jung, as we learn from Ernest Jones (1955, 382), who brought Jensen's[1] book to Freud's notice, and Freud is reported to have written the present work especially to please Jung. This was in the summer of 1906, several months before the two men had met each other, and the episode was thus the herald of their five or six years of cordial relations. Freud's study was published in May, 1907 and soon afterwards he sent a copy of it to Jensen. A short correspondence followed, which is referred to in the 'Postscript' to the second edition (p. 85); Jensen's side of this correspondence (three shortish letters, dated May 13, May 25 and December 14, 1907) has since been published in the *Psychoanalytische Bewegung*, **1** (1929), 207–211. The letters are most friendly in tone and give the impression that Jensen was flattered by Freud's analysis of his story. He appears even to have accepted the main lines of the interpretation. In particular, he declares that he has no recollection of having replied 'somewhat brusquely' when, as reported below on p. 82, he was asked (apparently by Jung) whether he knew anything of Freud's theories.

Apart from the deeper significance which Freud saw in Jensen's work, there is no doubt that he must have been specially attracted by the scene in which it was laid. His interest in Pompeii was an old-established one. It appears more than once in his correspondence with Fliess. Thus, as an association to the word '*via*' in one of his dreams[2], he gives 'the streets of Pompeii which I am studying'. This was on April 28, 1897 (Freud, 1950*a*, Letter 60), several years before he actually visited Pompeii, in September,

[1] Wilhelm Jensen (1837–1911) was a North German playwright and novelist, respected but not regarded as of very great distinction.
[2] The 'Villa Secerno' dream. It is also reported in *The Interpretation of Dreams*, *Standard Ed.*, **4**, 317; but the Pompeii association is not mentioned there.

1902. Above all, Freud was fascinated by the analogy between the historical fate of Pompeii (its burial and subsequent excavation) and the mental
events with which he was so familiar—burial by repression and excavation by analysis. Something of this analogy was suggested by Jensen
himself (p. 51), and Freud enjoyed elaborating it here as well as in later
contexts.

In reading Freud's study, it is worth bearing in mind its chronological
place in his writings as one of his earliest psycho-analytic works. It was
written only a year after the first publication of the 'Dora' case history
and the *Three Essays on Sexuality*. Embedded in the discussion of *Gradiva*,
indeed, there lies not only a summary of Freud's explanation of dreams
but also what is perhaps the first of his semi-popular accounts of his
theory of the neuroses and of the therapeutic action of psycho-analysis. It
is impossible not to admire the almost prestidigital skill with which he
extracts this wealth of material from what is at first sight no more than an
ingenious anecdote.[1] But it would be wrong to minimize the part played
in the outcome, however unconsciously, by Jensen himself.

Psychopathic Characters on the Stage (Psychopathische Personen auf der Bühne)

(*a*) German Editions:

(1905 or 1906   Probable date of composition. Not hitherto, 1953,
                 published in German.)

(*b*) English Translation:
          'Psychopathic Characters on the Stage'
1942   *Psychoanal. Quart.*, **11** (4), Oct., 459–464. (Tr. H. A. Bunker.)

The present translation is a new one by James Strachey.

Dr. Max Graf, in an article in the *Psychoanal. Quart.*, **11**, (1942), 465,
relates that this paper was written by Freud in 1904 and presented to him
by its author. It was never published by Freud himself. There must be

---

[1] In his *Autobiographical Study* (1925*d*), *Standard Ed.*, **20**, 65, Freud spoke a
little contemptuously of *Gradiva* as a work 'which has no particular merit in
itself'.

some mistake about this date (the MS. itself is undated), for Hermann Bahr's play, *Die Andere*, which is discussed on p. 93, was first produced (in Munich and Leipzig) at the beginning of November, 1905, and had its first Vienna performance on the 25th of the same month. It was not published in book form till 1906. The probability is, therefore, that the present paper was written late in 1905 or early in 1906. Our thanks are due to Dr. Raymond Gosselin, editor of the *Psychoanalytic Quarterly*, for supplying us with a photostat of Freud's original manuscript. The hand-writing is in places difficult to decipher, which accounts for a few divergences between the two English translations.

The Antithetical Meaning of Primal Words (Über den Gegensinn der Urworte)

(*a*) German Editions:

1910   *Jb. psychoan. psychopath. Forsch.*, **2** (1), 179–184.
1913   *S.K.S.N.*, **3**, 280–287. (2nd ed. 1921.)
1924   *G.S.*, **10**, 221–228.
1943   *G.W.*, **8**, 214–221.

(*b*) English Translation:
    ' "*The Antithetical Sense of Primal Words*" '
1925   *C.P.*, **4**, 184–191. (Tr. M. N. Searl.)

The present translation with a modified title, 'The Antithetical Meaning of Primal Words', is a new one by Alan Tyson.

We are told by Ernest Jones (1955, 347) that Freud came across Abel's pamphlet in the autumn of 1909. He was particularly pleased by the discovery, as is shown by the many references he made to it in his writings. In 1911, for instance, he added a footnote on it to *The Interpretation of Dreams* (1900*a*), *Standard Ed.*, **4**, 318, and he summarized it at some length in two passages in his *Introductory Lectures* (1916–17), Lectures XI and XV. The reader should bear in mind the fact that Abel's pamphlet was published in 1884 and it would not be surprising if some of his findings were not supported by later philologists. This is especially true of his Egyptological comments, which were made before Erman had put Egyptian philology for the first time on a scientific basis. The quotations from Abel which are made here are translated without any modification in the spelling of his examples.

The Occurrence in Dreams of Material from Fairy Tales (Märchenstoffe in Träumen)

(*a*) German Editions:

1913	*Int. Z. Psychoanal.*, **1** (2), 147–51.
1918	*S.K.S.N.*, **4**, 168–76. (1922, 2nd ed.)
1925	*G.S.*, **3**, 259–66.
1925	*Traumlehre*, 3–10.
1931	*Sexualtheorie und Traumlehre*, 308–15.
1946	*G.W.*, **10**, 2–9.

(*b*) English Translation:

'The Occurrence in Dreams of Material from Fairy Tales'

1925   *C.P.*, **4**, 236–43. (Tr. James Strachey.)

The present translation is a slightly amended reprint of that published in 1925.

The second of the two examples reported in this paper was derived from the analysis of the case of the 'Wolf Man', who was still under treatment with Freud at the time of its publication. The whole of this part of the paper was included verbatim in the case history, which was written in 1914 but only published four years later—'From the History of an Infantile Neurosis' (1918*b*). The analysis of the dream is there carried much further (*Standard Ed.*, **17**, 29 ff.).

The Theme of the Three Caskets (Das Motiv der Kästchenwahl)

(*a*) German Editions:

1913	*Imago*, **2** (3), 257–66.
1918	*S.K.S.N.*, **4**, 470–85. (1922, 2nd ed.)
1924	*G.S.*, **10**, 243–56.
1924	*Dichtung und Kunst*, 15–28.
1946	*G.W.*, **10**, 24–37.

(*b*) English Translation:
 '*The Theme of the Three Caskets*'
1925 *C.P.*, **4**, 244–56. (Tr. C. J. M. Hubback.)

The present translation is based on that of 1925.

Freud's correspondence (quoted in Jones, 1955, 405) shows that the underlying idea of this paper occurred to him in June, 1912, though the work was only published a year later.

<h2 style="text-align:center">The Moses of Michelangelo (Der Moses
des Michelangelo)</h2>

(*a*) German Editions:

1914 *Imago*, **3** (1), 15–36.
1924 *G.S.*, **10**, 257–86.
1924 *Dichtung und Kunst*, 29–58.
1946 *G.W.*, **10**, 172–201.
   '*Nachtrag zur Arbeit über den Moses des Michelangelo*'
1927 *Imago*, **13** (4), 552–3.
1928 *G.S.*, **11**, 409–10.
1948 *G.W.*, **14**, 321–2.

(*b*) English Translation:
 '*The Moses of Michelangelo*'
1925 *C.P.*, **4**, 257–87. (Tr. Alix Strachey.)
   '*Postscript to my Paper on the Moses of Michelangelo*'
1951 *Int. J. Psycho-Anal.*, **32**, 94. (Tr. Alix Strachey.)

The present translation is a corrected version of those published in 1925 and 1951.

Freud's interest in Michelangelo's statue was of old standing. He went to see it on the fourth day of his very first visit to Rome in September, 1901, as well as on many later occasions. He was already planning the present paper in 1912, but it was not written until the autumn of 1913. An account of his long hesitations over its publication and of his final decision to have it printed anonymously will be found in the second volume of Dr. Ernest Jones's biography of Freud. The paper appeared in *Imago* as 'by ***', and the disguise was not lifted until 1924.

Some Character-Types Met with in Psycho-analytic Work
(Einige Charakertypen aus der psychoanalytischen Arbeit)

(*a*) German Editions:

1916	*Imago*, **4** (6), 317–336.
1918	*S.K.S.N.*, **4**, 521–552. (1922, 2nd ed.)
1924	*G.S.*, **10**, 287–314.
1924	*Dichtung und Kunst*, 59–86.
1925	*Almanach 1926*, 21–6. (Section I only.)
1935	*Psychoan. Pädagog.*, **9**, 193–4. (Section III only.)
1946	*G.W.*, **10**, 364–391.

(*b*) English Translation:
> '*Some Character-Types Met with in Psycho-Analytic Work*'

1925   *C.P.*, **4**, 318–344. (Tr. E. C. Mayne.)

The present translation is based on the one published in 1925.

These three essays were published in the last issue of *Imago* for the year 1916. The third of them, although the shortest, has produced as many repercussions as any of Freud's non-medical writings, for it has thrown an entirely fresh light on the problems of the psychology of crime.

Extracts from the translation of this work published in 1925 were included in Rickman's *A General Selection from the Works of Sigmund Freud* (1937, 111–17).

On Transience (Vergänglichkeit)

(*a*) German Editions:

1916	In *Das Land Goethes 1914–1916*. Stuttgart: Deutsche Verlagsanstalt. Pp. 37–8.
1926	*Almanach 1927*, 39–42.
1928	*G.S.*, **11**, 291–4.
1946	*G.W.*, **10**, 358–361.

(*b*) English Translation:

     '*On Transience*'

1942   *Int. J. Psycho-Anal.*, **23** (2), 84–5. (Tr. James Strachey.)

1950   *C.P.*, **5**, 79–82. (Same translator.)

The present translation is a very slightly altered reprint of the one published in 1950.

This essay was written in November, 1915, at the invitation of the Berliner Goethebund (the Berlin Goethe Society) for a commemorative volume they issued in the following year under the title of *Das Land Goethes* (Goethe's Country). This elaborately produced volume included a large number of contributions from well-known writers and artists past and present, such as von Bülow, von Brentano, Ricarda Huch, Hauptmann and Liebermann. The German original (apart from the picture it gives of Freud's feelings about the war, which was then in its second year) is excellent evidence of his literary powers. It is of interest to note that the essay includes a statement of the theory of mourning contained in 'Mourning and Melancholia' (1917*e*), which Freud had written some months before, but which was not published until two years later.

A Mythological Parallel to a Visual Obsession
(Mythologische Parallele zu einer plastischen Zwangsvorstellung)

(*a*) German Editions:

1916   *Int. Z. Psychoanal.*, **4** (2), 110.

1918   *S.K.S.N.*, **4**, 195 (1922, 2nd. ed.).

1924   *G.S.*, **10**, 240.

1946   *G.W.*, **10**, 398

(*b*) English Translation:

     '*A Mythological Parallel to a Visual Obsession*'

1925   *C.P.*, **4**, 345. (Tr. C. J. M. Hubback.)

The present translation is based on the one published in 1925.

A Childhood Recollection from *Dichtung und Wahrheit*
(Eine Kindheitserinnerung aus *Dichtung und Wahrheit*)

(*a*) German Editions:

1917   *Imago*, **5** (2), 49–57.
1918   *S.K.S.N.*, **4**, 564–77 (1922, 2nd. ed.).
1924   *G.S.*, **10**, 357–68.
1924   *Dichtung und Kunst*, 87–98.
1947   *G.W.*, **12**, 15–26.

(*b*) English Translation:
    'A Childhood Recollection from Dichtung und Wahrheit'
1925   *C.P.*, **4**, 357–67. (Tr. C. J. M. Hubback.)

The present translation is a considerably modified version of that published in 1925.

Freud gave the first part of this paper before the Vienna Psycho-Analytical Society on December 13, 1916 and the second part before the same society on April 18, 1917. The paper was not actually *written* by him until September, 1917, in the train on his way back from a summer holiday in the Tatra Mountains in Hungary. The date of publication is uncertain, since *Imago* appeared very irregularly at that time, owing to war conditions. A summary of his conclusions will be found in a long footnote which he added in 1919 to Chapter II of his study of a childhood memory of Leonardo da Vinci's (1910*c*).

The 'Uncanny' (Das Unheimliche)

(*a*) German Editions:

1919   *Imago*, **5** (5–6), 297–324.
1922   *S.K.S.N.*, **5**, 229–73.
1924   *G.S.*, **10**, 369–408.
1924   *Dichtung und Kunst*, 99–138.
1947   *G.W.*, **12**, 229–68.

(*b*) English Translation:
   'The "Uncanny"'
1925   *C.P.*, **4**, 368–407. (Tr. Alix Strachey.)

The present translation is a considerably modified version of the one published in 1925.

This paper, published in the autumn of 1919, is mentioned by Freud in a letter to Ferenczi of May 12 of the same year, in which he says he has dug an old paper out of a drawer and is re-writing it. Nothing is known as to when it was originally written or how much it was changed, though the footnote quoted from *Totem and Taboo* on p. 217 below shows that the subject was present in his mind as early as 1913. The passages dealing with the 'compulsion to repeat' (p. 214 ff.) must in any case have formed part of the revision. They include a summary of much of the contents of *Beyond the Pleasure Principle* (1920*g*) and speak of it as 'already completed'. The same letter to Ferenczi of May 12, 1919, announced that a draft of this latter work was finished, though it was not in fact published for another year. Further details will be found in the Editor's Note to *Beyond the Pleasure Principle*, Standard Ed., **18**, 3.

The first section of the present paper, with its lengthy quotation from a German dictionary, raises special difficulties for the translator. It is to be hoped that readers will not allow themselves to be discouraged by this preliminary obstacle, for the paper is full of interesting and important material, and travels far beyond merely linguistic topics.

Dostoevsky and Parricide (Dostojewski und die Vatertötung)

(*a*) German Editions:

1928   In *Die Urgestalt der Brüder Karamasoff*, ed. R. Fülöp-Miller and
        F. Eckstein, Munich. Pp. xi–xxxvi.
1929   *Almanach 1930*, 9–31.
1934   *G.S.*, **12**, 7–26.
1948   *G.W.*, **14**, 399–418.

(*b*) English Translations:

    'Dostoevski and Parricide'

1929   *The Realist*, **1** (4), 18–33. (Tr. D. F. Tait.)

    'Dostoevsky and Parricide'

1945   *Int. J. Psycho-Anal.*, **26** (1 & 2), 1–8. (The above very considerably revised and with a slightly modified title.)

1945   *Partisan Review*, **12** (4), 530–44. (Reprint of above.)

1947   In F. M. Dostoevsky, *Stavrogin's Confession*, trans. V. Woolf and Koteliansky, New York: Lear Publications, 87–114. (Reprint of above.)

1950   *C.P.*, **5**, 222–42. (Further revision of above.)

The present translation is a very slightly corrected reprint of that of 1950.

From 1925 onwards, Fülöp-Miller and Eckstein began issuing a series of volumes supplementary to the great complete German edition of Dostoevsky which, edited by Moeller van den Bruck, had been completed a few years earlier. The new volumes, uniform with the complete edition, contained posthumous writings, unfinished drafts and material from various sources throwing light on Dostoevsky's character and works. One of these volumes was to contain a collection of preliminary drafts and sketches relating to *The Brothers Karamazov* and a discussion of the book's sources; and the editors were anxious to persuade Freud to contribute an introduction dealing with the psychology both of the book and of its author. They seem to have approached him early in 1926 and he had begun writing his essay by the end of June of that year. He was deflected from it, however, by the urgent necessity for producing his pamphlet on lay analysis (1926*e*) in view of the proceedings which had been begun against Theodor Reik (*Standard Ed.*, **20**, 180). Thereafter he seems to have lost interest in the Dostoevsky essay, particularly, as Ernest Jones tells us (1957, 152), after he had come across a book on the same subject by Neufeld (1923), which, as he says in a footnote (p. 252)—with considerable modesty, it must be remarked—, contained most of the ideas that he himself was putting forward. It is not clear when he took the essay up again. Jones (loc. cit.) suggests that it was finished early in 1927; but this seems scarcely likely, since Stefan Zweig's story with which the later part of the essay is concerned only appeared in 1927. The volume to which Freud's essay served as an introduction (*The Original Version of the Brothers Karamazov*) was not published until the autumn of 1928.

The essay falls into two distinct parts. The first deals with Dostoevsky's character in general, with his masochism, his sense of guilt, his 'epileptoid' attacks and his double attitude in the Oedipus complex. The second discusses the special point of his passion for gambling and leads to an account of a short story by Stefan Zweig which throws light on the genesis of that addiction. As will be seen from a subsequent letter of Freud's to Theodor Reik which we print as an appendix (p. 253), the two parts of the essay are more closely related than appears on the surface.

The present essay may show signs of being an 'occasional' piece, but it contains much that is of interest—for instance, Freud's first discussion of hysterical attacks since his early paper on the subject written twenty years before (1909*a*), a restatement of his later views on the Oedipus complex and the sense of guilt, and a sidelight on the problem of masturbation which is not to be found in his earlier account of the question (1912*f*). But above all, he had an opportunity here for expressing his views on a writer whom he placed in the very front rank of all.

The Goethe Prize (Goethe-Preis, 1930)

(*a*) German Editions:

    Brief an Dr. Alfons Paquet

1930   *Psychoanal. Bewegung,* **2** (5) (Sept.–Oct.), 419.
1934   *G.S.,* **12**, 406–7.
1948   *G.W.,* **14**, 545–6.

    Ansprache im Frankfurter Goethe-Haus

1930   *Psychoanal. Bewegung,* **2** (5) (Sept.–Oct.), 421–6.
1934   *G.S.,* **12**, 408–11.
1948   *G.W.,* **14**, 547–50.

The present translation, the first into English, is by Angela Richards.

In 1927 the City of Frankfurt founded the 'Goethe Prize', which was to be awarded annually to 'a personality of established achievement whose creative work is worthy of an honour dedicated to Goethe's memory'. The first three awards were made to Stefan George the poet, Albert

Schweitzer the musician and medical missionary, and Leopold Ziegler the philosophical writer. The amount of the prize was 10,000 Reichsmark—worth at that time about £500 or $2500.

At the suggestion of Alfons Paquet, a well-known man of letters who was Secretary to the Trustees of the Fund, it was decided to award the 1930 prize to Freud. This was announced to Freud (who was on holiday at the time in the Salzkammergut) in a letter from Paquet dated July 26, 1930 (printed in the *Psychoanalytische Bewegung*, **2**, 417–18), to which Freud replied on August 3.[1] It was the practice, as Paquet explained in his letter, for the prize to be presented each year on August 28 at a ceremony in the house in Frankfurt where Goethe was born, and for the recipient to give an address there, illustrating his own inner relation to Goethe. Owing to his illness, Freud was unable to do this himself, but the address which he prepared was read by Anna Freud at the ceremony in the Goethe House on August 28.

Medusa's Head (Das Medusenhaupt)

(*a*) German Editions:

1940   *Int. Z. Psychoanal. Imago* **25**, 105 (posthumous publication).
1941   *G.W.*, **17**, 47.

(*b*) English Translation:
      'Medusa's Head'
1941   *Int. J. Psycho-Anal.*, **22**, 69. (Tr. James Strachey.)
1950   *C.P.*, **5**, 105. (Reprint of above.)

The present translation is the one published in 1941.

The manuscript is dated May 14, 1922, and appears to be a sketch for a more extensive work.

[1] The date is given as August 5 in the two later German editions.

Works Cited

The entries reproduce the data given in the bibliographies appended to the volumes of *The Standard Edition*. The italic letters used to distinguish works by a particular author published in the same year (e.g., 1909*a*, 1909*b*) are those used in *The Standard Edition*. The short forms of journal titles are in accordance with the *World List of Scientific Periodicals* (London, 1952). Numerals in boldface type are volume numbers; numbers in ordinary type are page numbers. The following abbreviations are used:

G.S.	Freud, *Gesammelte Schriften*. 12 vols. Vienna, 1924–34.
G.W.	Freud, *Gesammelte Werke*. 18 vols. London, 1940—.
C.P.	Freud, *Collected Papers*. 5 vols. London, 1924–50.
Standard Ed.	Freud, *Standard Edition*. 24 vols. London, 1953–74.
S.K.S.N.	*Sammlung kleiner Schriften zur Neurosenlehre*. 5 vols. Vienna, 1906–22.
S.P.H.	*Selected Papers on Hysteria and Other Psychoneuroses*, 3rd ed. New York, 1920.

Abel, K. 1884. *Über den Gegensinn der Urworte*. Leipzig.
——. 1885. *Sprachwissenschaftliche Abhandlungen*. Leipzig.
Baillet, A. 1691. *La View de Monsieur Des-Cartes*. 2 vols. Paris.
Binet, A. 1888. *Etudes de psychologie expérimentale: le fétichism das l'amour*. Paris.
Bleuler, E. 1906. *Affectivität, Suggestibilität, Paranoia*. Halle. Trans. *Affectivity, Suggestibility, Paranoia*. New York, 1912.

Brandes, G. 1896. *William Shakespeare*. Paris.

Burckhardt, J. 1927 [1st ed. 1855]. *Der Cicerone*. Leipzig.

Darmesteter, J., ed. 1881. *Macbeth*. Paris.

Dostoevsky, A. 1921. *Fyodor Dostoyevsky*. London.

Ferenczi, S. 1912. 'Über passagere Symptombilding während der Analyse.' *Zbl. Psychoan.* **2**, 588. Trans.: 'Transitory Symptom-Constructions During the Analysis.' In *First Contributions to Psycho-Analysis*. London, 1952, chap. 7.

———. 1923. 'Zur Symbolik des Medusenhauptes.' *Int. Z. Psychoanal.*, **9**, 69. Trans.: 'On the Symbolism of the Head of Medusa.' In *Further Contributions to the Theory and Technique of Psycho-Analysis*. London, 1926, chap. 66.

Freud, S. 1895*b*. 'Über die Berechtigung, von der Neurasthenie einen bestimmten Symptomenkomplex als "Angstneurose" abzutrennen.' *G.S.*, **1**, 306; *G.W.*, **1**, 315. Trans.: 'On the Grounds for Detaching a Particular Syndrome from Neurasthenia Under the Description "Anxiety Neurosis."' *C.P.*, **1**, 76; *Standard Ed.*, **3**.

———. 1895*d*. With J. Breuer. *Studien über Hysterie*. Vienna. *G.S.*, **1**, 3; *G.W.*, **1**, 77 (omitting Breuer's contributions). Trans.: *Studies on Hysteria*. *Standard Ed.*, **2** (including Breuer's contributions).

———. 1896*b*. 'Weitere Bemerkungen über die Abwehr-Neuropsychosen.' *G.S.*, **1**, 363; *G.W.*, **1**, 379. Trans.: 'Further Remarks on the Neuro-psychoses of Defence.' *C.P.*, **1**, 155; *Standard Ed.*, **3**.

1900*a*. *Die Traumdeutung*. Vienna. *G.S.*, **2–3**. *G.W.*, **2–3**. Trans.: *The Interpretation of Dreams*. London and New York, 1955; *Standard Ed.*, **4–5**.

———. 1901*a*. *Über den Traum*. Wiesbaden. *G.S.*, **3**, 189; *G.W.*, **2–3**, 643. Trans. *On Dreams*. London and New York, 1951; *Standard Ed.*, **5**, 633.

———. 1901*b*. *Zur Psychopathologie des Alltagslebens*. Berlin. 1904. *G.S.*, **4**, 3; *G.W.*, **4**. Trans.: *The Psychopathology of Everyday Life*. *Standard Ed.*, **6**.

———. 1905*c*. *Der Witz und seine Beziehung zum Unbewussten*. Vienna. *G.S.*, **9**, 5; *G.W.*, **6**. Trans.: *Jokes and Their Relation to the Unconscious*. *Standard Ed.*, **8**.

———. 1905*d*. *Drei Abhandlungen zur Sexualtheorie*. Vienna. *G.S.*, **5**, 3; *G.W.*, **5**, 29. Trans.: *Three Essays on the Theory of Sexuality*. London, 1949; *Standard Ed.*, **7**, 125.

———. 1905*e* [1901]. 'Bruchstück einer Hysterie-Analyse.' *G.S.*, **8**, 3; *G.W.*, **5**, 163. Trans.: 'Fragment of an Analysis of a Case of Hysteria.' *C.P.*, **3**, 13; *Standard Ed.*, **7**, 3.

——. 1907*a*. *Der Wahn und die Träume in Jensens 'Gradiva.'* Vienna. *G.S.* **9**, 273; *G.W.*, **7**, 31. Trans. *Delusions and Dreams in Jensen's 'Gradiva.' Standard Ed.*, **9**, 3.

——. 1907*b*. 'Zwangshandlungen und Religionsübung.' *G.S.*, **10**, 210; *G.W.*, **7**, 129. Trans.: 'Obsessive Actions and Religious Practices.' *C.P.*, **2**, 25; *Standard Ed.*, **9**, 116.

——. 1907*d*. Antwort auf eine Rundfrage *Vom Lesen und von guten Büchern*. Vienna. Trans.: Contribution to a Questionnaire on Reading. *Int. J. Psycho-Anal.* **32**, 319; *Standard Ed.*, **9**, 245.

——. 1907*e*. Prospectus for *Schriften zur angewandten Seelenkunde*. In Freud, 1907*a*, 82. Trans. *Bull. Am. Psa. Ass.* **8** (1952): 214; *Standard Ed.*, **9**, 248.

——. 1908*e* [1907]. 'Der Dichter und das Phantasieren.' *G.S.*, **10**, 229; *G.W.*, **7**, 213. Trans.: 'Creative Writers and Day-Dreaming.' *C.P.*, **2**, 100; *Standard Ed.*, **9**, 143.

——. 1909*a*. 'Allgemeines über den hysterischen Anfall.' *G.S.*, **5**, 255; *G.W.*, **7**, 235. Trans.: 'Some General Remarks on Hysterical Attacks.' *C.P.*, **2**, 100; *Standard Ed.*, **9**, 229.

——. 1909*b*. 'Analyse der Phobie eines fünfjährigen Knaben.' *G.S.*, **8**, 129; *G.W.*, **7**, 243. Trans.: 'Analysis of a Phobia in a Five-Year-Old Boy.' *C.P.*, **3**, 149; *Standard Ed.*, **10**, 3.

——. 1909*d*. 'Bemerkungen über einen Fall von Zwangsneurose.' *G.S.*, **8**, 269; *G.W.*, **7**, 381. Trans.: 'Notes upon a Case of Obsessional Neurosis.' *C.P.*, **3**, 293; *Standard Ed.*, **10**, 155.

——. 1910*c*. *Eine Kindheitserinnerung des Leonardo da Vinci*. Vienna. *G.S.*, **9**, 371; *G.W.*, **8**, 128. Trans.: *Leonardo da Vinci and a Memory of His Childhood. Standard Ed.*, **11**.

——. 1912*e*. 'Über neurotische Erkrankungstypen.' *G.S.*, **5**, 400; *G.W.*, **8**, 322. Trans.: 'Types of Onset of Neurosis.' *C.P.*, **2**, 113; *Standard Ed.*, **12**.

——. 1912*f*. 'Zur Onanie-Diskussion.' *G.S.*, **3**, 324; *G.W.*, **8**, 332. Trans.: 'Contributions to a Discussion on Masturbation.' *Standard Ed.*, **12**, 243.

——. 1912–13. *Totem und Tabu*. Vienna, 1913. *G.S.*, **10**; *G.W.*, **9**. Trans.: *Totem and Taboo*, London, 1950; *Standard Ed.*, **13**.

——. 1913*f*. 'Das Motiv der Kätschenwahl.' *G.S.*, **10**, 243; *G.W.*, **10**, 244. Trans.: 'The Theme of the Three Caskets.' *C.P.*, **4**, 244; *Standard Ed.*, **12**, 291.

——. 1913*j*. 'Das Interesse an der Psychoanalyse.' *G.S.*, **4**, 313; *G.W.*, **8**,

390. Trans.: 'The Claims of Psycho-Analysis to Scientific Interest.' *Standard Ed.*, **13**, 165.

———. 1914*b*. 'Der Moses des Michelangelo.' *G.S.*, **10**, 257; *G.W.*, **10**, 172. Trans.: 'The Moses of Michelangelo.' *C.P.*, **4**, 257; *Standard Ed.*, **13**, 211.

———. 1914*e*. 'Zur Einführung des Narzissmus.' *G.S.*, **6**, 155; *G.W.*, **10**, 138. Trans.: "On Narcissism: An Introduction.' *C.P.*, **4**, 30; *Standard Ed.*, **14**.

———. 1914*g*. "Weitere Ratschläge zur Technik der Psychoanalyse: II, Erinnern, Wiederholen und Durcharbeiten.' *G.S.*, **6**, 109; *G.W.*, **10**, 126. Trans.: 'Recollecting, Repeating and Working Through (Further Recommendations on the Technique of Psycho-analysis, II).' *C.P.*, **2**, 366; *Standard Ed.*, **12**.

———. 1915*b*. 'Zeitgemässes über Krieg und Tod.' *G.S.*, **10**, 315; *G.W.*, **10**, 324. Trans.: 'Thoughts for the Times on War and Death.' *C.P.*, **4**, 288; *Standard Ed.*, **14**.

———. 1915*e*. 'Das Unbewusste.' *G.S.*, **5**, 480; *G.W.*, **10**, 264; Trans. 'The Unconscious.' *C.P.*, **4**, 98; *Standard Ed.*, **14**, 161.

———. 1916*a*. 'Vergänglichkeit.' *G.S.*, **11**, 291; *G.W.*, **10**, 358. Trans.: 'On Transience.' *C.P.*, **5**, 79; *Standard Ed.*, **14**, 305.

———. 1916*b*. 'Einige Characktertypen aus der psychoanalytischen Arbeit.' *G.S.*, **10**, 287; *G.W.*, **10**, 364. Trans.: 'Some Character-Types Met with in Psycho-Analytic Work.' *C.P.*, **4**, 318; *Standard Ed.*, **14**, 311.

———. 1916–17. *Vorlesungen zur Einführung in die Psychoanalyse.* Vienna. *G.S.*, **7**; *G.W.*, **11**. Trans.: *Introductory Lectures on Psycho-analysis*, rev. ed. London, 1929; *A General Introduction to Psychoanalysis.* New York, 1935; *Standard Ed.*, **15–16**.

———. 1917*b*. 'Eine Kindheitserinnerung aus *Dichtung und Wahrheit.*' *G.S.*, **10**, 357; *G.W.*, **12**, 15. Trans.: 'A Childhood Recollection from *Dichtung und Wahrheit.*' *C.P.*, **4**, 357; *Standard Ed.*, **17**, 147.

———. 1917*e* [1915]. 'Trauer und Melacholie.' *G.S.*, **5**, 535; *G.W.*, **10**, 428. Trans. 'Mourning and Melancholia.' *C.P.*, **4**, 152; *Standard Ed.*, **14**, 239.

———. 1918*b* [1914]. 'Aus der Geschichte einer infantilen Neurose.' *G.S.*, **8**, 439; *G.W.*, **12**, 29. Trans.: 'From the History of an Infantile Neurosis.' *C.P.*, **3**, 473; *Standard Ed.*, **17**, 3.

———. 1919*h*. 'Das Unheimliche.' *G.S.*, **10**, 369; *G.W.*, **12**, 229. Trans.: 'The Uncanny.' *C.P.*, **4**, 368; *Standard Ed.*, **17**, 219.

———. 1920*g*. *Jenseits des Lustprinzips.* Vienna. *G.S.*, **6**, 191; *G.W.*, **13**, 3. Trans.: *Beyond the Pleasure Principle*, London, 1950; *Standard Ed.*, **18**.

———. 1921*c*. *Massenpsychologie und Ich-Analyse.* Vienna. *G.S.*, **6**, 261;

G.W., **13**, 73; Trans.: *Group Psychology and the Analysis of the Ego.* London, 1922; New York, 1940; *Standard Ed.*, **18**, 67.

——. 1922*a*. 'Traum und Telepathie.' *G.S.*, **3**, 278; *G.W.*, **13**, 165. Trans.: 'Dreams and Telepathy.' *C.P.*, **4**, 408; *Standard Ed.*, **18**, 197.

——. 1923*b*. *Das Ich und das Es.* Vienna. *G.S.*, **6**, 353; *G.W.*, **13**, 237. Trans.: *The Ego and the Id.* London, 1927; *Standard Ed.*, **19**.

——. 1923*e*. 'Die infantile Genitalorganization.' *G.S.*, **5**, 232; *G.W.*, **13**, 293. Trans.: 'The Infantile Genital Organization of the Libido.' *C.P.*, **2**, 244; *Standard Ed.*, **19**.

——. 1925*d* [1924]. *Selbstdarstellung.* Vienna, 1934. *G.S.*, **11**, 119; *G.W.*, **14**, 33. Trans.: *An Autobiographical Study.* London, 1935; *Autobiography.* New York, 1935; *Standard Ed.*, **20**, 3.

——. 1925*h*. 'Die Verneinung.' *G.S.*, **11**, 3; *G.W.*, **14**, 11. Trans.: 'Negation.' *C.P.*, **5**, 181; *Standard Ed.*, **19**.

——. 1926*d*. *Hammung, Symptom und Angst.* Vienna. *G.S.*, **11**, 23; *G.W.*, **14**, 113. Trans. *Inhibitions, Symptoms and Anxiety.* New York, 1936; *Standard Ed.*, **20**, 77.

——. 1926*e*. *Die Frage der Laienanalyse.* Vienna. *G.S.*, **11**, 307; *G.W.*, **14**, 209. Trans.: *The Question of Lay Analysis.* London, 1947; *Standard Ed.*, **20**, 179.

——. 1927*b*. 'Nachtrag zur Arbeit über den Moses des Michelangelo.' *G.S.*, **11**, 409; *G.W.*, **14**, 321. Trans.: 'Supplement to "The Moses of Michelangelo."' *Standard Ed.*, **13**, 237.

——. 1927*d*. 'Der Humor.' *G.S.*, **11**, 402; *G.W.*, **14**, 383. Trans.: 'Humour.' *C.P.*, **5**, 215; *Standard Ed.*, **21**, 159.

——. 1928*b*. 'Dostojewski und die Vatertötung.' *G.S.*, **12**, 7; *G.W.*, **14**, 399. Trans.: 'Dostoevsky and Parricide.' *C.P.*, **5**, 222; *Standard Ed.*, **21**, 175.

——. 1930*a*. *Das Unbehagen in der Kultur.* Vienna. *G.S.*, **12**, 29; *G.W.*, **14**, 421. Trans.: *Civilisation and Its Discontents.* London and New York, 1930; *Standard Ed.*, **21**, 59.

——. 1930*d*. Letter to Dr. Alfons Paquet. *G.S.*, **12**, 406; *G.W.*, **14**, 545. Trans.: *Standard Ed.*, **21**, 207.

——. 1930*e*. Ansprache im Frankfurter Goethe-Haus. *G.S.*, **12**, 408; *G.W.*, **14**, 547. Trans.: Address delivered in the Goethe House at Frankfort. *Standard Ed.*, **21**, 208.

——. 1930*f* [1929]. Letter to Theodor Reik, in Reik 1930. Trans.: in Reik 1940; *Standard Ed.*, **21**, 195.

——. 1931*d*. 'Das Fakultätsgutachten im Prozess Halsmann.' *G.S.*, **12**,

412; *G.W.*, **14**, 541. Trans.: 'The Expert Opinion in the Halsmann Case.' *Standard Ed.*, **21**, 251.

——. 1933*d*. Preface [in French] to Marie Bonaparte's *Edgar Allan Poe*. London. 1949; *Standard Ed.*, **22**.

——. 1936*a*. Letter to Romain Rolland: 'Eine Erinnerungsstörung auf der Akropolis.' *G.W.*, **16**, 250. Trans.: 'A Disturbance of Memory on the Acropolis.' *C.P.*, **5**, 302; *Standard Ed.*, **22**.

——. 1939*a* [1937–39]. *Der Mann Moses und die monotheistische Religion*. *G.W.*, **16**, 103. Trans. *Moses and Monotheism*. London and New York, 1939; *Standard Ed.*, **23**.

——. 1942*a* [1905–6]. 'Psychopathic Characters on the Stage.' *Standard Ed.*, **7**, 305. Trans. of the unpublished 'Psychopathische Personen auf der Bühne.'

——. 1950*a* [1887–1902]. *Aus den Anfängen der Psychoanalyse*. London. Trans.: *The Origins of Psycho-Analysis*, London and New York, 1954.

Fuchs, E. 1908. *Geschichte der erotischen Kunst*. Berlin.

Fülöp-Miller, R., and Eckstein, F., eds. 1925. *Dostojewski am Roulette*. Munich.

Graf, M. 1942. 'Reminiscences of Professor Sigmund Freud.' *Psychoanal. Quart.* **11**, 465.

Grimm, Brothers. 1918. *Die Märchen der Brüder Grimm* (complete ed.). Leipzig.

Grimm, H. 1900. *Leben Michelangelo's*. 9th ed. Berlin and Stuttgart.

Grimm, J. and W. 1877. *Deutsches Wörterbuch*, vol. 4. Leipzig.

Guillaume, E. 1876. "Michel-Ange Sculpteur.' *Gazette des Beaux-Arts*, 96.

Hauser, F. 1903. 'Disiecta membra neuattischer Reliefs.' *Jh.österr. archäol. Inst.* **6**, 79.

Jekels, L. 1917. 'Shakespeares Macbeth.' *Imago* **5**, 170. Trans.: 'The Riddle of Shakespeare's *Macbeth*.' In *Selected Papers*. New York, 1952.

——. 1926. 'Zur Psychologie der Komödie.' *Imago* **12**, 328. Trans.: 'On the Psychology of Comedy.' In *Selected Papers*. New York, 1952.

Jensen, W. 1903. *Gradiva: ein pompejanishes Phantasiestück*. Dresden and Leipzig.

Jentsch, E. 1906. 'Zur Psychologie des Unheimlichen.' *Psychiat.-neurol. Wschr.* **8**, 195.

Jones, E. 1955, 1957. *Sigmund Freud: Life and Work*, vols. 2 and 3. London and New York. [Page references are to the London ed.]

Jung, C. G. 1906, 1909. *Diagnostische Assoziationsstudien.* 2 vols. Leipzig. Trans.: *Studies in Word-Association.* London, 1918; New York, 1919.

Justi, C. 1900. *Michelangelo.* Leipzig.

Kammerer, P. 1919. *Das Gesetz der Serie.* Vienna.

Knackfuss, H. 1900. *Michelangelo.* 6th ed. Bielefeld and Leipzig.

Knapp, F. 1906. *Michelangelo.* Stuttgart and Leipzig.

Lloyd, W. Watkiss. 1863. *The Moses of Michael Angelo.* London.

Lübke, W. 1863. *Geschichte der Plastik.* Leipzig.

Mach, E. 1900. *Die Analyse der Empfindung.* 2nd ed. Jena.

Miller, O. 1921. 'Zur Lebensgeschichte Dostojewskis.' In F. M. Dostojewski's *Autobiographische Schriften.* Munich. Russian original first published 1883.

Müntz, E. 1895. *Histoire de l'Art pendant la Renaissance: Italie.* Paris.

Neufeld, J. 1923. *Dostojewski: Skizze zu seiner Psychoanalyse.* Vienna.

Preller, L., ed. Robert, C. 1894. *Griechische Mythologie.* 4th ed. Berlin.

Rank, O. 1909. *Der Mythus von der Geburt des Helden.* Leipzig and Vienna. Trans.: *The Myth of the Birth of the Hero.* New York, 1914.

——. 1912*a*. 'Völkerpsychologische Parallelen zu den infantilen Sexualtheorien.' *Zbl. Psychoan.* **1**, 69.

——. 1912*b*. *Das Inzest-Motiv in Dichtung und Sage.* Leipzig and Vienna.

——. 1914. 'Der Doppelgänger.' *Imago* **3**, 97.

Reik, T. 1929. Article on S. Freud's 'Dostojewski und die Vatertötung' (see above, Freud 1928*b*). *Imago* **15**, 232.

——. 1930. *Freud als Kulturkritiker.* Vienna.

——. 1940. *From Thirty Years with Freud.* New York; London, 1942.

Roscher, W. H. 1884–1937. *Auführliches Lexikon der griechischen und römischen Mythologie.* Leipzig.

Sanctis, Sante de. 1899. *I sogni.* Turin. German trans.: *Die Träume.* Trans. O. Schmidt. Halle, 1901.

Sanders, D. 1860. *Wörterbuch der Deutschen Sprache.* Leipzig.

Schubert, G. H. von. 1814. *Die Symbolik des Traumes.* Bamberg.

Seligmann, S. 1910–11. *Kriegsneurosen und psychisches Trauma.* Munich.

Springer, A. 1895. *Raffael und Michelangelo*, vol. 2. Leipzig.

Steckel, W. 1911*b*. 'Zur Psychologie des Exhibitionismus.' *Zbl. psychoanal.* **1**, 494.

Steinmann, E. 1899. *Rom in der Renaissance.* Leipzig.

Stekel, W. 1911*a*. *Die Sprache des Traumes.* Wiesbaden.

Strakhov, N. 1921. 'Über Dostojewskis Leben und literarische Tätigkeit.'

In F. M. Dostojewski's *Literarische Schriften.* Munich. Russian original first published 1883.

Stucken, E. 1907. *Astralmythen der Hebraeer, Babylonier und Aegypter.* Leipzig.

Thode, H. 1908. *Michelangelo: kritische Untersuchungen über seine Werke,* vol. 1. Berlin.

Wilson, C. Heath. 1876. *Life and Works of Michelangelo Buonarroti.* London.

Wölfflin, H. 1899. *Die klassische Kunst: eine Einführung in die intalienische Renaissance.* Munich.

Zinow, A. 1881. *Psyche und Eros.* Halle.

Zweig, S. 1920. *Drei Meister* (vol. 1 of *Die Baumeister der Welt*). Leipzig. Trans.: *Three Masters.* New York and London, 1938.

——. 1927. *Die Verwirrung der Gefühle.* Leipzig. Trans.: *Conflicts.* New York and London, 1939.

MERIDIAN

Crossing Aesthetics

Library of Congress Cataloging-in-Publication Data

Freud, Sigmund, 1856–1939
  Writings on art and literature / Sigmund Freud : with a foreword
by Neil Hertz.
    p.   cm. — (Meridian: crossing aesthetics)
  Includes bibliographical references.
  ISBN 0-8047-2972-7 (cloth : alk. paper). — ISBN 0-8047-2973-5
(pbk. : alk. paper)
  1. Psychoanalysis and the arts. I. Title. II. Series: Meridian
(Stanford, Calif.)
NX180.P7F74 1997
700'.1'9—dc21   96-51922
                                                       CIP